Personalizing Education

Personalizing Education

Values Clarification and Beyond

112095

Leland W. Howe
Associate Professor, Temple University

Mary Martha Howe
Director, Philadelphia Center for Humanistic Education

HART PUBLISHING COMPANY, INC.
NEW YORK CITY

CONTENTS

5

Personalizing Education

Preface

Within the brief period of a few years, Values Clarification[1] (V.C.) has become an immensely popular teaching approach. All over the country, thousands of teachers, counselors, and administrators have either been trained to use the Values Clarification strategies in their schools, or have read the books *Values and Teaching* (Louis Raths, Merrill Harmin, and Sidney Simon)[2] and its sequel, *Values Clarification* (Sidney Simon, Leland Howe, and Howard Kirschenbaum).[3] The question we wish to address with this book is one that has been raised by both critics and supporters of the approach: "Is V.C. a fad? Or will it be as useful in ten years as it is today?"

Our belief is that Values Clarification is not "just another innovation," and that it can be an even more useful teaching tool in the years to come. Yet V.C. may indeed be discarded in the coming decade, unless teachers and educators come to understand the approach as more than games to be used on Fridays, or as a means of enlivening the classroom when students get bored or restless.

Our concern about the future of Values Clarification

arises mainly from our experiences with teachers who have been trained in or exposed to the V.C. approach. Although many times we are pleased to see that the strategies *are* being used, and used properly—that is to say, the teacher is not using the strategies to moralize or to teach his own values—we are often disappointed to see that Values Clarification as a teaching method has little relationship to the curriculum. Many teachers have told us that they simply set aside a period of time as "values time." When it is over, students and teacher go back to doing what they have always done. In other words, there is no relationship between what goes on during "values time" and what goes on during math, science, English, social studies, or the other areas of the curriculum.

The V.C. training methods may have contributed to this problem. Teachers love V.C. training because they go home from a workshop with something concrete to try in the classroom. What's more, they have had trial runs through the strategies and know first-hand the excitement and enthusiasm these generate. Quite a few teachers have said to us that they couldn't wait until Monday morning to try the strategies. But the very things that make V.C. training so appealing are also perhaps its greatest weakness. The fact that teachers can attain visible *results* after such a short period of time (most training sessions are less than a week in duration) can effectively prevent the participant teachers from understanding the true potential and power of the V.C. process.

Those who have written about the V.C. approach may also have contributed to the problem. This is especially true with regard to *Values Clarification*, the popular handbook by Simon, Howe, and Kirschenbaum. Teachers love it because "it doesn't have so much theory," and the strategies "really work." The book tends to be viewed as a very useful handbook of 79 teaching strategies rather than as an integrated approach to teaching, which it is.

Perhaps another part of the problem is that there has been little attempt to articulate just how the valuing process can be made to pervade the total educational process. Harmin, Kirschenbaum, and Simon have made a good start at this with their book entitled *Clarifying Values Through Subject Matter.*[4] Included in the book is one brief chapter which states the need for integrating the valuing approach with other humanistic approaches—such as the informal and open classroom, group dynamics, etc.—but one is left wondering how this can be done.

What is needed, then, is a book which (1) is useful and practical, (2) stresses the process of valuing, (3) extends the valuing process to other aspects of the classroom, such as interaction, organization, management, and so on, and (4) shows how V.C. can be used with other humanistic methods.

The aim of our book is to do just this, to make Values Clarification an integral part of every dimension of the classroom. What teachers and administrators must come to see is that valuing is not a gimmick of limited usefulness, but a way of thinking about teaching, a way of relating to students, a way of *personalizing* education so that every student can achieve his or her full potential.

LELAND W. HOWE
MARY MARTHA HOWE

Philadelphia
June, 1974

Notes

1. *See page 19,* "What is Values Clarification?"
2. Columbus, Ohio, Charles E. Merrill, 1966. For full bibliographical material of the works cited in this book, consult the Bibliography at the rear.
3. New York, Hart, 1972.
4. Minneapolis, Minn., Winston Press, 1972.

Acknowledgments

We wish to thank:

Edward Betof, for the many hours he spent listening to ideas, making suggestions, writing strategies, and editing this book.

Fred Harwood, for sharing the "nuts and bolts" of managing a choice-centered classroom and for making personalized education work in urban schools.

Merrill Harmin, for introducing us to Values Clarification, to new directions in education, and to each other.

Margaret Hazzard, for so beautifully preparing the manuscript —typing, drawing, proofing, and making sense out of some very rough drafts.

Howard Kirschenbaum, for supporting our work and sharing his ideas on ways to personalize education.

Liesl and Peter, for being so patient with Mom and Dad for so long.

Robert Muschlitz, for his dedication to the cause of

personalizing education and his contributions to this book.

Louis Raths, for his pioneer work in Values Clarification and humanizing education.

Sidney Simon, for "turning on" thousands of educators to Values Clarification.

John Thorn, for a superb job of editing the book.

INTRODUCTION

1. The Values Clarification Approach

Our values are the things that we are for and the things we are against. They give purpose and direction to our lives. If our values are clear, consistent, and soundly chosen, we tend to live our lives in meaningful and satisfying ways. If we lack values, or our values are confused and conflicted, we tend to live our lives in troubled and frustrating ways.

Today, more and more people—especially the young— seem to be living their lives without clear purpose and direction, unable to decide what they are for or against. Bewildered by the choices that confront them daily, some withdraw and attempt to shut the confusion out. Some conform and become only too willing to let others tell them exactly what to believe and do. Still others lash out at the confusion, trying to smash anything that troubles them.

It is little wonder, then, that the largest single complaint voiced by teachers is that "today's students are so unmotivated and difficult to work with." Unfortunately, the impersonal nature of many of our schools is not helping this situation. Students who lack values, or hold confused values, are likely to see little or no relevance in their lessons no matter what the teacher does. Thus, schools which continue to stress only academic goals are wasting their efforts, to say the least; in many cases, the schools may actually be serving to heighten the students' confusion regarding values.

Neither is the answer for these schools to try to teach values through such means as moralizing, lecturing, reward and punishment, or any of the other methods which attempt to impose values externally. This, too, is likely to compound frustration and lead ultimately to resentment of the well-meaning teacher.

If students are to become motivated and receptive to learning, what the schools must do is to personalize the educational process, to place prime emphasis on the students' *personal* growth rather than merely their intellectual development. The schools must begin to teach students the *skills* they need to sort out the confusion and conflict in their lives, and to find the things that they value. Time must be spent in the classroom to help students learn to set and achieve goals that will bring meaning and satisfaction to their lives. What teachers will find, if our own experience can be generalized, is that when students' lives gain purpose and direction, the students actively seek knowledge that is relevant to their purposes and goals. The problem of "how to motivate students" disappears.

The difficult question, of course, is, "How to do it?" What are the really useful teaching tools for personalizing education? These are the questions this book is designed to answer. While we offer many practical approaches and strategies, one approach plays a larger role in the book than others. It is the Values Clarification approach developed by Raths, Harmin, and Simon. In our minds, this approach provides the key to personalizing education.

WHAT IS VALUES CLARIFICATION?

Values Clarification is not an attempt to teach students "right" and "wrong" values. Rather, it is an approach designed to help students prize and act upon their own freely chosen values. Thus, V.C. is concerned with the process by which students arrive at their values rather than the content of these values. To implement the V.C. approach in the classroom, the teacher uses strategies which help students learn to:

1. Choose their values freely.

2. Choose their values from alternatives.

3. Choose their values after weighing the consequences of each alternative.

4. Prize and cherish their values.

5. Share and publicly affirm their values.

6. Act upon their values.

7. Act upon their values repeatedly and consistently.

These seven steps have come to be known as the valuing process of *choosing, prizing,* and *acting.*[1] For a detailed discussion of this valuing process and the Values Clarification approach which grows out of it, consult *Values and Teaching* by Raths, Harmin, and Simon or *Readings in Values Clarification* by Kirschenbaum and Simon.[2]

p. 97

Notes

1. In *Values and Teaching*, Raths, Harmin, and Simon state these seven steps as criteria which define a value.

2. *Op. cit.*

2. Personalizing Education

A LITTLE GIRL'S DREAM[1]

I went for another walk today. Only it was raining a little. I walked down the road to an old underground playhouse we had. It was where an old house used to stand. I like to walk in the rain and things like that. I like to wish upon stars and I like to be alone to get my head straight. Everything was all right except our neighbor had just spread cow manure in the field in front of our house.

As I walked further down the road everything was kind of quiet. The rain was getting stronger and beating against my face. I just held my head up and let the rain fall on me. The flowers were drinking the water to stay alive. The animals were trying to get out of the rain.

When I got to the woods where the playhouse and rock pile was, I noticed someone had put a fence up. We used the rocks for tables and chairs in the playhouse. I wanted to go inside but the fence had me blocked out; I couldn't get through. So I just stood next to the fence and stared into the playhouse. As I stared, I just let my mind go free. I let it go back to when I was a little girl. I could see myself as a little girl playing in the playhouse. . . .

I was swinging on our home-made swings which were in the basement. And I was playing in the playhouse with my toys, but I was all alone. No one would play with me unless I had a cigarette. Then I stopped and wondered, they weren't my friends at all, were they? . . .

When I was little I liked to be alone a lot of the time, I would go for walks or for a ride on my pony just to get away from everyone. I would go down to the creek. I would sit and cry because I didn't have a daddy like all of my friends. I always wondered why mommy never got married. I was afraid of that thought, afraid to face that as a great big problem in my life.

I had a dream one night about this. I was sitting on my mommy's knee and I told her these words: "Mommy, I love you and all of my toys, but I want a daddy like the other girls and boys. And I'll give you my pennies, my nickels and dimes, but buy me a daddy. Please, he don't have to be new just as long as he loves me—any daddy will do. But mommy, please make him promise that he won't go away. Mommy please let's go get one today." After she heard this she started to cry and then I woke up crying for her.

I always went away to cry, because I didn't want Mom to know what I was crying about. But as I grew up, I thought I would get over it. After I found out why. But I guess I never will. I sleep alone, so I can cry without anyone hearing me. I won't ever say anything to her about it in fear that she would be badly hurt.

When I started dating, Mom would never let me go. Linda and I had to sneak out. One night we got caught and Mom yelled at us. I was mad at her until I realized what she was trying to do. I was going to ask her one night why she never got married. The next day I was looking in her bureau and found a picture of my father. I went down to the creek and cried most of the day.

I'm afraid in life today, will I ever end up that way. Will my children run and hide to cry from me and my mistakes? I wish that I could go back into the past and start all over again. Is all of my past and present a part of which makes me a lonely person? I never like to talk of this, but I had to get it out. It makes me cry when I even think about it. I'll never blame Mom for this, I can't.

"A Little Girl's Dream" was written by a ninth grade girl whom we'll call Julie (that is not her real name). Having read her sensitive and moving theme, we might expect that Julie was a student in an advanced-placement English class. Rather, from fourth grade on, Julie had a history of failure and behavior problems in school. By eighth grade, she was averaging 30 days of absence per year. Her academic record was dismal. Disciplinary action was frequent. Her high school vice-principal characterized her attitude toward school as one of "perpetual anger." This anger was manifested in numerous physical encounters with both students and teachers.

However, in ninth grade, Julie was placed in a special classroom where she received personalized attention. Within a few short months, her anger and anti-social behavior dissipated, and in its place a new creativity and sensitivity were born.

What turned Julie on to learning after five years of

rebellion and stagnation in school was personalized education. Instead of being told what, when, and how she had to
learn, Julie was encouraged to discover herself, explore her
values and her goals in life, decide what things she needed to
learn, and learn them in ways that were meaningful to her.
She began working on projects that she was interested in and
at which she could succeed. She had a chance to talk to other
students and to teachers whenever she felt the need. She
began to learn new ways to make decisions and sort out her
confusing world. She began to find things about herself of
which she could be proud, and she was encouraged to share
these with others. Her teachers constantly supported her and
made her feel she was a truly worthwhile, capable person.
For the first time in her life, school became an enjoyable,
meaningful, and successful experience.

We would like to share with you some of the things that
made Julie's learning experience so special. But before
sharing our strategies and techniques for personalizing classrooms, we would like to identify briefly the characteristics
that personalized classrooms seem to have in common and
that make them different from and, we think, better than
other kinds of classrooms. (A simple definition of a personalized classroom is one in which a high priority is placed on
facilitating personal growth. This involves helping the *whole*
child or adolescent grow—physically, intellectually, emotionally, socially, and morally.)

PERSONALIZING HUMAN RELATIONSHIPS

As we visited and observed personalized classrooms, the first
thing that was evident upon entering was that the climate was

relaxed, friendly, and cooperative. Teachers and students felt good about themselves and what they were doing. They were supportive of each other, freely offering and accepting each other's help and encouragement. Interpersonal competition was absent from the classroom: students respected each other's differences; the emphasis was on helping each person grow and achieve his or her full potential, regardless of the capabilities and performance of others.

As we observed the teachers in these classrooms, we noted that they acted more as friends, helpers, and resource persons, and less as experts and dispensers of information. A major portion of their efforts was directed toward letting their students know that they cared about them very deeply. These teachers listened to students attentively. They provided encouragement. They validated student strengths and accomplishments. They offered challenges and helped students meet those challenges.

In short, these teachers and students were able to build a classroom climate that met student needs for acceptance, love, and respect, and that created the conditions for learning and personal growth to occur.

PERSONALIZING GOALS

In so many classrooms, instruction seems totally unrelated to the concerns, interests, and goals that the students bring to class. In personalized classrooms, however, the students' concerns, interests, and goals were used as the primary basis for instruction. To facilitate this, much time was devoted to helping students identify their concerns, clarify their values, set their own learning goals, that take responsibility for their own learning and behavior in the classroom. The instructional emphasis was not on meeting certain content objectives, but on teaching students the skills and processes that they needed to *learn how to learn*. Teachers would schedule, on a regular basis, small and large group sessions to work on Values Clarification, decision making, and goal setting strategies; the purpose of such sessions was to aid students in raising and answering the questions, "What is worth learning?" and "What is worth doing?" Student answers were then used as the basis for setting the instructional goals and objectives of the class. Teachers who felt strongly about certain content or cognitive skill objectives generally found that they could mesh these objectives with the goals that students set.

PERSONALIZING CURRICULUM

A third aspect of the personalized classrooms we observed was that the curriculum actually emerged from students' interests, concerns, and goals, or was modified in ways which served to help students identify and deal with their concerns, clarify their values, and achieve their own learning goals. Teachers often started with student interests and concerns as a basis for building a unit of study. What is more, they encouraged students to participate in formulating the important questions to be asked in the unit, and in developing the means for finding the answers.

Even teachers who were "locked" into a curriculum that had to be covered found creative ways to relate the content to student interests and concerns. For example, in a science unit on the telephone, students would not only learn how the telephone was invented and how it worked, but would also explore how their lives would be different without telephones, whether the telephone has been a negative or positive influence in our society, or how much value they place on the telephone. As a sample activity, students might go for a week without using a telephone and then record how their lives were changed, and whether they liked the results. Or, in a history unit on the Civil War, which is perhaps more remote from student interests and concerns, students would not stop with learning the causes of the Civil War, but might go on to explore the causes of conflict as it relates to their own lives. Many teachers who were compelled to teach certain content areas also used Values Clarification strategies[2] as an integrating device to make their subject matter come alive and at the same time involve students in the seven-step valuing process *(see page 19).*

In either case, whether the curriculum emerged from student interests and concerns or was adapted to meet them, it served to provide students with the knowledge and cognitive skills they needed to achieve their own learning goals.

PERSONALIZING CLASSROOM ORGANIZATION AND MANAGEMENT

In personalized classrooms, the teachers used organization and management as tools to build a climate of trust, meet student needs, help students clarify their values and become self-directed, and provide for individual learning differences.

Building a Climate of Trust

For instance, even in the first few weeks of class, teachers would try to provide some measure of choice to indicate their confidence in the students' ability to make decisions about their own learning. Thus, by simply giving students a chance to choose with whom they worked, or which of two tasks they performed, the teachers moved a long way toward building a sense of trust and acceptance in the classroom.

Meeting Student Needs

These teachers also used various classroom structures and management techniques to help students meet their needs for security, approval, belonging, prestige, achievement, and self-esteem. For example, room dividers were used to give students places where they could have some privacy if they wished it. Points and tokens were used with students who needed constant approval and reinforcement. Group work, support groups, and classroom meetings were used with students who needed affiliation and group identification. Students who needed prestige and status were given important classroom tasks like record keeping, or were designated as student experts in some aspect of the curriculum or classroom operation.

Clarifying Values

Teachers in personalized classrooms, especially those who had been trained in Values Clarification, also used organization and management procedures to facilitate students' choosing, prizing, and acting upon their values. For example, these teachers provided many opportunities for students to *make choices from alternatives*—one of the seven critical dimensions of the valuing process. In fact, one of the most characteristic features of the personalized classroom was that many alternative activities and ways of learning were available for student choice. Classrooms at both the elementary and secondary levels were filled with plants, animals, games, maps, audio-visual materials, books and magazines, and junk of every type and description—all tied into a variety of learning activities. The alternatives often extended beyond the classroom as well, in the form of field trips, community experiences, outdoor activities, and resource people from the community. Such a diversity of alternative learning activities exposed students to a variety of value positions from which to finally choose their own values.

Because the alternative learning activities were usually written up in a self-instructional task card format and posted around the classroom, students were encouraged to *make their choices freely* without undue pressure from the teacher or their peers. Learning to choose freely is, of course, another important dimension of the valuing process. Students who were unable to make sound choices freely received assistance from the teacher. But as these students' decision-making skills increased and they became better able to make choices, they were provided with the opportunities to take more responsibility for their own learning.

Another important dimension of the valuing process which was facilitated by the use of a choice-centered classroom organization is the process of *choosing after carefully weighing the consequences of each alternative*. Not only did students in personalized classrooms have their choice of activities and ways of learning, they were also presented with alternative ways of behaving in the classroom. For example, many of the teachers used learning contracts to help students set and achieve their own learning goals. Once the contract was negotiated and agreed upon by both the student and the teacher, the student was responsible for fulfilling the specifications of the contract by a certain date. The student was then free to use his or her class time as he or she saw fit as long as other students were not disturbed. If students decided to use their class time to socialize, and then failed to fulfill the contract by the due date, they had to live with the consequences of their behavior—that is to say, they did not receive the payoff, whether it be in the form of points which eventually contributed to passing the course, or some other tangible form of positive reinforcement. In this way, students were allowed to experience the logical consequences of their own behavior. Even students who for several years or perhaps all their lives had been protected from experiencing the consequences of their behavior did not take long to understand the concept of consequences. The end result was that students learned to think about the consequences of their decisions and actions before they made a choice, thus making them better choosers.

The choice-centered classroom also facilitates the processes of *prizing* and *public affirmation*, two other important dimensions of the valuing process. Since students in these classrooms were encouraged to learn and work on projects of their own choosing, they usually selected things that they considered important and at which they could succeed. When they completed their task or project, they were usually proud of what they had done. By the end of the school year, they had undertaken and done many things which they could prize. Students were also provided with an opportunity to publicly affirm the things which they prized. The unrestricted movement and interaction that was characteristic of these classrooms allowed students to share their successes with each other and the teacher whenever they wished, rather than waiting until after school or some later time. Many times we walked into a personalized classroom and had a student come up to us after a few minutes and ask with a proud gleam in his or her eye, "Want to hear me read?" or "Want to see the project I did?" In addition, the bulletin boards, walls, and room dividers provided opportunities for public affirmation since student work was displayed.

These choice-centered classrooms also facilitated the valuing processes of *acting upon one's values* and *acting repeatedly and consistently*. Many of the projects that students undertook were action-oriented projects. For example, if students were studying a unit on consumer protection, they did consumer surveys in their local communities, compiled and analyzed the results, made their own assessments of what laws or enforcement changes were needed, and then wrote letters to their government representatives encouraging passage or enforcement of the laws. Thus, students were not expected to learn for tomorrow and put their insights and learnings into practice after graduation; rather, students were encouraged to take repeated and consistent action on their values and test out their learning in the real world.

Helping Students Become Self-Directed

The teachers we observed who had personalized their

classrooms held as one of their primary aims to help students become self-directed, autonomous persons who had learned how to learn. To accomplish this aim, they used a continuum of classroom organization and management styles *(see page 460)*. At one end of the continuum was a style that could be called totally teacher-directed—that is, the teacher made all of the planning, execution, and evaluation decisions in the classroom. At the other end of the continuum was a management style that could be called student free choice— that is, the student rather than the teacher made all of the planning, execution, and evaluation decisions. In between were several additional management styles, each of which varied in the amount of student decision making that was encouraged.

Accordingly, we saw teachers using different teaching styles with different students in the same classroom, depending upon how self-directed each student was. The objective was to encourage the student to become more self-directed by gradually turning over more and more decision-making responsibilities. It appeared to be a successful strategy, since we observed students who in September could not function in the classroom unless they were told every move to make, and who by April were able to successfully initiate, plan, execute, and self-evaluate their own learning projects.

Providing for Individual Learning Differences

Last but not least, we noted from our observations that teachers who used a personalized, choice-centered organization and management system seemed to do an excellent job of providing for the varied learning needs of individual students. For example, students were encouraged to use self-paced instructional materials to learn at their own rate. Kinesthetic, auditory, and visual materials which ranged from very simple to complex were available and used by students as they chose.

ORGANIZATION OF THE BOOK

We have organized the book into four parts to reflect the four dimensions that we believe are critical in personalizing the classroom. Each part contains a variety of practical strategies designed to help the teacher personalize that particular dimension of his or her classroom.

In choosing the strategies for this book, we have tried to accomplish two objectives. One, we selected only those strategies whose usefulness has been demonstrated in the classroom and have been used or adapted successfully by teachers at a variety of grade levels. Second, we selected a number of the strategies for the express purpose of introducing teachers to the wide variety of approaches which can be used to personalize education. Although most of the strategies in this book arise from our work in Values Clarification—which we think is an extremely viable approach to personalizing education—we have included many other methods and approaches which can be used in conjunction with the V.C. approach to do an even more effective job of personalizing education.

The following chart provides a listing of these approaches and how we see each facilitating the process of personalizing

Approaches and Methods Which Can Be Used to Personalize Education[3]

PERSONALIZING HUMAN RELATIONSHIPS	PERSONALIZING GOALS
Developing a Climate of Trust, Acceptance, and Open Communication	*Helping Students Develop and Clarify Their Values, Purposes, and Goals*
1. Teacher Effectiveness Training (Gordon)	1. Values Clarification (Raths, Harmin, Simon)
2. Human Development Program (Bessell & Palomares)	2. Gestalt Awareness (Perls)
3. Transactional Analysis (Berne & Harris)	3. Confluent Education (Brown)
4. Enhancing Self-Concept (Canfield & Wells)	4. Achievement Motivation (Alschuler)
5. Reality Games (Sax)	5. Re-evaluation Counseling (Jackins)
6. The Classroom Meeting Model (Glasser)	
7. Natural and Logical Consequences (Dreikurs)	

NOTE: The sources on these two pages are not meant to be inclusive; rather, they are simply the approaches with which we are most acquainted.

PERSONALIZING THE CURRICULUM	PERSONALIZING CLASS-ROOM ORGANIZATION AND MANAGEMENT
Making Knowledge and Cognitive Skills Serve Students' Values, Purposes, and Goals	*Using Classroom Organization and Management to Facilitate Learning and Personal Growth*
1. Values Clarification Through Subject Matter—Three Levels Approach (Harmin, Simon & Kirschenbaum) 2. Student Concerns Curriculum (Borton & Newberg) 3. Developing Curriculum From Student Concerns (Harwood & Howe) 4. Simulation and Games	1. The Choice-Centered Classroom Approach (Harwood & Howe) 2. Schools Without Failure (Glasser) 3. British Informal Education Approaches 4. Open Education Approaches

education. We have selected what we consider to be the fundamental ideas, skills, or processes of the approach, created one or two strategies which are consistent with our theme of personalization, and included them in the appropriate sections of this book. In no way, however, should you consider these short encounters as more than an invitation to do more reading in the appropriate sources, and to gain further experience and training in the approaches.

Notes

1. Used with permission of the author.
2. See the strategies in Part II of this book or the strategies provided in *Values Clarification* and *Values and Teaching*.
3. For a list of specific sources, consult the Bibliography at the conclusion of this book.

PART I

PERSONALIZING HUMAN RELATIONSHIPS IN THE CLASSROOM

3. Introduction to Part I

If we teachers are to reach our goal of helping every student learn the skills and self-confidence needed to achieve his or her fullest potential as a person, it is vital that human relationships be personalized in the classroom. No dimension of teaching is more critical. Meaningful learning and personal growth cannot take place in a climate of competition, hostility, and misunderstanding. Learning and personal growth require people to take risks, to see and think of things in new ways, to try different means of relating and behaving. People do not take risks when they fear that failure will mean rejection. Rather, meaningful learning, personal growth, and creativity flower in a warm, accepting, and supportive climate.

The strategies included in this first part of the book have been selected because they quickly develop just such a climate. As this climate of trust and acceptance builds in the classroom, students will become more and more interested in learning, think and act more creatively, and grow toward the kinds of persons they can potentially become.

We have divided Part I into two sections. In the first

section, we have included strategies designed primarily to develop within students and teachers an open, accepting, and non-judgmental attitude—the kind of attitude which says, "I don't necessarily agree with everything you think, but I totally respect your right to think it." This kind of an attitude builds trust because students realize that they can be open and honest and not be judged or "put down" by others. Some of the strategies actually teach students the "skills" of non-judgmental acceptance. Other strategies in this section increase students' communication skills, such as active listening, drawing out, and focusing on the speaker, which are essential in the creation of a supportive, accepting climate.

In the second section, the strategies deal primarily with helping students build self-concept. We believe that when a student feels really good about himself, not only does his learning ability increase tremendously, but he is also able to care more deeply about others. Some of the strategies in this section help build self-concepts from within by having students find things about themselves which they can prize. Some strategies help to do this from the outside, by having students and the teacher give feedback on and validate each other's strengths and good points. Other strategies simply make students aware of self-concept—ways we unintentionally destroy it, and ways of building it.

4. *Developing a Climate of Acceptance, Trust, and Open Communication*

Values Name Game

PURPOSE

When people come together for the first time, there is usually a period of uneasiness or apprehension. An enjoyable and useful way to relieve this feeling of awkwardness is the *Values Name Game*. The game also helps students identify some of the things they enjoy doing and brings out some things they might like to try doing. An interesting side effect is the way the game builds self-concept.

PROCEDURE

Depending on the age of the individuals, divide the class into groups of from four to twelve people (the younger the class, the fewer in the group). The group members should sit in a circle so that every person can see and speak without being obstructed. Request a volunteer or designate someone to start the game by saying his name and telling the group about something that he likes to do (in just a few words). For example, "My name is Ed and I like to play baseball." Moving in a clockwise direction, the next person repeats the preceding name(s) and what those people like to do. The speaker then gives his or her name and what he or she likes to do. For example: "His name is Ed and he likes to play baseball. My name is Joan and I like to sing." This process continues until the original starter repeats all the names and "likes."

If someone cannot remember a person's name or what a person likes, he or she should be helped by the rest of the group. This is not a contest, but a chance to begin to develop helping relationships.

Some teachers use the *Values Name Game* to begin new classes at the start of a term. Others have told us that their students enjoyed it even after several months together because they learned new things about their classmates.

VARIATIONS

The game can be varied in a number of ways. Some teachers prefer to use smaller groups (four or five people) and increase the number of items that individuals can learn about each other. For instance: "His name is Bob, he likes to paint, he has three brothers, and he lives on Main Street."

Still another variation would be to vary the members of the groups at each succeeding meeting. In this way, a teacher can provide the opportunity for every member of a new class to learn each other's name and something about that person. Within a few class meetings, there will have developed a closer rapport between the students as well as a sense of belonging.

Another fun variation is to have each person pantomime the things people like to do, rather than saying them.[1]

Biographies[2]

PURPOSE

The purpose of *Biographies* is to help students get better acquainted. This strategy also aids in the initial stages of trust building, which is so necessary to an open and free values-clarifying environment.

PROCEDURE

Divide the class into groups of three. The purpose of biography triads is best served when the participants do not know each other or at least know very little about one another.

Participants decide who will go first. That person then tells as much about himself as he can in one minute (observe the time limit strictly). The other two participants also take one minute apiece for their biographies.

Together, participants 2 and 3 take two minutes to tell participant 1 what they heard him say. Afterwards, participants 1 and 3 repeat the process for No. 2, and participants 1 and 2 repeat the process for No. 3.

VARIATIONS

After the above procedure has been completed, take three minutes for the three participants to informally ask questions of each other or to comment on what was said.

Another possible variation is for participants, at their own option, to each take one additional uninterrupted minute to continue their biographies or to expand on a particularly important point of their lives.

Values Get-Acquainted

PURPOSE

This is a good strategy for helping people get to know each other quickly. It also helps students find others with interests and values similar to theirs, and, more important, helps them realize that some people may have interests and values very different from theirs. This is one way of raising new alternatives for them to consider.

PROCEDURE

Provide students with a worksheet like the one below. (Make up the items to fit your group.) Their task is to mill around the room, meeting and talking with each other, until they have completed the worksheet. The worksheet is complete when they have placed a name beside each description.

Worksheet

Instructions: Find a person in the room who fits one of the descriptions below. Place his or her name on the worksheet in the appropriate space provided. Continue until all blanks are filled. Each name may appear only one time.

FIND A PERSON WHO:	NAME:
1. Has read a book just for fun in the last 2 weeks.	_____
2. Plays a musical instrument.	_____
3. Would be in favor of a law to limit couples to two children.	_____
4. Has been camping recently.	_____
5. Loves to go horseback riding.	_____
6. Has ever written a "letter to the editor."	_____
7. Has an unconventional hobby or pastime.	_____
8. Has worked for a candidate running for political office.	_____
9. Thinks school attendance should be completely voluntary after grade six.	_____
10. Thinks women with small children should not work outside the home.	_____

ADDITIONAL ITEMS FOR WORKSHEET

Find a person who:

1. Learned a new skill in the past two weeks.

2. Has a friend who is a celebrity.

3. Thinks children should not work for their allowance.

4. Has a close friend from another country.

5. Has had someone from another race (religion) to their home for dinner or to play.

6. Is planning to vote the same political party as his or her parents.

7. Is planning to go into politics someday.

8. Is in favor of a law to ban guns in the U.S.

9. Has had a scary dream recently.

10. Is a ski buff.

11. Wears seat belts when riding in a car.

12. Would be willing to donate his or her body to science after death.

13. Has recently written a letter to his or her congressman or some other governmental representative.

14. Would like to retire at age 40.

15. Has taken or is now taking karate lessons.

16. Thinks students should pay their own way through college.

Introductions[3]

PURPOSE

Introductions gives students a chance to get to know other students better by exploring with them their viewpoints on a particular issue. In addition, this strategy is an important aid in developing students' listening ability. But most importantly, it facilitates the development of a sense of interdependence that is crucial if the valuing process is to function in a group setting. This game can be used at the beginning of a term for helping people to get acquainted, or it may be used later in the term as deeper personal ties are being developed.

PROCEDURE

Form groups of four people who do not know each other well. One person volunteers to be questioned by the three other participants about anything that he feels proud of or good about. The person who is being questioned *always* picks the discussion topic. At the outset, he may take as much as two uninterrupted minutes to explain his thoughts and feelings about the topic. The topic may be as big as capital punishment or as small as a funny incident that happened recently.

After the initial explanation, it becomes the responsibility of the three questioners to learn as much about the volunteer's topic as they can. It is important that the volunteer have control over the game. If he feels that there is no more that he wishes to reveal, or that the topic is being changed, he should tell this to the questioners.

The questioners should be given five minutes to ask about the volunteer's topic. At that point, one representative of each of the questioning triads introduces his or her group's volunteer to the entire class. The introduction should begin with the volunteer's name and as much information about his or her topic as can be remembered. The two other questioners can help in the introduction if the representative forgets any important points. The volunteer can opt to clear up any points that may have been forgotten or confused by the representative(s) introducing him. The volunteers in each of the other groups should be introduced to the class in the same fashion, as time permits.

VARIATIONS

A large block of time can be taken so that everyone gets a chance to be introduced with his topic. Or, the teacher or class may decide to do only one round of introductions a day, but to continue *Introductions* on successive class meetings until each student has been introduced to the large group. The four group members should remain constant each day.

A difficult, sometimes frustrating, but valuable lesson can be had if *Introductions* is used later in the term to help students to understand points of view with which they disagree. In this variation, the groups of four can be made up of students who disagree on a given topic that may have been discussed in class. Two rounds of *Introductions* should be included within the group with two different viewpoints being explored *one after the other* and then presented to the class.

My Secret Pal[4]

PURPOSE

This simple, fun game can go a long way toward building positive, supportive relationships in the classroom.

PROCEDURE

Have students draw names from a basket, hat, whatever. The name each student draws is his or her secret pal for the week. Students are not to reveal their secret pals to anyone. During the week, students must do or give at least five nice or special things to their secret pals, but they must do or give them in such a way that their secret pals do not know or find out who their benefactors are.

For example, a student might write a note to his secret pal telling him some special things that he likes about his pal. He could then slip it into his secret pal's desk or cubby when he isn't looking. Or, a student might give her secret pal a gift. It might be a poem, a stick of gum, or something homemade. The gift could be sent secretly by having a friend deliver it.

At the end of the week, have students reveal their secret pals.

VARIATION

Have students keep their secret pals for longer periods of time. Students can then give their secret pals birthday gifts, Christmas gifts, Valentine cards, and so on.

COMMUNICATION-SKILLS LADDER

The following eight strategies, when used in sequence, form a communication-skills ladder. The first four strategies, *Non-listening, Two Ships Passing in the Night, The Happy Hooker,* and *In/Out Discussion Groups* help students become aware of some of the dysfunctional skills and behaviors they and others use to block meaningful communication. The next four strategies are designed to teach, one step at a time, the skills, attitudes, and behaviors students need if communication in the classroom is to become fully functional and effective. *The Positive Focus Game* teaches students how to ask helpful questions and to listen non-judgmentally. *I Messages* teaches students how to share their feelings and give feedback to others non-judgmentally. *Active Listening* teaches students how to listen to others empathetically. And *Conflict Resolution* teaches students how to resolve interpersonal conflict on a no-lose basis.

Non-Listening[5]

PURPOSE

There are many obstacles that prevent people from communicating effectively. These barriers or "dysfunctions" tend to disrupt both the flow of words and the understanding between people. This strategy, like the two that follow, points out just a few of the many problems that can arise when people talk *at* instead of *with* others. This strategy is effective when done in one session with the two that follow.

PROCEDURE

Divide the class into groups of six, sitting in circles. Each group should select one of its members to present a one-minute autobiography, a quick summary of his life from birth to present. The autobiographer should do everything in his power to make the other five people listen to him. The five "non-listeners" should do everything they can *not* to listen. The only ground rule is that no one may leave the circle.

It is not uncommon to see students climbing on chairs, shaking people, kneeling beside non-listeners, etc., in order to have someone listen to them during this exercise. Play it a second time, giving another member of the group a chance to present an autobiography and to feel the frustration of saying something important and not having anyone listen. This also gives the first autobiographer a chance to try active non-listening himself.

Two Ships Passing in the Night[6]

PROCEDURE

Often when two individuals are speaking to one another about an issue, and each is very concerned about getting his or her point across, an outsider listening to them can readily see that they are neither listening carefully to each other nor responding to each other's statements. Each is plowing forward with his or her own agenda seemingly oblivious to the other, like two ships unknowingly passing side by side in the night.

Another appropriate analogy for this type of miscommunication might be two televisions placed face to face and tuned in to different channels—having a "duelogue" rather than a "dialogue."

Have students form pairs. Each person in the pair should take several minutes to write a list of ten phrases or short sentences about any topic of his or her choice. The sentences do not have to be sequential but should all be on one topic. The paired students should not know what their partner is writing. When the lists are completed, partners should alternate reading one sentence at a time with all of the dramatic flavor that they can muster.

The Happy Hooker[7]

PROCEDURE

Another communication problem that frequently occurs is one that can be called *The Happy Hooker*. This happens when a listener interrupts a speaker by "hooking" onto a word or phrase in order to discuss something of interest to the listener instead.

Have students form groups of six. Have one person in each group begin discussing the topic "Something exciting that has happened to me recently." As soon as another member of the group hears a word that reminds him of something in his life, he "hooks" into the conversation by interrupting with a "hooking phrase." This second member then talks about his topic until a third member "hooks" into his story, and so on. The topic of the conversation may change any number of times after the original speaker—it will probably end up a long way from where it began.

Before beginning the exercise, you might have the students compile a short list of "hooking phrases" they have heard. Here are some starters:

1. Speaking of that . . .

2. That reminds me of . . .

3. Glad you mentioned that . . .

4. Oh, right, remember the time . . .

5. Just as you were saying . . .

6. That's like . . .

7. Oh, that's nothing! Let me tell you . . .

FOLLOW-UP

These three strategies are most effective when the teacher makes no comment at all on what happens and doesn't use them as an opportunity to moralize. Instead, ask the students to share some "I learned . . ." statements of what they learned about communication and themselves through the series of strategies.

In/Out Discussion Groups

PURPOSE

This strategy helps students improve their communication skills, increases students' awareness of the parts they play in a discussion, and strengthens the ability of the group to hold meaningful, effective small group discussions.

PROCEDURE

Divide the class into groups of six or eight students each. Divide these groups in half, one half forming a circle with their chairs, and the second half forming an outer circle with their chairs around the first half.

The "in" group (inner circle) is then given a topic to discuss for ten minutes (for possible topics, see below). The "out" group (outer circle) is not allowed to speak *at all* during these ten minutes. Their task is to observe the communication process of the in group. They are asked to notice what kinds of things people do that block communication and what kinds of things they do that facilitate communication.

POSSIBLE TOPICS FOR DISCUSSION

1. What causes communication problems between people?

2. Is there a generation gap between students and teachers?

3. What can be done to make schools more meaningful places for students and teachers?

4. Use one of the value dilemma topics, *pages 251-279.*

5. Use one of the "Dear Abby" discussion topics, *pages 279-289.*

6. Use a topic related to subject matter, e.g., "What do you think were the causes of the Civil War?" (Make sure topics do not call for objectively right and wrong factual answers.)

At the end of ten minutes, each person in the out group reports his or her observations to the in group, by whipping around the outer circle in turn. During this time, the in group must remain completely silent.

When the out group is finished, the groups change seats and the process is repeated, either with the same topic or with a new one. After the second round, the ins and the outs may want to form one big group to discuss either the original topic or the communication process.

FOLLOW-UP

Have the students make a list of what helps and what hinders communication in a small group discussion. The list might include such things as: listen carefully and build on what has been said before; give everyone who wants to talk a chance to do so; respect other people's right to feel different about some things.

VARIATION

The structure of *In/Out Discussion Groups* can also be used very effectively without giving students the task of observing communication processes. The in group can discuss a topic or problem and the out group can simply listen, without comment, to what is being said. They have their chance to discuss the topic or problem when the groups reverse.

Positive Focus Game[8]

PURPOSE

The Positive Focus Game is an extremely useful technique for helping students understand and develop some of the basic communication skills so important in a personalized classroom. Through this game, students learn to focus their attention completely on the person who is talking, to hear everything he has to say without interrupting or disagreeing, to respect his rights to feel differently about things, and to try to really understand how he feels. In addition, this strategy goes a long way toward building self-concept because it gives students a chance to receive total attention, to feel that what they have to say is important.

PROCEDURE

Have each student write his reaction to a values question, problem, controversial statement, or some other values-related stimulus. (See strategies in Part II.) Then divide the class into trios.

Within each trio, one person volunteers to be the focus of the group for five minutes. The focus person briefly reads or states his reaction to the stimulus. Then the other two people in the group try to find out more about what the focus person thinks by following these three rules:

1. *Rule of Focusing:*   The focus person is to be the absolute center of attention for the entire five minutes. The other two group members must do nothing to turn the group's attention to themselves. This means they cannot debate, disagree, express their opinion, or talk about their experiences. They must hold in all their ideas and opinions, and express them when they are the focus person.

2. *Rule of Drawing Out:*   The other two people should do everything they can to draw out the focus person and find out as much as possible about what he thinks, and why he thinks this. This can be done primarily by asking questions. The questions should be ones that help the focus person clarify his ideas for himself and for the rest of the group; they should not probe to find out more than the person evidently wants to reveal. The questions also should not be designed to lead the focus person in a direction that the questioner thinks he *should* go, rather than in a direction that really helps the focus person clarify his thinking. If the focus person feels the questions are too probing, or lead him in a

direction he doesn't want to go, he should state this.

3. *Rule of Acceptance:* The two questioners should try to accept the focus person completely and let him know that they are trying hard to understand his point of view. They do not have to agree with what the person says, but they must agree with his right to say it. Even if they disagree with what he is saying, they should only give the focus person positive feedback by saying things like "I understand what you are saying," or "I can see how you feel that way" or just nodding and smiling. The only time to disagree with what the person has said is when it becomes your turn to be the focus person. It is difficult not to give negative feedback to someone when you strongly disagree with him, but it becomes easier each time you play this game. The questioners should be careful that they don't give subtle negative feedback through frowns, tone of voice, and the way questions are worded.

At the end of five minutes, the teacher stops the groups and asks them to do a brief evaluation of how well they are following the rules of the game. Each person draws three continuums on his paper, one continuum for each of the three rules. The continuums range from 1 (low) to 10 (high). Then each person places the two questioners' initials on the continuums to represent how well each questioner followed the rules. (Since the focus person was not supposed to follow any rules, his initials are not on the continuums.) The focus person rates the two questioners, and each questioner rates himself and the other questioner. For example, on the continuums below Billy was a questioner, so he rated himself and Susie, but not Jack, the focus person.

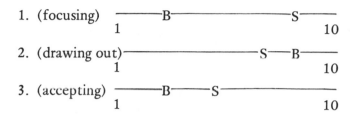

1. (focusing)
2. (drawing out)
3. (accepting)

These continuums are not discussed at this time, but should be put aside for later.

Another person then volunteers to be the focus person and the game is played for another five minutes. At the end of that time, the teacher again stops the groups and asks them to do three evaluation continuums. When these are completed, allow ten minutes for each group to share both sets of evaluation continuums.

After these discussions are complete, the third person in each group should have five minutes to be the focus person.

VARIATION

Game of It[9] :   This is a simplified version of *The Positive Focus Game*, designed for early elementary students. The focus person is "it" for two minutes. The other two people are asked to really listen to the "it" person, not to talk except to ask questions, and not to criticize or disagree with the "it" person. At the end of the two minutes, the other two people try to remember what the "it" person has said and repeat it back to him.

FURTHER SUGGESTIONS

This game is so important that we recommend that it be played on a regular basis, at least once every two weeks, with a different discussion topic each time. After the students really understand the rules and have become skilled at following them, the evaluation part of the game can be eliminated.

When a classroom discussion becomes a heated debate in which everyone seems to want to talk at once, suggest that the class form trios and play *The Positive Focus Game* for fifteen minutes so that everyone gets a chance to be heard.

Also, the structure of this game can be very effectively used to discuss content-area topics. For example, the focus person might discuss his interpretation of a poem, what caused a particular war, or even how to solve a written problem in math.

SOLVING HUMAN RELATIONS PROBLEMS IN THE PERSONALIZED CLASSROOM[10]

The next three strategies are designed to help both students and teachers to learn to use "I messages," active listening, and no-lose conflict resolution. Even though our limited treatment will serve only as a brief introduction, we feel that these ideas and skills are so important in personalizing human relationships in the classroom that we could not leave them out of this book. We strongly urge those who find these strategies to be useful to read Thomas Gordon's *Parent Effectiveness Training*[11] (PET), from which the ideas and skills come, and seek training in these methods from the appropriate sources.

PET theory states that whenever a problem arises between two or more persons, someone in the relationship owns the problem. There are three possibilities: it is either *mine, yours,* or *ours*.

When the problem is *mine*, I am the one who feels bothered. The other person or persons who bug me do not feel that there is any problem. They are not bothered. For example, let's say several students are working together very noisily on a group project. The noise that they make does not bother them, but it does bother me, as the teacher, because I find it difficult to concentrate and talk quietly with other students. The problem is *mine*. Instead of ordering the noisy students to "be quiet," which Gordon says is a "You message," the teacher would be more effective sending an "I message." In this case, he might say to the group, "I realize you are really involved in what you are doing, but when you talk so loud, I can't concentrate on what I'm doing." By so doing, he avoids placing blame and making them feel guilty or defensive, which would probably have been the result had he said, "Will you *please* be quiet?!"

When a person is:

1. *Put down* ("You're just trying to see how far you can push me.")

2. *Preached or Moralized to* ("You ought to know better.")

3. *Ridiculed* ("You dummy.")

4. *Criticized* ("You never get anything right.")

5. *Given Solutions* ("This is the way you ought to do it.")

6. *Ordered* ("Do your homework!")

the chances of that person modifying his or her behavior is reduced.

An "I message" lets the other person know in a non-judgmental way how *you feel* because of his or her behavior. "You are just plain lazy" is a "You message." "*I* feel disappointed when you miss our meetings because I count on your advice," is an "I message."

The reason that "I messages" are usually more successful than "You messages" is because "I messages" accurately and honestly reflect the effect of the other person's behavior on *you*. This is far less threatening than suggesting that there is something wrong or bad about the other person because his or her behavior upsets you. "I messages" place the responsibility for altering behavior on the other person. "I feel disappointed when you miss our meetings because I count on your advice," gives the other person the opportunity to change his behavior, if he chooses, without having to defend himself.

When the problem is *yours, you* are the one who feels bothered by our relationship. I (or others) do not feel that there is any problem. When I become aware that you feel there is a problem, the most effective thing I can do is to use active listening. For example, several students might feel that I, as the teacher, am demanding too much work from them.

Rather than defend my position or ignore the students, each of which will probably serve only to intensify the students' feelings of frustration, Gordon suggests that I try to actively listen to their feelings by reflecting back to them my understanding of what they say and feel. By so doing, I set the stage for resolving the problem on a no-lose basis.

When the problem is both yours and mine—that is to say, *ours*—no-lose conflict resolution is the most effective strategy. This avoids the resentments that often build up when someone loses and someone wins.

As a teacher, you should make a habit of using these strategies in appropriate situations. Students will tend to follow your example. But don't be discouraged if they do not learn them quickly. "I messages," active listening, and no-lose conflict resolution are difficult skills and processes to learn. They require a good deal of understanding and lots of practice. This is why we so strongly suggest that after trying out these strategies, you seek further experience and training from a certified PET/TET[12] trainer.

Worksheet

Instructions: Use this worksheet when you feel that there is a problem in your relationship with another person(s) and/or when you become aware that someone else is feeling upset.

1. What is the problem? Briefly state the problem in such a way that the blame is not placed on anyone. Instead, talk about your feelings in relation to the problem.

2. Who owns the problem? (Check one of the following.)

    _____ A. The problem is *mine*. I am the one who is upset. No one else in the relationship feels upset.

    _____ B. The problem is *yours*. You are the one(s) who feel(s) upset. I (and others) do not feel upset.

    _____ C. The problem is *ours*. We both (all) feel upset by what is going on (or has taken place) in our relationship.

If you check Item A, and feel that you must attempt to modify the other person's (or persons') behavior,[13] try sending an "I message." *See page 65* for further instructions.

If you checked Item B, try to use active listening with the other person(s) who feel(s) upset. *See page 70* for further instructions.

If you checked Item C, try to use no-lose conflict resolution with the other person(s) involved in the relationship. *See page 75* for further instructions.

"I Messages"[14]

PURPOSE

When one person wants to modify another's behavior, "I messages" let the other person know (1) how his or her behavior makes you feel, and (2) that you trust him or her to respect your needs by modifying his or her behavior appropriately. "You messages" tend to teach students that they are not responsible for changing their behavior, while "I messages" make it clear that such responsibility really rests with the persons who have received the "I message" rather than with the sender.

This strategy is designed to help students learn to make and send "I messages" when they own the problem.

PROCEDURE

Introduce students to "I messages" with a brief discussion of who owns the problem; *see page 61* of this book or pages 63-64 of *Parent Effectiveness Training*. Give several examples of the difference between "I messages" and "You messages."

Then, pass out the worksheet on *page 66* and have students complete it alone.

When students finish, follow up the activity in one or both of the following ways:

One, have students form pairs, trios, or small groups and share and compare their responses. Suggest that students try to put themselves in the shoes of those involved in the conflict situations.

Two, have students role play the conflict situations, first using "You messages," then using "I messages." Afterwards, have them make "I learned . . . " statements and discuss their learnings.

VARIATIONS

Have students brainstorm a list of conflict situations in which only one person owns the problem. Place these on a worksheet and follow the above procedure.

Some teachers like to schedule on a regular basis "I message" circles. During this period, students and teacher pull their chairs into a circle and for ten minutes anyone may give someone else an "I message." The messages, however, must be positive "I messages." For example, John might say to Paul, "I felt really good when you offered to help me with my homework because I feel you want to be my friend," and so on.

Worksheet[15]

Instructions: The chart below lists conflict situations (Column I) in which only one person owns the problem. In Column II, for each solution, write a typical "You message" that might be sent in that situation. See the example provided for Situation 1. In Column III, write an "I message" for each situation. See the example provided for Situation I.

If you have trouble phrasing "I messages," try using the following sentence construction by filling in the appropriate blanks. "I feel_____when you_____ because I_____."

Avoid "I messages" that are really disguised "You messages." In Situation 1 below, "I feel nervous about your safety, so you'd better be in by 12:00, *or else*," is as much a "You message" as "You'd better be in by 12:00, *or else*.

I. CONFLICT SITUATION	II. YOU MESSAGE	III. I MESSAGE
1. A father is upset because his daughter often arrives home after her midnight curfew.	*"You'd better* be in by 12:00, *or else.*	"I would feel better if you would be home by midnight *because I'm concerned about your safety* late at night."
2. A child is upset because an older brother refuses to share the family bicycle.		
3. A mother is upset with her son when he sits down to watch TV because she feels his chores should come first.		
4. The teacher is talking with a student when another student interrupts the conversation for the third time.		

5. Sharon promises to return a book to Helen. After a friendly reminder, she again forgets the book.

6. John makes plans to meet his friend Peter at the park. John shows up 40 minutes late and offers no excuse or apology.

7. Linda leaves her older sister's room a mess after playing with her stuffed animals.

8. The teacher promises to keep an eye on Janet's lunch while she runs an errand for her. When Janet returns, the teacher has stepped out of the room and part of Janet's lunch is missing.

9. Students working on a team project are so loud that others in the room are having difficulty working.

When you complete the worksheet, compare your responses with the ones in the Key below.

KEY

YOU MESSAGE	I MESSAGE
2. "You hog! You never let me use the bike."	"I feel angry when you don't share our bicycle."
3. "You lazy bum! All you ever do is watch football. Now take out the trash this minute!"	"I get angry when you watch TV before you do your chores because it makes me feel that all the responsibility of the house is on me."
4. "Will you *please* stop interrupting us!"	"I get upset when you keep interrupting because it makes us take longer to finish."
5. "I'll never lend you a book again if you don't remember to return it."	"I feel irritated when you forget to return my book because I need it to finish a report."
6. "Where have you been?! I've been waiting here for over 40 minutes! You're never on time!"	"I feel frustrated when you show up 40 minutes late because I have many other things to do this afternoon."

7. "Linda, you're a slob! That is the last time I'm letting you play in my room."	"Linda, when you leave my room messy, I get angry because I have to clean it up."
8. "You *promised* to watch my lunch!"	"I know you are very busy, but when you didn't keep an eye on my lunch, I felt let down."
9. "Will you kids quiet down? You are acting like wild animals."	"I know you are really involved, but when you talk so loud, I have trouble concentrating on my work."

Active Listening[16]

PURPOSE

When someone else in the relationship owns the problem, active listening is one of the most effective strategies to use. It differs from passive listening in that instead of remaining silent when the other person is talking about his or her concern, the listener periodically reflects back to the speaker in a few words his or her understanding of the speaker's words and feelings. Active listening often works like magic: when the speaker has a chance to voice his or her feelings, the problem may simply disappear. In cases where the problem still remains, active listening helps the speaker on the way to a solution.

Active listening also serves to help create a climate of trust and acceptance in the classroom.

PROCEDURE

Provide students with a copy of the worksheet below. Their first task is to complete it alone.

Then, divide the class into groups of four or five. In these groups, they are to share and compare their individual responses, and try to arrive at a consensus response for each of the given comments. When they finish, distribute the key of suggested answers.

Worksheet

Instructions: Read each of the following comments and circle the response below it which comes closest to what you think you would say to this person. Then check the key on *pages 73-74* to see what kind of a response you chose.

COMMENT 1

Why do some people talk all the time in class when they have nothing to say? It makes me angry. I wish they would just shut up! They're only trying to impress the teacher.

1. You really shouldn't be so critical of others. What is apparent to you might not be apparent to them.

2. You think some people talk in class to win points with the teacher.

3. I get pretty dismayed by some of the things people say in class, too.

4. You think some people talk unproductively in class and it makes you angry.

5. Do you also get the impression that a lot of this kind of business goes on after class around the teacher's desk?

COMMENT 2

I always seem to do the wrong thing. I'm just a jerk.

1. You feel like the worst person in the whole world.

2. How long have you felt this way?

3. You feel you never do anything right.

4. I feel that way sometimes, too.

5. You should know better than to run yourself down. You'll never get anywhere that way.

COMMENT 3

Just leave me alone! I don't want to talk with anyone or do anything with anybody. No one cares about me.

1. I felt just like that one time.

2. That's a stupid thing to say.

3. You're upset and you don't want to talk with anyone because you feel no one cares about you.

4. Has someone hurt you badly?

5. You feel like people hate you.

COMMENT 4

I don't want to play with Jim anymore. He's a dummy, and he's selfish and mean.

1. You are threatened by him so you don't want to play with him anymore.

2. It isn't nice to call someone a *dummy*.

3. You're angry with Jim because you feel he is selfish and mean.

4. I know how you feel.

5. What did you do to him?

KEY

❶		❷		❸		❹	
1.	E	1.	I	1.	S	1.	I
2.	I	2.	P	2.	E	2.	E
3.	S	3.	U	3.	U	3.	U
4.	U	4.	S	4.	P	4.	S
5.	P	5.	E	5.	I	5.	P

E = Evaluative: a remark that classifies and places some kind of a label on a statement.

S = Supportive: a remark which says "I agree with you" or "I feel that way too."

I = Interpretive: a response that goes beyond what is included in the original remark. It attempts to place the speaker in a position he may not feel he belongs in.

P = Probing: a response which attempts to find the reasons for the original remarks.

U = Understanding: a response which reflects back to the speaker what he has said and/or what he feels and indicates that the listener understands and accepts the information conveyed, without trying to go beyond it, investigate it, or label it.

FOLLOW-UP

Hold a discussion among the entire class in which you present the idea of active listening. (For more information on this, consult Thomas Gordon's *Parent Effectiveness Training*, pp. 29-84.) Follow up the discussion of active listening in one or both of the following ways:

1.   Have students choose one of the situations on the worksheet, or create one of their own, and write a dialogue in which one person actively listens to the other. Then, have them evaluate each other's dialogues by placing the appropriate codes used in the key next to each statement by the active listener. An effective dialogue should be coded with mostly U's.

2.   Have students choose one of the situations on the worksheet, and in pairs, role play the persons involved. One student is to role play the person with the problem. The other is to use active listening. Students can tape their role plays and code the tape-recorded conversation as above.

As a teacher, you should use active listening as much as possible when students express their feelings and concerns. They will tend to follow your example and use active listening more themselves.

Conflict Resolution[17]

PURPOSE

When both or several people involved in a relationship "own the problem," no-lose conflict resolution is one of the most effective strategies for insuring that each person involved in the conflict is satisfied with the solution. No-lose conflict resolution helps to create a classroom climate where both students and teacher feel respected and in control of their lives. It does away with the power struggle which is characteristic of so many classrooms.

PROCEDURE

Divide students into pairs, and provide each pair with a dittoed sheet of the sample conflict situations on *page 76.* Each pair selects one of the conflict situations with one student role playing one side of the conflict while the second student plays the other side. Their goal is to resolve the conflict by using the five-step process below so that each feels happy or satisfied with the mutually agreed-upon solution. (A person who is not involved in the conflict is sometimes helpful in this strategy as a "process observer" who later reports to the pair on their method of conflict resolution.)

We also suggest that you provide students with a copy of the five steps as outlined on *page 77,* and that you lead the pairs through each step by (1) introducing and explaining what is involved in the step, (2) giving an example of what might take place in the pairs, (3) checking to make sure the instructions are clear, (4) answering any questions students might have, and (5) setting a time limit for each step.

Sample Conflict Situations

1. Mr. Tate thinks Sharon will slough off and stop working if he grades her too easy. Sharon thinks Mr. Tate expects too much and grades her unfairly.

2. Mrs. Harris feels that John will take advantage of her if she is not tough on him in class. John feels that Mrs. Harris is too strict and is forcing him to find devious ways to meet his needs for independence and autonomy.

3. Linda and Anne share a locker together. Linda likes to keep all of her books and projects, a change of clothing, make-up, and other assorted items in her locker because it is so handy. Anne likes to keep only a few essential books and her coat in the locker so it won't be so messy. Each is upset by the other.

4. Mary and Bill are working together on a project. Mary feels that Bill is not contributing his share to the project. Bill feels that Mary is too "bossy" and won't let him contribute to the project in the way he thinks is best. They are at an impasse.

5. Jill and Larry both need to use the tape recorder for

several days. Each has selected a project which involves interviewing a number of students in the class and taping their responses. Jill wants to find out how her classmates feel about ecology. Larry wants to find out how his classmates feel about population control. There is not time enough before the projects are due for each of them to have a turn at the tape recorder. Thus they have decided to do a joint project which combines questions about ecology and population control. However, Jill feels that Larry's questions are too detailed. Larry feels that Jill is just skimming the surface. Each is upset with the other and valuable time is passing by quickly.

A Five-Step Process for Resolving Interpersonal Conflicts

Step 1:   *Formulating a Statement of the Problem.*   Each person involved in the conflict makes (or writes) a statement about the conflict as he or she views it. Most important, students should avoid blaming, criticizing, judging, ridiculing, shaming, or name-calling. The statement should take the form of an "I message." See the *"I Message"* strategy, *pages 65-70,* for details. Each person takes a turn making (or reading) his or her statement while the other person uses active listening *(see pages 70-74).*

Step 2:   *Clarifying the Dimensions of the Conflict.*   After each person has made his or her statement, the pair try to define the dimensions of the conflict, noting the specific areas of agreement and disagreement. Questions are allowed during this step, but they should be of a clarifying nature; probing questions are not allowed. "I messages" and active listening are to be used during this phase of the process.

Step 3: *Brainstorming All the Possible Solutions to the Conflict.*   When the dimensions of the conflict have been defined, the two students are then to brainstorm—shoot out ideas as fast as they can think of them—as many possible solutions to the conflict as they can think of in the time limit set by the teacher. Evaluation of the alternative solutions is not permitted.

Step 4: *Identifying the Consequences.*   Once the brainstorm of alternative solutions is completed, the pair turns its attention to identifying the consequences of each of the most viable solutions. Both the pros and the cons of each alternative should be listed.

Step 5: *Choosing a Mutually Acceptable Solution.*   Finally, the two evaluate each of the alternative solutions and attempt to select one that they can each be satisfied with. If the students cannot find a solution that is mutually acceptable, they are to return to Steps 2 and 3 above and repeat the process until they can arrive at a mutually acceptable solution.

FOLLOW-UP SUGGESTIONS

When students finish their role play, have them form into groups or re-form the whole class. Each pair should share the conflict situation they selected, the solutions they considered, and the one they finally arrived at, if they did. Then, have students share "I learned . . . " statements about the activity.

The *Five-Step Process for Solving Interpersonal Conflicts* can also be used when real conflict situations arise in the classroom. If students have previously been through the process in a role-play situation, it is then a matter of getting the persons involved calmed down so that they can rationally go through each of the above steps. Do not attempt to get students together when their tempers are still flaring. Chances are, they won't stick to the rules and the process will deteriorate into a name-calling session which won't help anyone.

Notes

1. This idea was passed on to us by Leonard Berman.
2. By Edward Betof.
3. By Edward Betof.
4. We learned this strategy from Jim Wilson, Associate Professor of Urban Education, Temple University.
5. By Edward Betof.
6. By Edward Betof.
7. By Edward Betof.
8. Developed by Saville Sax, co-author of *Reality Games*, New York, Popular Library, 1972.
9. Our thanks to Elliott Seif for the idea behind this variation.
10. Our thanks to Edward Betof for his early work in developing the strategies included in this section.
11. New York, Wyden, 1970.
12. Gordon offers workshops in both parent effectiveness training (PET) and teacher effectiveness training (TET).
13. Gordon suggests two additional ways to deal with the situation when one owns the problem; either to modify the environment or to modify oneself. See pages 107 and 139-143 in *Parent Effectiveness Training* for more on these strategies.
14. Gordon, *op. cit.*
15. Developed by Edward Betof.
16. From the work of Thomas Gordon and Carl Rogers.
17. This strategy is a synthesis of several conflict-resolving strategies, most notably Saville Sax's "Conflict Resolution Game" in *Reality Games* (*op. cit.*), Gordon's Six Step "no-lose" method for resolving conflicts in *Parent Effectiveness Training* (*op. cit.*), and Merrill Harmin's "Game for Resolving Conflicts," available from the NEXTEP Program, Southern Illinois University, Edwardsville, Ill.

5. Building Students' Self-Concepts

IALAC[1]

PURPOSE

The IALAC Story, developed by Sid Simon, is the basis for this strategy, which is designed primarily to focus attention on self-concept. A student's self-concept is perhaps the most important single factor in determining the extent to which he or she becomes a self-actualizing person, to use Abraham Maslow's term for one who has fulfilled his basic needs and is able to live to achieve his human potential. Developing a good self-concept in each student, then, must be a primary focus of personalized education. This strategy helps students and teachers recognize the many ways we unconsciously affect each other's sense of self-worth by the little things we say and do each day.

PROCEDURE

Explain to students: "As each of us wakes up each morning, we pin on a big IALAC sign, proclaiming to the world, "*I Am*

Lovable And Capable." As we go through the day, our sign gets bigger or smaller depending on how others treat us. Each time someone says or does something that makes us feel good about ourselves, our sign grows a little bigger. Each time someone says or does something that makes us feel less lovable or less capable, a piece of our sign gets ripped off."

At this point, you might read all or part of Simon's *IALAC Story*, if you have it available. If not, create and tell a short story of your own, about a day in the life of a student, illustrating various ways that his IALAC sign is reduced or enlarged by different things that happen to him during the day. Or, use or adapt the one we have provided *(page 83)*. Then ask students to give some more examples of ways that people build or tear each other's signs.

Next, hand out uniform pieces of manila paper and ask each student to make an IALAC sign for himself. Explain that for the rest of the day, students are to wear these signs, putting them on with masking tape. The tape should be centrally located in the room, along with some scraps of manila, so that it is readily available for this strategy. Any time during the day that something happens to make them feel less lovable and capable, they are to rip a piece from their sign. If something happens to make them feel more lovable and capable, they can add to their signs. At the end of the day, the students can divide into small groups and discuss their day's experiences.

By the way, the teacher should not forget to wear a sign himself. It is amazing to see the effective feedback one can give without moralizing, judging, or saying a word—simply by ripping a piece of your sign!

VARIATION

When a student wishes to build on another student's IALAC sign, he or she may write a positive message on the sign and initial it.

NOTE: We feel very strongly that the message of the *IALAC Story* is so important that it should be required reading for anyone who deals with children or adolescents. The story is available in bulk (10 copies or more) from Argus Communications, 7440 Natchez Ave., Niles, Ill. 60648. Individual copies may be obtained by sending 50 cents per copy to the Philadelphia Humanistic Education Center, 8504 Germantown Avenue, Phila., Penna. 19118.

THE STORY OF WALTER KELLER

Walter Keller is a 7th grader. This is a story of what happens during a typical day to Walter's IALAC sign. At 7:15 A.M., Walter awakens to the sound of his mother's voice, "Walter! You lazy bum! Get down here this minute! You're going to miss the bus." (*Rip.*) Walter hurriedly gets ready for school. At 7:30, he sits down to breakfast and tips over his milk. It looks like another bad day ahead for Walter. (*Rip.*)

At 7:36, Walter boards the school bus. Two neighbor girls laugh at his new haircut as he sits down in the seat in front of them. (*Rip.*) At 8:24, the school bus arrives at school. Walter takes a minute to go to the bathroom before rushing to his first-hour class. However, just before he gets to the classroom door, the late bell rings. Mr. Williams says he's late—15 minutes detention. (*Rip.*) Furthermore, Mr. Williams announces a spot quiz over the assigned chapter on India; last night Walter had decided to watch a CBS Special on Africa instead of doing his geography homework. (*Rip.*)

It's 9:15, math class. Mrs. Dunlow gives Walter back a test with a big red 97 at the top. As she hands it to him she says, "You got three wrong, Walter." (*Rip.*)

At 10:00, there is a special honors assembly. Walter sits for 45 minutes watching his friends receive awards for things he just can't seem to do as well, no matter how hard he tries. (*Rip.*)

Science class is at 10:45. Mr. Peters, the science teacher, is also the baseball coach. Walter wants to make the baseball team and feels he might improve his chances if he made a good impression in Mr. Peters' class. He has decided to try harder, even though he hates science. Today, Mr. Peters asks the class a question. Walter raises his hand. Mr. Peters responds, "Walter, put your hand down or I might have to call on you; I don't want you to make a fool of yourself." (*Rip.*)

Lunch comes at 11:30. Walter wants to impress a new girl who has just enrolled in school. As he walks by her table, a buddy sticks out his foot, sending Walter and his lunch sprawling to the floor. (*Rip.*)

Gym class is at 12:05 P.M. Walter tries to run five laps around the gym on a full stomach. It gives him heartburn. (*Rip.*)

One o'clock is art class. Mrs. Goldman tells Arthur Dillman that she likes his painting of a fruit basket better than Walter's sculpture of a swastika. (*Rip.*)

English class is at 1:45. Mrs. Tanner makes everyone who missed a spelling word on the spelling test write the word 100 times. Walter missed 13. (*Rip.*)

Two-thirty is detention. (*Rip.*) At 2:47, Walter arrives in the locker room to suit up for baseball try-outs. Coach Peters tells Walter not to bother. "If you can't make it on time, the team doesn't need you," he says. (*Rip.*)

At 5:15, Walter arrives home on the late bus. His mother, who has had her IALAC sign ripped to shreds at a department-store clearance sale, yells as he enters the door, "Walter, don't slam the door! I have a terrific headache." (*Rip.*) The rest of the evening doesn't go any better. At 8:45, Walter climbs into bed and falls asleep. And wouldn't you know it—even his dreams are trouble. He dreams that he is being chased by a mad dog. (*Rip.*)

Some days are just like that. Maybe tomorrow will be different.

My Time[2]

PURPOSE

One of the most important lessons that a student can learn in school is that he is capable and worthy enough to have some class time devoted completely to him. This lesson is simple in structure but powerful in its effect on the building of self-concept. In addition, it allows students to make choices that are important to them, and to act on those choices by sharing something of themselves with classmates. The sharing also makes this strategy useful in developing a sense of community within the class or group.

PROCEDURE

Class or group time should be planned so that opportunities are set aside for *My Time*. This is a chance for students to voluntarily lead the whole class, or a group of students, in any activity of his or her choice. For instance, one student may use the time to relate a story that is important to him, while another student may explain a project that she is working on so that other students can evaluate it. A third student may teach other students the rules of a game or the method of origami.

The ways that *My Time* can be used are endless. The most important rule to follow as a teacher is that *you provide the time* and the student *decides how to use it*. In order to allow all students an equal opportunity to use the time that is provided, we suggest the following:

1. Schedule *My Time* on a regular basis.

2. Schedule it so that at least once every few weeks each student has an opportunity to lead *My Time*.

3. No student should be given a second opportunity to lead until every other student who wants to has had a chance.

4. Leading *My Time* should be a voluntary activity. A schedule should be made where students can sign up ahead of time to be the leader. This will enable the student to plan the time usefully.

5. The amount of time that is provided should be adapted to grade level so that *My Time* can be used with children of all ages.

6. In an open, or choice-centered classroom, *My Time* can be scheduled by the students themselves whenever they have something to share.

VARIATIONS

Use *My Time* with smaller groups of students.

Or, use it as a tutoring experience: allow students to pick a subject that they are good at and to "practice teach" students who need help in that area.

"I Can..." Statements[3]

PURPOSE

"I Can..." Statements is one of those very simple but powerful strategies that can be used over and over again in the classroom to build up students' feelings of "I can-ness."

PROCEDURE

On one of those rainy, dreary days when everyone seems to be feeling down, stop everything and do *"I Can..." Statements*. Explain to the class that whenever anyone thinks of something that he or she can do, they are to call it out.

Example: "I can tie my shoes by myself!" If students have trouble thinking of things, have them sit quietly for a minute or two and write down at least one thing they can do before calling out; also place several examples of things they can do on the chalkboard. Let the calling out go on until just before students tire of the activity. Notice how *"I Can..." Statements* lift the class spirits.

VARIATION

Have students keep a list in their notebooks of all the things they can do. Every time they learn to do something new, they are to add it to the list.

Strength Lists and Whips

PURPOSE

The purpose of *Strength Lists and Whips* is to help students focus on their assets; the ultimate goal is to build their self-concept.

PROCEDURE

Ask students to take out a sheet of paper and, in the next five minutes, list as many of their strengths as they can. Or, have them list things that they really like about themselves. Explain that the list is to be private; no one else will see it unless the student wishes to share something on his list.

When students finish, ask them to put their lists in their notebooks or folders, but to keep the lists handy because they will be recording new assets every week.

Then, have students pull their chairs or desks into a circle or several small circles. Whipping around the circle, each student takes the opportunity to share something he wrote on his strength list, or to pass. When the strength whip is completed, volunteers may talk more about what they wrote and why. No one in the group should be put on the spot, however. This should be a sharing experience, not a defending one.

At first students may be reluctant to share their strengths. Part of this may be due to the fact that to do so might be considered bragging, which they have been taught is wrong. Explain the difference between a boastful, competitive kind of pride, and the kind of pride that says, "Hey, I'm good at this and I'd just like to have you know it." Another reason for some students' reluctance may be a feeling that they do not have any strengths. However, as time goes on, students will begin to find something they can become good at just so they can be part of the whip. Accordingly, fewer passes may indicate increases in self-concept.

VARIATIONS

Have students make a collage of their strengths using drawings, clippings from newspapers, or pictures from magazines.

Or, have students make up an advertisement or commercial about themselves in which their strengths and assets are portrayed.

"Mirror, Mirror"

PURPOSE

This is a variation on the previous strategy, but it is so useful that we want to emphasize it by setting it off as a separate strategy. Its purpose is to build a strong feeling of self-worth within the student.

PROCEDURE

Find a mirror. The round one by Creative Playthings made from metal with a wood frame is perfect, but any small mirror that can be easily passed around a group will do. Ask the class to form into a circle. Introduce the strategy by recalling the story of Snow White and the magic mirror:

> *Mirror, Mirror on the wall,*
> *Who's the fairest one of all?*

Explain that you have a mirror very much like that mirror, but with this one you must say:

> *Mirror, Mirror, say what you see,*
> *Say what you like the best about me.*

Each student in turn is to hold the mirror up to his ear and think what he likes best about himself; it is as if the mirror were really telling him. He puts the mirror down and reports to the group what the mirror said. The mirror is then passed to the next student. The process is repeated until all students in the circle have had a turn or have passed.

VARIATIONS

Have students pass the mirror around the circle asking the same question, but rather than putting it to their own ear, they put it to the ear of their neighbor. He thinks of something he likes best about the person holding the mirror and reports this to the group. The process is repeated by passing the mirror on to the next person.

Or, you can attach the mirror to the wall (a larger one can be used) and place above it a sign that reads:

Mirror, Mirror on the wall,
What about me do you like best of all?

Students are then to look into the mirror and make a list of the things they like best about themselves. This variation can be used in a choice-centered classroom; *see page 460.*

Strength Sharing

PURPOSE

Strength Sharing provides a way for students to openly share all the good things about each other that they can think of, thus building self-concept. It is also a valuable tool for dealing with the honest acceptance of praise.

PROCEDURE

Divide the class into groups of six to nine people. One member volunteers to be the focus. Each student writes all the complimentary things that he can think of about the focus person. After a few minutes, students tell the focus person some of the good things that they have written about him. Repetition of compliments should not be discouraged, because it tends to reinforce the original compliments. Stress that one rule should never be compromised: students *must* believe what they say. Repeat the process until each group member has been the focus.

When the last person has taken his turn at the focus, have the students talk about how they felt when they were the focus. Was it difficult? Embarrassing? Enjoyable?

NOTE: This strategy can be successful only after the students have been together long enough to really know each other. Also, don't use the strategy if there is a chance that one of the students won't be given any strengths.

Strengths Game

PURPOSE

In this game, the student gets in touch with some things about himself that he prizes or feels good about. Others in the group give him positive feedback by trying to guess what he wrote. This often results in a strengthened self-concept.

PROCEDURE

Students divide into groups of six to eight of their own choosing. Provide each student with a 3 x 5 card and a grid upon which to copy his responses *(see page 94).* Have them complete the following steps:

1. Complete the sentence stem, *My two greatest strengths are. . . .* Write it on your 3 x 5 card. Do not let others in the group see the card.

2. Someone in the group should now collect the 3 x 5 cards. Hand them to the collector with the writing face down. The collector should now shuffle the cards.

3. Each group member draws a card. It does not matter if you receive your own card in the draw. Keep it, and do not reveal that you are the author.

4. Going around the group, each member reads the response to the unfinished sentence which appears on his card. If you have trouble making out the words or handwriting, do the best you can; and do not ask for help. The person who wrote the response should not reveal himself even if the response is read wrong. If the response is incomprehensible or blank, simply note it and go on to the next person.

5. As the responses are read, each group member should copy them or the key words onto the grid which has been provided. They should be placed in Column No. 1.

6. Privately guess the name of the person in your group who wrote each response. Keeping your grid covered, enter this in Column No. 2.

7. Now you are ready to play the guessing part of the game. As a group, discuss who thinks who wrote each

Grid for the

	1. 3 X 5 CARD RESPONSES	2. FIRST GUESS
1.		
2.		
3.		
4.		
5.		
6.		
7.		
etc.		

response and why. The why is important because this is the feedback part of the game. You are telling the person how you view him or her. It is important to discuss the items randomly so that no one is revealed. This can be done by focusing on one response at a time, making such comments as, "I think 'persistence' is Frank." "I disagree; I think it is Laura because. . ." and so on. If your classmates correctly guess you as the author, you can throw them off the track by sug-

Strengths Game

3. REVISED GUESS	4. REAL AUTHOR

gesting that you think it might be someone else in the group.

8.   When all of the responses have been discussed, each group member makes another private assessment and revises his first list if he feels it is necessary. Enter your revised guesses in Column No. 3.

9.   Now go around the group; each member is to reveal his identity. It is important that when you reveal, you

discuss some of the reasons for your response if you have any.

10.   Discuss the feedback you received. Did people in the group see you the same way you see yourself? What were the similarities? What were the differences?

VARIATIONS

Complete the following sentence stem to read as a metaphor. For example, *I feel best when I am a rose.*

I feel best when I am. . .

Or, complete the sentence stem below:

Two things I do very well are:

Or, complete the sentence stem below:

Two famous people I identify with are:

One of our favorite variations is called *Student of the Week*. Each week (or day) the teacher chooses a different student in the class and makes a list of his or her strengths, talents, and other positive qualities. The list is posted so students can guess who the student is by writing their guess below the attributes. At the end of the week, the teacher reveals the true identity of the student.

A "Me Tree"

PURPOSE

This strategy is designed to help students identify their strengths and accomplishments as a means of promoting their feelings of self-worth.

PROCEDURE

Have students draw large "Me Trees" on newsprint, or provide them with a smaller dittoed copy of a Me Tree *(see page 98)*. On the roots, students write, draw symbols, or paste pictures of all of their strengths and talents/abilities—one strength or talent per root. On the branches, students write, draw symbols, or paste pictures of all of their accomplishments and successes—one per branch. Some roots and branches should be left empty so that new elements can be added as they happen in the future.

Then, students place their names on the trunks of the Me Trees and post the completed trees around the room. Students may fill in the empty roots and branches whenever they develop a new strength or accomplish something new. Encourage students to point out each other's strengths and talents.

VARIATIONS

Once each week, take five to ten minutes to whip quickly around the class, giving each student a chance to share something that he has added to his Me Tree that week. Students should be allowed to pass.

Another option is to pair students and have them do Me Trees for each other.

Or, one student each week can be selected to be the "Me Tree Student of the Week." Each student in the class writes, draws a symbol, or pastes a picture of at least one strength, ability, or accomplishment they think belongs on that student's Me Tree.

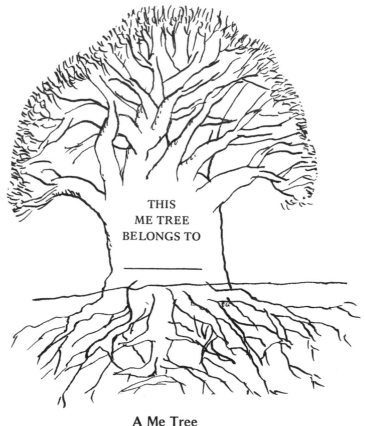

THIS
ME TREE
BELONGS TO

_____

A Me Tree

Messages About Me

PURPOSE

This activity has proven very successful in strengthening feelings of self-worth. It also provides an opportunity for students to decide what they prize about others and to publicly affirm these feelings.

PROCEDURE

Have one student lie on a piece of paper that is large enough for an outline of his body to be traced (or lean on paper that has been affixed to a wall). Trace the outline with a thick crayon or marking pen. Next, ask the class to write comments about the person on his outline which demonstrate a quality of the person that we *like, prize,* or *respect.* If the students cannot write, they should share their contribution verbally with the group, and let the teacher write it.

Stress that students should think about the outlined person's human qualities or characteristics, not about possessions of the student or his family. All comments should include the contributor's name. Stress that no negative comments are allowed.

Some examples of positive contributions are:

Johnny shares his toys.—BILLY

Johnny runs real fast.—SUZY

Johnny reads well.—WENDY

When the silhouette is filled with contributions, post it in the room.

NOTE: Always permit students to "pass" if they do not wish to be written about. Also, the teacher should not choose the order of students to be focused on in *Messages About Me*. Some method of random selection, such as picking numbers out of a hat, should be used to determine the order. Don't use the strategy if there is any possibility that one of the students would not receive any positive messages.

I'm Proud to Be Me—a Song

PURPOSE

An old camp song is the basis of this strategy. The goal is to help students focus on some of the things they like and are proud of about themselves. At the same time, the strategy helps them recognize that other people may be proud of different things for different reasons—hopefully, this recognition helps them accept and respect such differences.

PROCEDURE

Teach students the song, *I'm Proud to Be Me* (see below). Used by itself, without any follow-up, the song makes students feel it is okay to be proud of themselves for what

I'M PROUD TO BE ME

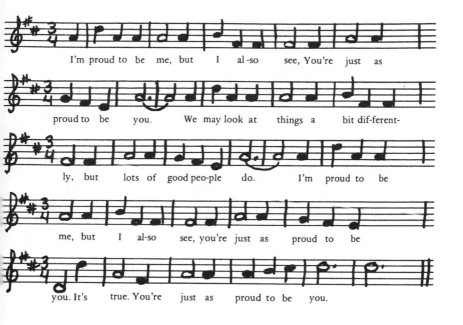

they are. Used with follow-up, the song helps set the stage for some very powerful self-image building activity.

For follow-up, stop the singing and ask five students to quickly share one thing that each likes about himself or is proud of, by completing the sentence stem "I'm proud to be me because. . . ." Then do another round of singing, share, sing again, and so on. Don't try to do the whole class in one session; fifteen students, five per round, is plenty. Hold another singing session later in the week and have the rest of the class share their "I'm proud to be me's."

Validation Statements[5]

PURPOSE

In our society, affirming publicly what we are proud of or what we do well is a difficult task. We learn early in life that it is risky to reveal the positive side of ourselves, especially in front of peers.

This strategy aids in removing some of the limits that people face in the prizing phase of the valuing process. It also helps people to distinguish between a healthy public affirmation of pride and bragging, a competitive type of pride where one sees oneself as better than others. Validation statements can also be an important method in building community trust and personal self-esteem.

PROCEDURE

Divide the class into groups of from six to ten people. Explain that validation time is set aside in order to assist each other in talking about things of which we are proud or skilled. During validation time, only positive things are to be discussed.

Within each group, one individual should have the attention of everyone else. He or she is called the focus person. The focus person begins with a statement that reflects some character trait or skill which he or she is proud of. For example, Sally might say: "I'm proud of the way I can control my temper." Henry might say: "I think that my athletic achievements are something to be proud of."

The other people in the group then validate the person's

statements by making comments which honestly reinforce the focus person's original statement. For the examples above, some validating statements might be: "Sally, when you were called a name last week, you just turned your back and walked away." Or, "You sure can hit a ball hard, Henry." After one person's statement has been validated, proceed so that everyone in the group has a chance.

NOTE: The teacher should discourage the use of negative statements ("I'm proud that I'm not fat."). Comments that are bragging in nature should be restated. A useful rule of thumb to differentiate between prizing and bragging is that bragging statements compare oneself to others in order to show superiority: e.g., "I can play the piano better than anyone in the class."

The option to pass is very important when a student's turn comes to be validated.

The teacher should make validating statements himself.

Validating statements should be used to reinforce the group trust level after the group knows each other well. It should not be an introductory strategy.

VARIATIONS

Have several people being validated at the same time if embarrassment is a problem.

Have large-group or whole-class validation sessions.

Post validation statements on the board.

In a group of students who don't know each other outside the classroom situation, you may need to narrow the topic to "things I'm proud of about the way I relate to other people," or a similarly circumscribed topic.

Animal Farm[6]

PURPOSE

This strategy is designed to help students get in touch with what they value about themselves by identifying with and acting out animal roles.

PROCEDURE

Tell the students that they are to choose the animal that they like best; if they have trouble thinking of animals, list some on the board. When they have selected their animal, they are to write about and/or share the following things:

1. What do I like best about this animal? (The way it looks, moves, what it represents, etc.)

2. How am I most like this animal?

3. How would I like to be more like this animal?

Then, let students volunteer to role play their animal in front of the group. This often gives students a chance to affirm a behavior pattern they like or try out some new behavior that is not typical of them but which they would like to adopt; for example, a shy student might choose to be a tiger and try out being more aggressive.

VARIATION

Have students select a famous person they like best. Students then answer the following three questions.

1. What do I like best about this famous person?

2. How am I most like this famous person?

3. How would I like to be more like this famous person?

Students then voluntarily role play the famous person they have selected.

Notes

1. IALAC is an acronym for I Am Lovable And Capable, created by Sidney B. Simon in his book *I Am Lovable and Capable*, Niles, Ill., Argus Communications, 1973.
2. By Ed Betof.
3. We thank Donna Lydick for the idea behind this strategy.
4. Our thanks to Sylvia Rae for her contributions to this strategy.
5. The idea of validating was learned from Marianne Simon and comes out of Harvey Jackins' work in Re-evaluation Counseling. This strategy was written by Edward Betof.
6. The idea for this strategy came from Stuart R. Shafer.

PART II

PERSONALIZING GOALS IN THE CLASSROOM

6. *Introduction to Part II*

In a personalized classroom, the students *own* the goals. The teacher does not force his or the school's goals upon the student. This is a dramatic shift from what goes on in most conventional classrooms in our country. Traditionally, curriculum experts or textbook writers have been called upon to write the objectives for schools. In this arrangement, teachers are viewed as instructional agents who work in such a way that these objectives are achieved.

The difficulty with this view of teaching and learning is that students become simply the recipients of instruction aimed at achieving X number of objectives. In most cases, the students have little or no understanding of what the goals are, or why these are important, or how achieving them will help them become better persons or thinkers or whatever. As a result, students often have very little motivation for achieving the objectives and thus developing the skills and concepts associated with them. Perhaps this is one of the major reasons why students today retain so little of what they are taught in our schools.[1]

In the personalized classroom, students are the source of

their own learning goals and objectives. Their concerns, needs, interests, and values are the basis for learning and teaching. This is not to say that the goals of the teacher, school, or community do not enter into the picture. They do, and should; however, these goals are important in directing learning only to the extent that they mesh with or actually become the students' own goals.

The problem faced by teachers who are committed to personalizing goals in the classroom is that many students come to school without clear and consistent goals, or without any goals at all. The job then becomes one of helping these students sort out their confusing and conflicted world and make some sense out of their lives. Thus, much attention must be paid in the classroom to helping students learn to clarify their values and to find out what is worth learning, doing, and living for. Only when students have done this can they begin to set and achieve their own learning goals.

This part of the book provides a number of strategies which the teacher can use to help students learn to clarify their values, make better choices and decisions, set their own learning goals, and take action to become the persons they want to become.

We have divided this part of the book into three sections to correspond with the valuing process of *choosing, prizing,* and *acting.*[2] Since such skills as decision making, risk taking, goal setting, and action planning are a vital part of the valuing process, we have not included specific sections or strategies to teach these skills. However, we have noted in the *Purpose* of the strategies when these skills are also being taught.

One of the major reasons we have divided Part II into the three sections of *choosing, prizing,* and *acting* is to emphasize that each strategy has a purpose directly related to the valuing process. This kind of division, however, presents a problem since a number of the strategies serve to teach more than one set of skills. We have placed the strategies where we think they best belong and have noted the other valuing skills which they also serve to develop.

We cannot stress enough that the strategies included in this part of the book are only a beginning. Although they are designed to teach students a process of valuing, this process must become a living part of the classroom if it is really to become effective. Using the strategies as an isolated segment of a school program, or simply as games, is not sufficient to help students develop clear, strong, and sound values.

Most of the strategies presented here are new strategies, and in part represent an attempt to fill some holes in the original V.C. publications. For example, only a few strategies found in either *Values and Teaching* or *Values Clarification* focus on the area of *choosing freely*. We have tried to remedy this situation by providing numerous strategies dealing with making free choices. Moreover, a few of the strategies presented here are important variations upon previously published strategies. These strategies are not designed to replace the originals, but to supplement them.

A WORD ABOUT USING THE STRATEGIES

The strategies can be used with the whole class, in small groups, or given as individual assignments. By posting the instructions, the strategies can be used in a self-instructional setting *(see page 547)*. A number of the strategies, like *My*

Personal Plan of Action (page 342), can be used again and again. Others, like *The Kidney Machine (page 243)*, are one-time strategies, although variations on the strategy can be created and used again. Also, most of the strategies are applicable to any grade level, and in some cases can be used with pre-school children. For use at the lower grades, the teacher will have to modify the language and simplify the instructions, and with a number of strategies, like *Let's Build a City (page 193)*, the whole task will have to be simplified. Finally, the strategies can be used to help teach subject matter *(see page 418)*.

The fact that we state the purpose of each strategy does not mean that the strategies cannot serve other purposes which may be unrelated, or indirectly related, to developing the valuing process. Our objective in the *Purpose* section is to show that each strategy is a small part of a whole process, but this should not prevent teachers from modifying or adapting the strategies to fit other educational objectives.

GUIDELINES FOR USING THE STRATEGIES[3]

The following guidelines must be followed if the strategies are to be used successfully:

1. The teacher must be accepting and non-judgmental of student responses. Nothing kills personal inquiry quicker than verbal or non-verbal indications that the teacher is looking for and willing to accept only "right answers." The teacher must never use values clarification strategies to moralize or teach "correct values."

2. The teacher must encourage other students to be accepting and non-judgmental, thus promoting a climate of respect, trust, openness, and diversity in the classroom.

3. The teacher must respect, and demand that others respect, individual privacy. He must allow students to "pass" or not participate in any personal inquiry and values activities.

4. The teacher must not grade students on the personal or values content of their written and verbal responses.

5. The teacher must respect and protect the confidentiality of student responses and not report personal information gained via the strategies to individuals outside the classroom.

6. The teacher must model the behavior he hopes to elicit from students and be willing to open himself to personal inquiry even if the questions that students ask are difficult. Of course, the teacher also has the right to "pass." The teacher should participate in the strategies whenever possible. Frequently, particularly in the lower grades, she may need to wait until all the students have answered before giving her own answer, because many students will have trouble accepting the idea that the teacher is not necessarily supplying the "right" answer. The teacher may need to repeat each time she answers, "This is my value but it doesn't have to be your value. I believe that each person has a right to hold his own values, even if they are very different from mine."

Notes

1. Some researchers estimate that most students retain as little as 5 percent of what they are taught in school.

2. For a discussion of the valuing process of choosing, prizing, and acting, *see page 19.*

3. We strongly recommend that teachers secure training in the use of these strategies. For a list of training centers and other materials available, write: The Philadelphia Center for Humanistic Education, 315 Wadsworth Avenue, Philadelphia, Pennsylvania 19119.

7. *Helping Students Become Aware of, Prize, and Publicly Affirm Their Values*

Dream House

PURPOSE

There are lots of ways we can gather data about ourselves to begin to answer the question, "What do I value?" One rather enjoyable, as well as productive way is to think about our dream house—what kind of a house would we really like to live in—and compare it with the dream houses of others. By thinking about what our house says about us, as well as by learning from others what they think it says about us, we can often learn a great deal about what we value and how we present ourselves to others. We can then decide whether we like what we see, or whether some changes are in order.

PROCEDURE

Introduce the strategy as a long-term, in-class project which students can work on periodically, or as a long-term homework assignment. The task is for students to design their ideal house. If they could live in any kind of house, large or small, new or old, fancy or rustic, "way out" or traditional, what kind of house would it be? They are to make two drawings of the house; one is to be an outside view and the other a floor plan. Stress that the drawings do not have to be elaborate, or even very good, just as long as students know what they mean by them. However, students can put as much creativity into their designs as they want by using colored inks, textures, models, etc.

Students are also to furnish the house by locating and arranging simple drawings of furniture on their floor plan. Squares can represent chairs, circles can represent tables, rectangles can represent beds, and so forth.

When students finish, they are to get together in pairs, trios, or small groups and compare their dream houses. The dream houses can then be posted around the room for all to see. After looking at the houses, students might note which houses, or parts of houses, they like better than their own, or changes they would now like to make in their own houses, having seen all the others.

As an optional follow-up activity, have students write statements of what they think their houses say about them—who they are and what they stand for. If students are not very sophisticated at this kind of analysis, give them several continuums and have them place themselves on each according to where they think they are. Use the following continuums or make up your own:

What does your dream house say about you in terms of your being a:

loner_____ grouper

optimist_____pessimist

conservative_____radical

free-wheeling sort _____orderly type

leader_____follower

city lover_____country lover

Students can also place their classmates' initials on the continuums to indicate what they think each dream house says about its designer; however, this alternative should be avoided unless the participants are volunteers who have developed considerable trust and concern for one another. Forcing students into this kind of activity, even though you feel it might be helpful, often does far more harm than good.

ADDITIONAL SUGGESTIONS

Young children, or students who do not draw very well, may like thumbing through magazines (or pictures of houses, floor plans, and furniture which you have already cut out) to find and put together their dream houses.

The activity is quite adaptable to teaching math skills such as measuring, computation, ratios, percentages, etc. For example, students can draw their dream houses to scale, compute the square footage of floor space, figure the percentage of floor space each room occupies in relation to the total floor space, etc. Or, home economics teachers might use a Sears catalog and have students try to furnish the house on a budget of so many dollars. Color coordinating and interior decorating can also become topics of discussion. English teachers might have students write themes about *My Dream House*. Social studies teachers might get into such topics as the history of Western architecture, the houses of different cultures around the world, how man's self-image affects the kind of house he builds and vice versa. The ideas seem limitless.

VARIATION

Have several students form a group and cooperatively design their dream house by following these rules:

> *Rule 1:* No one in the group is allowed to talk during the drawing of the house.
>
> *Rule 2:* Only one group member at a time may work on the house. He or she is to draw only one line and then pass the paper and pencil to another group member. The line must be continuous, and not double back upon itself.
>
> *Rule 3:* Each member of the group is to have a turn before any member has a second turn.

Following the completion of the house, each group member is to put pluses beside the things he likes about the house and minuses beside the things he dislikes. Then the group is to review the process and discuss their feelings and ratings of the house. Group members might wish to note times when they were frustrated because others were not picking up on their ideas, or angry because someone put something in the house that they didn't want or like, or happy because someone completed a line just as they wanted, and so on. If two or more groups do the activity, they may wish to compare their houses as well as the process that they each went through to draw them.

Values Lists

PURPOSE

"What do I value?" The answers we give to this question often give purpose and direction to our lives. If our answers are confused and conflicting, chances are that we are living confused and conflicted lives. If our answers lack quality and substance, chances are that our lives also lack quality and substance. One way of examining these matters is to make a list of what we value and then analyze it for personal meaning.

PROCEDURE

Introduce the activity by talking briefly about its purpose. Ask students to make a list of the things they value (prize or cherish). The list is to be private, unless they wish to share it with others. Sometimes it is helpful to specify the number of items, "In the next ten minutes, see if you can come up with

25 or more items." If the list is given as a take-home assignment, you may want to make it 50 or more items. Explain that the student can put anything he wishes on the list. To get students started, give a few examples of the items that might appear on *your* list, or make your list on the chalkboard while students are making theirs on paper.

When students finish, ask them to code their lists by placing the following symbols beside all items that apply.

1. (*) beside all items that are possessions.

2. (L) beside all items that are living things.

3. (P) beside all items that are persons.

4. ($) beside all items that cost a lot of money. You must decide what "a lot of money" means.

5. (V) beside all items that are values like *freedom, national security,* etc.

6. (C) beside all items that are character traits like *honesty, humbleness, forgiveness,* etc.

7. (M) beside all items that you think your mother also values.

8. (F) beside all items that you think your father also values.

9. (W) beside all items that you have worked hard to obtain.

You may wish to modify the above list so that it is more

applicable to the age and characteristics of your students by adding your own coding and dropping others.

More than one symbol may be placed beside an item. The coding can be done in the margin of the list. Or, you might facilitate the process by providing students with a dittoed form as illustrated.

ITEM	CODINGS									
1.										
2.										
3.										
4.										
5.										
6.										
etc.										

The activity may be followed up in several ways. Privately, students can look over their lists and codings, noting things they learned about themselves. These can be written out by completing several times the sentence stem, "I learned that I. . . . " Or, you may wish to call upon a few volunteers to share some of the items that appear on their lists, as well as something they learned about themselves. A third way is to divide the class into small groups and let them share as much or as little of their lists and findings as they wish.

VARIATIONS[1]

There are a number of other ways you can work this strategy. For example, students might keep a running list of all the things that they do over a two week period that they are proud of having done, or all the things they have done in their life of which they are proud. The list can be developed around such themes as:

"Things I prize about myself."

"Things I prize about my classmates."

"Things I'd like to buy."

"Things I love to give others."

"Things others can give me that I prize."

"Things I prize that I have made."

You might assign a different kind of list periodically until students tire of the activity.

A particular values list which can be very revealing, especially for the teacher, deals with what students like and dislike about school. Ask students to make two separate lists, one containing all the things they like about school, and the other containing all the things they dislike about school. When they finish, have them code their lists with the following symbols:

1. (T) beside all the items that have mostly to do with teachers.

2. (S) beside all the items that have mostly to do with your fellow students.

3. (L) beside all the items that have to do with your lessons or schoolwork.

4. (E) beside all the items that have to do with extra-curricular activities like sports, plays, the school newspaper, student government, etc.

Follow up with a discussion or have several students conduct a poll by compiling all the lists and codings, and report the results to the class. Be prepared for some harsh criticism of schools.

A values list that often fits in with a Thanksgiving unit is a list of "Things I'm Thankful For." Some codings students could use on this are:

1. (F) beside something connected with your family.

2. (M) beside a material possession.

3. (G) beside something which has been given to you.

Values lists can be used in conjunction with academic activities. For example, students studying the American Revolution might make up a list of all the things a typical American soldier of that period might have cherished, and then compare it with their own lists. This often serves to increase interest and involvement with the subject matter, as well as to give students a different perspective from which to view their own lives.

Marie Oehler, an elementary teacher, used a bulletin board on which her students could post things which they were proud of or valued. She described the activity as follows:

"One large classroom bulletin board was designated as *It's Your Choice*. The children were allowed and encouraged to bring in anything that interested them. The only rule was that they tell the class what they brought in and why they brought it in. I went on the premise that if they wanted to bring it in and hang it up, they must be proud of it.

"This idea went over big with the children. They brought in many and varied things. Some of these 'treasures' included hand colored drawings, optical illusion designs, articles about Michael Jackson, comics, cards, newspaper articles, etc.

"I felt that this activity was a huge success. All of the children were involved. And the bulletin board had to be extended to the surrounding walls. The children eagerly looked forward to the time when they would show their 'prized possessions.' "

Teachers: By yourself, or with several other teachers from your subject area, brainstorm a list of all the possible ways you could use the *Values List* strategy. You'll be surprised by the length of the list.

Here's one for you:

What do you like about your job? Make a list. Place the following symbols beside the appropriate items to identify how you feel concerning the item:

1. (M) beside any items you want to do more of on the job.

2. (X) beside any items you performed but were not required to do.

3. (+) beside any items you really enjoy doing.

4. (S) beside any items that directly involve students.

What do you dislike about your job? Make a list. Review the list and indicate how you feel by using the following symbols:

1. (U) beside any items which you consider unimportant in performing your duties.

2. (O) beside those items that others expect you to do.

3. (E) beside those items which are essential to carrying out your duties.

4. (R) beside those items which you are required by policy to do.

5. (T) beside those items you think you may be expected or required to do, but are unsure about.

Here's another:[2]

Make a list of the people whom you telephone most frequently. Now code the list with the following:

R = relative

B = business

F = friend

L = local call

LD = long distance call

X   =   you would like to remove this number from your list if you could

☺   =   you feel good when you call this number

★   =   you haven't called for some time but you would like to

♀   =   female

♂   =   male

M   =   you have this number memorized

Values Categories[3]

PURPOSE

This is an adaptation of a game that children have played for years called "Categories." Its purpose is to help students become more aware of some of the things they value, how they might have developed these preferences, and how these compare to the valued things of others.

PROCEDURE

Provide students with a copy of the worksheet on *page 127.* (For older students, you may wish to add to or modify the categories on the grid. For younger children, you may want to simplify as well as reduce the number of categories.) Their task is to fill in the boxes in the grid. Thus, by reading item number one on the vertical axis—"my favorite now"—and completing it with item number one on the horizontal axis—"food"—the student writes in the appropriate box his or her favorite food at the present time, and so on for the rest of the items on the grid.

Worksheet No. 1

	MUSIC	MOVIE	BOOK(S)	SPORT	HOBBY	WAY TO TRAVEL	PLACE TO BE ALONE	PLACE TO VISIT	FOOD	ENTERTAINMENT	ANIMAL (PET)	COLOR
My favorite now												
My favorite five years ago												
My best friend's favorite												
My mother's favorite												
My father's favorite												
If I had $5 to spend, I'd buy or spend it on												
The person I most like to do or share this with												
The last time I did or had this												

Worksheet No. 2

	SINGER(S)	SPORTS FIGURE(S)	AUTHOR(S)	FEMALE HERO(ES)	MALE HERO(ES)	TV STAR(S)	MOVIE STAR(S)	ROCK GROUP(S)	POLITICAL FIGURE(S)	TEACHER(S)	ARTIST(S)	FICTIONAL CHARACTER(S)
My favorite now												
My favorite 5 years ago												
My best friend's favorite												
My mother's favorite												
My father's favorite												
What I most admire about my favorite												
How I would like to be more like my favorite												
How this person came to be my favorite												
My teacher's favorite												

When students finish their grids, they can form small groups to share and compare their responses. The grids can also be posted if students wish to do so. In either case, encourage students to write down and share some of the things they learned about themselves or others as a result of the activity.

Values Scavenger Hunt

PURPOSE

By sharing ideas on what physical things best represent certain values, students should develop an awareness of and clarify some of the values they and others hold.

PROCEDURE

Divide the class into groups of three or four. Tell the students they are going on a values scavenger hunt. The values scavenger hunt differs from a regular scavenger hunt in that students are given a list of values to find instead of a list of things; their job is to find something that represents each value on the list and bring it back to class.

Provide each student with a copy of the worksheet on *page 130.* Then assign the activity as homework, or take the class to the park or some other suitable outdoor location so that they can carry out the assignment. Each group must agree on one item for each value, so if this strategy is given as homework, the groups will need class time to decide on one item for each value. Remind students about preserving the natural environment wherever possible and suggest that they just describe, rather than remove, any living things.

Follow up the scavenger hunt with a discussion in which the students in each group present the things they found and explain (1) why they chose each item and (2) what value each item represents.

Worksheet

Instructions: Below is a list of values. Your task is to find something that represents each value and bring it back to class. Example: for the value friendship you might bring back a stone—"good friendships are like stones in that they are indestructible even when placed under a great deal of stress."

VALUE	OBJECT	REASON YOU CHOSE IT
1. Beauty		
2. Love		
3. Friendship		
4. Truth		
5. Peace		
6. Equality		

VARIATIONS

Have students use a camera to photograph things that represent the values. Or, have students do the hunt individually, then discuss it in small groups.

A scavenger hunt can also be used for building students' self-concepts. For example, pair students up on the basis of how well they know each other—the more acquainted, the better. Then, individually—or with a student who is not his partner—each student is to go in search of five things that remind him of five of his partner's strengths. For example, a student might select a delicate flower because it reminds him of his partner's sensitivity to others. The students in each pair are then to share with each other what they found on the hunt and why they selected it.

A World of My Own Creation

PURPOSE

We are born into a world we did not help to create. If we feel self-confident and skillful, we may get a chance to help shape the world we live in and make it more like the kind of place we sometimes dream about. This strategy gives students a chance to play the "creator" for a while. Its purpose is to help students think about what kind of world would really be a better place in which to live.

PROCEDURE

Introduce the strategy with the following: "I want you to close your eyes and think about what it would be like if you could be the "creator of the world" for a while. What kind of world would you build? Would it have lots of people? Would there be wars? How would people make a living? Would there be schools? Would there be different races and religions? Would there be oceans and mountains? Would people own the land? Would there be nations and flags?"

Ask students to open their eyes and get together in small groups to discuss the kind of world they would like to create. Each small group is to make a list of the things it wants to include in its newly created world. Stress that everybody's ideas are to be included. If ideas conflict, the group must work out the conflict either by coming to a compromise or by coming up with a new solution. When the groups have finished, each is to present its ideas to the class as a whole. The similarities and differences are then compared.

Following the class discussion, each student is to write a theme entitled, "A World of My Choice," in which he is to put forth in considerable detail the kind of world he would create if he had the chance.

As an additional follow-up, have the students list the five to ten things about their "new world" that they like the most. Next to each thing, ask them to list several ways they might begin working right now to move our present world in that direction. They could then share these lists in small groups and make "contracts" to actually begin working on one of the items by a certain date. Or a group of students might begin a group "action project" as the result of a list.

VARIATION

Have students get together and think about creating a new school. For example, students could be given the following hypothetical situation:

Imagine that you have been called into a school district very much like the one you now go to school in. There have never been schools there. But the people there now want schools. They don't want just any school. They want the most advanced schools anyone can imagine. You are in a position to recommend what these schools should be like. What would you recommend?

Personal Interviewing

PURPOSE

Personal interviewing is a basic tool for collecting personal data. It can be used to help students identify the stands they hold on a range of political, social, and values issues. It further serves to help students clarify their thinking by comparing their own positions to those of others whom they interview. Finally, it gives students a chance to share and affirm their values positions.

PROCEDURE

Introduce interviewing by having students pair up and interview each other using the worksheet on *page 134*. One student should ask the questions on the worksheet and record the other student's answers, which should be as complete as possible. Then students are to switch roles. When the interviewing is complete, have students talk about the experience in a large or a small group, noting the problems encountered. Solutions to these problems should be talked through. Now students are ready to conduct interviews with persons outside of school.

Each student is to interview at least three people who are 18 years or older, who maintain a household, who are not students, and who are not members of their own family. The interviews can be conducted in person or over the phone. Set a deadline for the interviews to be completed.

When the interviews are completed, a committee should be formed to summarize the results of both the in-class and outside interviews. Then, students are to break into small groups and compare their own reactions to these summarized results.

Worksheet: Grading

Instructions: Introduce yourself and state your purpose for conducting the interview. Indicate that all information will be confidential.

1.   I'd like to find out some of your feelings about the grading practices that are in use in our schools today. For example, which of the following statements do you most agree with? Check that statement.

_____ A. Grades are generally helpful in stimulating learning in the classroom.

_____ B. Grades are sometimes helpful in stimulating learning in the classroom.

_____ C. Grades usually serve to inhibit learning in the classroom.

2. Which of these statements do you most agree with?

_____ A. Grades are very necessary to motivate students to learn.

_____ B. Grades are sometimes necessary to motivate students to learn.

_____ C. Grades are unnecessary to motivate students to learn.

3. Which of the following would you like to see?

_____ A. A complete change in the grading system.

_____ B. Some modification of the grading system.

_____ C. No change in the grading system.

4. If you favor a change, what would you favor?

_____ A. A pass/fail option.[4]

_____ B. Credit/no credit.

_____ C. Replace letter grades with written evaluations.

_____ D. Other_____

5. Do you agree or disagree with the following statement: "There is a high degree of correlation between academic performance and on-the-job performance; if an individual does well academically, it is likely that he or she will do well on the job."[5]

_____ A. Strongly Agree.

_____ B. Agree Somewhat.

_____ C. Not Sure.

_____ D. Disagree Somewhat.

_____ E. Strongly Disagree.

6. What is your level of education?

_____ A. 11th grade or below

_____ B. High school diploma

_____ C. Two years or less of college or business school, etc.

_____ D. B.A. from college or university

_____ E. Master's Degree

_____ F. Advanced degree or doctorate

Interviewer's Name _____

School _____

Date Completed _____

ADDITIONAL WORKSHEETS

Worksheets can be designed much more simply, especially for use by younger children. For example, the following worksheet was designed by an elementary teacher[6] in the Philadelphia school system following a long and bitter teachers' strike in the Spring of 1972. Its purpose was to (1) help students understand the strike and (2) aid them in thinking about the values issues involved.

Worksheet No. 1

Name of person interviewed _____

Name of interviewer _____

Position of that person _____

1. Do you think the teachers' strike was good?

2. Should schools have stayed open without all the teachers?

3. If you were a teacher and the schools had been opened, would you have reported to school despite the strike?

4. Should the teachers who refused to come to school be punished?

5. Was there a good reason for the strike?

6. Did teachers strike only for money?

7. Were the children hurt because of the strike?

8. Who was responsible for the strike?

9. If the strike had lasted longer what would you have done?

Worksheet No. 2[7]

Instructions: Place an X in the appropriate column below for each of the 17 items to indicate whether you think the particular item is (A) *morally wrong*, (B) *morally right*, or (C) *not a moral issue*. Then go back over the items marked as morally wrong and rank order them from the most important to the least important as a moral issue. Place a 1 in front of the most important item, a 2 in front of the next most important item, and so on.

RANK	ITEM	A. I FEEL THIS IS MORALLY WRONG.	B. I FEEL THIS IS MORALLY RIGHT.	C. I FEEL THIS IS NOT A MORAL ISSUE.
	1. Using an addictive drug			
	2. Smoking pot			
	3. Destroying public property			
	4. Destroying private property			
	5. Shoplifting			
	6. Having homosexual activity			
	7. Having children out of wedlock			
	8. Pushing heroin			
	9. Pushing pot			
	10. Having premarital sexual relationships			
	11. Having extramarital sexual relationships			
	12. Wife swapping			
	13. Having an abortion			
	14. Telling lies to protect friends			
	15. Telling lies to protect your own interests			
	16. Telling lies to protect your family			
	17. Using a "buyer beware" policy to make a profit			

A Me Box[8]

PURPOSE

Our lives can be thought of in terms of four cells.[9] In one cell is our public self: the "me" that everyone knows, the conscious image we project to the rest of the world. In a second cell is our private self: the "me" only we know, the part of us which we reveal to no one, except perhaps our most intimate friends. In the third and fourth cells are our blind areas: One contains the "me" that others see but of which we are as yet unaware; in the other is the "me" that neither we nor others know.

A primary goal of Values Clarification and personal inquiry is to reduce the size of the cells in our blind areas and move toward greater self-disclosure. *A Me Box* is a very simple and safe but effective means for helping students explore and reveal to others their beliefs, attitudes, values, and concerns.

PROCEDURE

For this activity, each student will need a box which he or she should select on the basis of individual taste. The box should have a lid or flaps and should be large enough so that things can be attached to both the inside and outside; otherwise, the box can be of any size, shape, color, and material.

On the outside of the box, each student is to make a public statement by making a collage of pictures, poems, photographs, quotations, drawings, newspaper clippings, etc.

The inside of the box is for revealing a more personal and private statement, also in the form of a collage. (Or, objects can be placed in the box.)

When students have finished their *Me Boxes*, the activity can be followed up in several ways. The boxes can be placed on display for other students to see. However, to see the inside of another student's box, permission must be obtained from that student. Students can form small groups to discuss the exteriors and interiors of their boxes. Small slots can be cut in the boxes so that students can slip in personal notes to the box's owner.

Hex Signs

PURPOSE

The Pennsylvania Dutch have long decorated their barns with colorful hex signs. The popular belief is that the hex sign wards off evil spirits.

For example, a hex sign with rain drops painted on it is believed to help insure crop abundance; a hex sign with hearts painted on it is thought to bring love and romance. Thus, a hex sign often reflects what the person who displays it values most.

This strategy provides students with an opportunity to design and make their own hex signs. While doing so, they are encouraged to think about what they value and would like to protect or insure.

PROCEDURE

Introduce the strategy by discussing hex signs, what they are and the purpose they serve. Then provide students with large sheets of oaktag.

Their task is to select three of the symbols or designs from the list on *page 143* and, by combining these three, design a hex sign which reflects some of the things they think are important in life. The symbols or designs can be repeated several times to provide balance and a pleasing appearance. A finished hex might look like this:

HEART FOR LOVE AND ROMANCE

BIRDS FOR HAPPINESS

CLOVER LEAF FOR GOOD
LUCK AND SUCCESS

For young children or students who cannot draw well, cut out the figures from cardboard and let them trace the designs.

When students finish, the hex signs can be posted for display.

Hex Designs

 = raindrops for abundance and prosperity

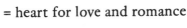 = oak leaf for strength to meet life's challenges

 = maple leaf for beauty

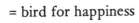 = bird for happiness

 = heart for love and romance

 = dove for peace and tranquility

 = tulip for religious faith

 = rosette for joy

 = eagle for independence

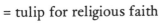 = star for success

= clover leaf for good luck

= unicorn for honesty and integrity

VARIATION

Have students invent their own symbols and designs to represent other things in life that they value.

Values Box

PURPOSE

Composition assignments need not be dull and uninvolving, as is the case in many classrooms. Writing about self and what one feels, believes, and values can be an exciting and meaningful experience for students. This strategy presents a method and many topics for helping students identify, write about, and clarify their values.

PROCEDURE

Get an index file and stack of 3 x 5 index cards. Read through the Values Activities on *pages 145-180* and select some that you think your students would enjoy. Place these on the 3 x 5 cards, one per card, and put them in a file box, the Values Box. The Values Box may then be used in any of the following ways:

1. Place the Values Box on your desk. When giving a writing assignment, pull one of the cards and read it to the class, or put the information on the chalkboard. Students then write about the activity.

2. Pull several of the cards and place them on the chalkboard. Let students come up and choose which activity to write about.

3. Select ten to fifteen activity cards and post them on a bulletin board or wall. Let students select their own writing assignments and complete them at their own

pace. (Use this format in the choice-centered classroom. *See page 460.*)

4. Place the Values Box on a table at the back of the classroom and let students select their writing assignments from it.

5. Use the cards to stimulate small or large group discussion with or without the writing assignment.

NOTE: It is important that you not grade the writing assignments given from the Values Box. Grading and negative feedback about one's own writing, especially when it deals with feelings, beliefs, and values can be damaging both to the student's self-concept and to the development of creative writing.

Values Activities

1. Out of all the places you have been, where would you take a person you love and why?[10]

2. Write a story about yourself using all of the following words. You can use the words more than once.

1. happiness		6. different	
2. proud		7. sixteen	
3. money		8. never	
4. best		9. love	
5. family		10. future	

3. Remember your last argument? How did you solve it? Did you fight or talk it over? Looking back, how would you solve it *now*?

4. What is success? List the ten biggest successes of your life. Discuss briefly any one success.

5. "Feelings exist, and that fact makes them right." Do you agree or disagree with this statement? Express some feelings that you experienced today. What did you do about them, if anything?

6. Write an essay: "If I Could Live for 200 Years. . . . "

7. What would you do if you had a car?
   1. Where would you go?
   2. How fast would you go?
   3. What would you do when you got there?
   4. What kind of car would you want?

8. What is more pleasing to you:
   1. Doing something for someone else?
   2. Having someone do something for you?
   Tell about times recently when each of these happened to you.

9. How have hair and clothing styles changed in your lifetime? What are your views toward these changes? Do you think our society has accepted any changes which have come about? Why or why not?

10. As a teenager, react to this statement: "Young people today are not responsible enough to drive. They do not think of their friends' lives, they just think about showing off."

11. Do you believe in sex before marriage? If so, under what circumstances? What are some of the consequences that you might possibly face? What would you do if you or, in the case of boys, your girl became pregnant? Would you consider marriage? Abortion? Giving up for adoption? Why or why not?

12. Do you think it is a good idea for teenagers to pay board to their parents? Would you expect your children to begin paying board at the age of 15 or 16? Explain your reasons.

13. "You can't be a truly religious person if you don't attend church services regularly." React to this statement.

14. What made last weekend memorable?

15. How would you spend $1,000?

16. Describe a world without love.

17. Take a desk to a corner of the room and write a story on what it is like to be all alone in the world.

18. Write your response to the following: "If you had to live for one year in a twelve-foot-square room with no windows, what would you put in it?"

19. "The Most Unforgettable Person I Ever Met"—write a theme about him or her.

20. Using your knowledge and/or imagination, describe a routine day for an average housewife with one child, age two. Do you like the day? How would you feel if you were this housewife?

21. Theme: "What I like best about me." Think about:
    1. What are my best points of character and personality;
    2. How can I use these good points to help me succeed?
    3. Will it take much effort to use these qualities to help me succeed? Is it worth it to try to be better?

22. What do you think was the greatest event in the history of the United States? Write a report giving your reasons for the choice.

23. Watch a show on T.V. or in a theater and tell what you liked or disliked about it. Also, tell how you would improve it.

24. You are a rocket going to the moon:
    1. How do you feel?
    2. What do you see?
    3. What will you do when you get there?
    4. Will you be glad or sad to get back home? What things did you miss most? What things least?

25. If you had to choose between something important and your boyfriend or girlfriend, which one would you choose? *Tell why.*

26. Write a story or theme about your most exciting summer vacation.

27. Make your own version of a "Peanuts" cartoon (in pictures). Try to get a message across.

28. Pick your favorite summer vacation month and write

about why it is your favorite and what you like to do then.

29. If you had the coolest car in town, what would you act like?

30. Select a picture from a book and write a poem about it.

31. Get a friend and make up a comedy skit about an important issue we face today. Act it out on tape or in front of the class.

32. Take a pencil and writing tablet, and go outside and start a conversation between two objects. They are having a disagreement.

33. What is death? What do you think it will be like?

34. What is a nightmare (in your own words)? Describe your worst nightmare.

35. What is failure? List the five most recent put-downs you've experienced. Discuss any one failure or put-down.

36. You are a salesman: try to sell me the car of your dreams. Be realistic in your prices. Take into consideration that you should make at least 20 percent of the total as profit. As your final selling point, show me the actual cost to you as compared to the price you're making me pay.

37. Write an essay on "The Apollo Project" and how you feel about it. Do you think it was money well spent?

38. If you didn't go to school what would you do? Tell about it.

39. If you could discuss any topic, what would you choose?
    1.
    2.
    3.
    4.
    5.

    How would you discuss them? Why do you want to discuss these topics?

40. What do you believe is the ideal age to get married for men? For women? Why?

41. What do you think about the war in Vietnam? Should we have stayed or were we right in getting out? Explain why you feel this way.

42. What kind of a job would you want after school? Why? What other alternatives have you considered?

43. Do you believe school causes emotional problems in teenagers? Why or why not?

44. Do you think drinking is a problem with teenagers? Why or why not? What do you do about drinking at parties?

45. Do you think that drugs are a big problem with teenagers? Elaborate on your answer.

46. Why do so many young girls become pregnant during the early years of high school? What could or should be

done to help decrease this number, or should nothing be done?

47. If you had the opportunity to quit school, would you? Why or why not? What would be the advantages of leaving school? Of staying in school? What would be the disadvantages of each?

48. Write an essay entitled "Lunch Time."

49. "Few teenagers in this school know what is going on in the world around them." Do you agree with this statement? If so, do you think something should be done about this problem? What?

50. "What is Happiness?"

51. Find a quiet spot. Make a list of some of your major problems. What can you do to help solve your problems?

52. Write an essay on something that made you sad this week.

53. Write a fictional story about your favorite sport.

54. Write a theme on your degree of freedom compared to that which your friends have.

55. Write a convincing argument about why your favorite model car is best.

56. Write a short story on "A Day in My Home."

57. Write a story on what you did after school yesterday. Was your time well spent?

58. Do you think teenagers should have to work for their allowances? Do you plan to make your children work for theirs? Explain.

59. How do you feel about deer hunting season?

60. What is temptation? Have you ever been tempted to do something wrong? If so, describe your temptation, tell how you handled the situation and what the final outcome was.

61. On the bookshelf are two Travel Guides from AAA. Using both of these, plan an itinerary for a week's vacation. List places you would like to visit, fishing or hunting spots where you would camp, and about how much money you would need to spend on your trip.

62. What does "going steady" mean to you? Discuss the pros and cons of going steady. Do you think you would ever want to go steady?

63. Cut out a picture and write a short story about it.

64. If you didn't go to school today, what would you do? Tell all about it.

65. Are you superstitious? Why or why not? If you are, what superstitions do you have?

66. Using pictures from magazines and your own captions, describe yourself.

67. What is freedom? Do students in our school have too much or too little freedom? In what ways?

68. Do you consider yourself a responsible person? What does responsibility have to do with being mature?

69. If you had to choose the style of clothes for the U.S., how would we all be dressed? Why did you choose this style?

70. What is maturity? Do you consider yourself mature? Explain why you think you *are* or *are not.*

71. Describe in detail your most terrifying experience. Try to use vivid, descriptive words.

72. Write a theme on "If I Were a Building. . . . " Think about what services you would provide, what materials you would be made from, what you would look like, where you would be located and why.

73. Using magazine pictures and your own commentary, create a story and put it into form.

74. What do you think is the biggest problem in families today? Who or what causes it? What can be done about it?

75. If I could pick any two people to be my parents (excluding your present parents), I would pick. . . . Tell why.

76. Write and photograph a short story.

77. Write about someone else in the room, but don't give his or her name.

78. Write about "If I Had a Car," or "If I Had a Motorcycle."

79. Write about "My Most Embarrassing Experience."

80. Discuss what you think might be an average day in the life of a mother or father.

81. You are a mechanic. You are very busy and you must close the garage in 10 minutes to attend a very good friend's wedding. One of your customers calls and asks you what he should check if he can't get his car started. The only thing he can tell you is that the car had started on three different occasions today, and he can't understand why it won't start now. What will you do?

82. Why do you think some teenagers would do just about anything to get their own car? Would you?

83. Describe what you think of a teenage girl who gets drunk? Do you believe it impresses guys or turns them off? Why?

84. What do you think is the right age for parents to allow their kids to go to drive-in movies? Why?

85. What does marriage mean to you? Are you anxious to get married? Why? Why not?

86. Describe you best friend but don't reveal who he or she is. Why is this person your friend?

87. If a class trip were planned, where would you like to go? Why? Is there anything special you would like to see? (Confine your travels to a 100-mile radius from the school.)

88. What is the No. 1 hit on the Top Ten this week? In your opinion, what made the record popular? Do you like it or dislike it? How do the words relate to you as a teenager?

89. You are going to apply for a job. (Name the job.) What preparations would you make before going for an interview? How would you dress?

90. Choose a record of a classical composition or a Broadway hit. Listen to it. Did you like it? Why or why not? Was the music relaxing? What impressions did you have while listening to the music? How would your friends react if you told them you liked this type of music?

91. If you could be an animal, what kind of animal would you like to be? Why?

92. If you could be reincarnated, what kind of person would you like to be? Why?

93. What is love? What do you love most?

94. What is hate? What do you hate most?

95. If you were 21 years old, what would you be doing right now?

96. You are in Death Row. Tomorrow you will die. There is no way out. Write what is going on in your mind.

97. "Boyfriends!" ("Girlfriends!") Write about it.

98. Draw a comic strip (at least three boxes) about school and write captions for each box.

99. Ask any three friends to join you in a circle. Individually list ten things you like to do. Explain why you like each thing, and ask if your friends have similar interests.

100. You have $200 to buy something. Look through the newspaper and magazine advertisements to see what you can afford. List up to five things in the order that you would buy them.

101. What is discipline (in your own words)? If you were a parent, how would you handle discipline? What might be the results?

102. If you had $4,000 to spend on a new car:
    1. Which would you buy, in order of preference?
       Rambler   Chevy   V.W.   Ford
       Oldsmobile   Buick   Dodge   Plymouth
    2. Why?
    3. State exact models of each.
    4. Show proof of price.
    5. Keep in mind the 6% sales tax on list price.
    6. State equipment included or extras for your new car.

103. Write a theme on how you would teach a class if you taught one of the following subjects:
    1. English
    2. Math
    3. Reading
    4. History
    5. Science

104. If your girlfriend or boyfriend were coming to your house for a dinner that you would prepare especially for her/him, what would she/he find when you answered the door? Describe the mood, setting, meal, etc.

105. Suppose our school had a hobby show. Would you enter? If so, tell about your entry. If not, tell what hobby you wish you had.

106. Name at least four events that can radically change a person's way of living. Describe how one, if any, has caused you to change.

107. Boys only: What is a girlfriend? What kind of girl do you want for a girlfriend? What would you do to keep her happy enough to be your steady girl?

108. Write about a current political issue found on the front page of the newspaper. Write about your feelings on the political issue. Ask your friends their feelings on the same issue and include that.

109. Pick a state that you would someday like to visit or live in. Give your reasons why. If you want to stay here, state why.

110. What does the word "democracy" mean to you? Write an essay about your feelings and meanings.

111. What are you going to do when you get out of school? Do you think your job will have any effect on anyone else? For example: You are a mortician. Without you, what would everyone do with all the dead bodies? You can see this job is certainly needed by everyone. Write a theme on the importance of *your* job.

112. What does the word "poverty" mean? What do you think of the government's policies on the problem of poverty? What would be your answer for a sure cure for poverty?

113. You are a worker in a steel factory. You decide that you need better working conditions and higher pay. What would you do to go about getting the things you want? Would you vote for a labor union or not? Give your reasons for wanting these better conditions and why your method would get you the things you want.

114. What do you think of women's liberation? Is it a political issue? Do you think that women are discriminated against? Do you think that women's lib has gone too far?

115. What do you think of Communist Party members running for President?

116. Answer these questions:
        What do you worry about most?
        What are the causes of your worries?
        Can any of your worries be eliminated?
        Which of them might you deal with first? How do you decide?
        Are there other people with the same problems? How do you know? How can you find out?

117. Answer these questions:
        What bothers you most about adults? Why?
        When you become an adult how do you want to be similar to or different from adults you know?

118. Answer these questions:
        What, if anything, seems worth dying for?
        How did you come to believe this?
        What seems worth living for?
        How did you come to believe this?

119. Answer these questions:

How can you tell the "good guys" from the "bad guys"?

How can "good" be distinguished from "evil"?

What kind of person would you most like to be?

How might you get to be this kind of person?

120. Answer these questions:

What is progress?

What is change?

What is the difference between the two?

List one of the important changes going on in our society which should be encouraged, and one which should be resisted. Why? How?

What would you change if you could?

Why would you do it?

How might you go about it?

121. Is it right for a man to give a woman his seat on the bus? Why or why not? Should a woman ever give a man her seat? If so, when?

122. Is it right for children to be allowed to stay out until 10:30 on weeknights? Why or why not? How late will you allow your children to stay out on weeknights? Explain.

123. Select one of the following and write a theme about it:

My Childhood

If I Had Three Wishes

I Have a Dream

Three Days to Live

Death

A Sad Day Remembered
Love
If I Were the American Flag
My Earliest Memory
If I Could Be
My Ideal Man
My Ideal Woman
A Happy Time Remembered
A Day in My Life
A Day in My Home
Going Steady
A World Without Love
Alone
Together
Darkness
When I Die
Hate
My Boyfriend
My Girlfriend
I'm Proud
If I Were Rich As Rich Could Be
If I Were Poor As Poor Could Be
My Friends
A Little Girl's Dream
If I Could Be a Child Again
My Secret Wish
The Me I Want to Be
A Monster I Can Be at Times
A Little Boy's Dream

124. What is your idea of a perfect weekend?[11]

125. If you could be anyone in the world, who would you be? What would it be like?

126. If you were the President, what would you change about your country?

127. You are the richest person in the world. What are you going to do with all your money?

128. Where is your most favorite place to be? What do you like best about it?

129. If you were a teacher, how would you run a classroom?

130. Write about a change that you'd make in this world.

131. Write about why you do or don't like war.

132. What would you do if you had one day left to live?

133. What would it feel like to be a movie star? Would you like to be one? What kind of movie star? How would your life be different?

134. What would it feel like to be a sports star? Would you like to be one? What kind of sports star? How would your life be different?

135. If you were a movie producer, what would your movie be about?

136. If you were a blackboard, what would you like to have written on you?

137. If you could change one thing in your classroom, what would it be? Why?

138. What is your favorite food? Write about it.

139. If you owned a castle, what would be in and around it?

140. Would you like to fly? Why or why not?

141. If you were Superman, what would you do?

142. If you were a star, what place in the world would you shine over? Describe the place.

143. How would you run your baseball team if you were a big league manager?

144. If you were a window, where would you like to be?

145. If you were a book, what would you like your pages to contain?

146. If you had the choice, what year would you like to be living in right now? Why?

147. If you could remove one thing from your classroom, what would it be? Why?

148. If you had one wish, what would it be? Why?

149. Write a story projecting yourself into the future in a time machine.

150. Write new words to a popular song.

151. Write an advertisement such as you would see in magazines, trying to sell yourself as the product. Make yourself interesting enough so that people will want to buy you.[12]

152. Write two paragraphs about any of the following

topics. The first paragraph tells why you love it. The second paragraph tells why you hate it:

    a. Getting up in the morning.
    b. Watching television.
    c. Taking care of brothers and sisters.
    d. Sports.
    e. Animals.
    f. Reading.

153. What's in a name? Look up your name in the dictionary and write down the definition you find. If you can't find your name, make up a meaning. Write how the definition does or does not describe you.

154. Write a brief "autobiography." Describe your life, what you look like, the things you do, what you like and hate, and what you want to be.

155. The Story Of: In order to write about another person (called a "biography"), you must learn about him or her. Make up some interesting questions to ask someone in the class. Then, interview that person and write his or her biography. In what ways is he or she like you? Different from you?

156. Find an article in the paper about someone who did a wonderful thing. Write about why you think it was wonderful.

157. Write about a movie or T.V. show telling why you *didn't* like it.

158. Express Yourself: Take a piece of paper and make a collage that tells about you. To do this you need to

paste pictures, drawings, and objects to form an interesting composition that shows what you are like, things you do, and things that you like.

159. Moving On: Suppose you had to move away right now to another neighborhood. What things at school and at home would you miss? What things would you remember best? What would you be glad to leave? Who would you want to say goodbye to?

160. If I had a magic pair of boots, I would . . .[13]

161. Cut five pictures from a magazine and write your own story.

162. Examine the neighborhood in which you live, paying particular attention to those things and people that you like or dislike there. Write an essay trying to make your readers feel the same way about the neighborhood as you do. Ask yourself: What is special about my block, what makes it different from others? Do the kinds of buildings or arrangements of buildings make it look different from other blocks or the same? Are there any yards, trees or flowers?

163. Select some object you like or dislike intensely in your neighborhood, home, city, or school. Select an object or place—not a person. Describe it. Why do I like or dislike it? How do I feel every time I see the object?

164. Describe an event. (First day of school, haircut, the birth of a younger brother or sister, a time when you got lost, etc.) Answer the following: Why was the event important? What actually happened? What did I learn

from the event? Did it change my life? How? Did it change my attitude toward people? If so, how? Did the event affect others? How? Did it change my behavior? How?

165. "Friends help us to enrich our lives." Do you agree or disagree? Write a paragraph on friendship, telling how you feel about this statement and/or telling how a person can make friends, keep friends, and be a good friend.

166. Did you ever do something wrong and, no matter what else you did or said, you kept making matters worse? Write a paragraph about "My Adventures in Blunder-Land," telling about an embarrassing blunder.

167. Finish this sentence: "If I were on good terms with Time, I'd ask him to _____." Write a story about it.

168. Would you want to feed a future family of yours the foods you generally eat? What would be similar or different?

169. Have you ever worn clothes that your group considered daring or different? If so, what happened to you? What did your friends and family say? If you haven't, how would you feel if you found yourself in a situation where your clothes were different from everyone else's? What do clothes mean to you?

170. If you had the power to correct one environmental problem, what would you choose?

171. Donna lost her pocketbook and you found it. What did you do?

172. Interview at least five class members. Find out their: names, addresses, favorite foods. How do they spend Saturday mornings, Sunday nights, etc. Compare them to yourself.[14]

173. Describe your room in detail, through drawing or writing about it. It should include measurements in feet and inches, furniture location, important items. What do you like best about it? Least about it?

174. Describe your favorite room in your house. What makes it so?

175. Describe your house in writing and/or drawing. If you use photos, also include a written description of the inside and outside. What do you like best about it? Least?

176. After having read several "little people's" books, make a little person's book to give to a "wee one" of your choice.

177. Spend a day with a member of your family and tell about it in your journal. What did you like most about that person's day? What did you like least about it?

178. Write a poem or short story or a collection of any such items and make a gift of it to a member of your family (maybe someone you rarely show your feelings to).

179. Write a short play or soap opera about a difficult decision or choice you have made.

180. Do research on possible alternative types of family structure or living units. Which alternative do you like best? Describe or depict through drawings what this alternative might be like.

181. Find a cardboard box. On the inside make a collage of your personal beliefs, values, and goals, the ones that only your close friends know about. On the outside of the box, make a collage of your personal beliefs, values, and goals that you are willing to share publicly with anyone. Use pictures from magazines, newspaper clippings, drawings, etc.

182. Select a famous person you want to be more like; read a book or article about him and write about it.[15]

183. Write down your ideas of an *ideal* person; what would he/she be like, where would he/she go, how would he/she look, what would he/she do?

184. Set up a conflict situation. How would your ideal person react? How would you react?

185. What three countries do you see as the most important in the world today? Why? Does their size have anything to do with their importance?

186. List the major world problems that are present now. Which do you feel is most important? Why? Is there anything you can do about it?

187. Should all people in the world have the same rights and freedoms? Explain.

188. Write about an environment that would be ideal for you; tell why you would like it.

189. If you had two wishes, what things would you like to see improved in the world? Explain.

190. As President of the U.S., what country would you deal with most severely concerning military strength? What would you do?

191. Rank these in order of importance and briefly describe why you ranked them that way.
    1. Clean air and water.
    2. World peace.
    3. Less arms.
    4. More personal freedom.
    5. Democracy over communism.
    6. Guaranteed income for all people.

192. Describe an ideal relationship with the following people:
    1. Mother.
    2. Father.
    3. Best friend.
    4. Teacher.
    5. Police.
    6. Sister or brother.

193. How would you try to create a perfect relationship? List the steps you would have to follow.

194. What things in your house or room are you most proud of?

195. If you get married and have a family, would you want to live in this area? Why or why not?

196. What changes would you like to see in your neighborhood in the next ten years?

197. Write a letter to the mayor suggesting an improvement in your city or neighborhood that you think needs to be made.

198. Take a survey of people in your neighborhood and find out what they like and dislike about the neighborhood.

199. Describe your family. [16]

200. Keep a diary of everything you do for one month. What did you learn about yourself? Is there anything you would like to change?

201. Write ten things you like to do with your family.

202. Describe the perfect vacation.

203. Should the government have the power to limit the size of your family? Support your stand with several reasons.

204. Write a "Dear Abby" about a problem you are having. Trade papers with a classmate so that each of you writes an answer to the other's problem.

205. Make a cookbook of your favorite foods and recipes. Collect recipes from your friends and classmates.

206. Imagine that you are getting married. Plan the perfect wedding.

207. Write a description of your ideal mate.

208. Write down some advice you'd give your younger brothers or sisters about getting along with parents.

209. Give the following interview to some members of your family. Answer the questions yourself, too. Compare your answers with theirs.

What is your favorite color?
Your favorite food?
Your favorite T.V. show?
Your favorite book?
Your favorite song?
What do you think of women's lib?
What three things do you like to do best?
What three things do you like to do least?
What is one thing you'd like to learn before you die?
What is your greatest achievement?
What person do you most admire?
What is your most prized possession?
What makes your best friend your best friend?
If you could visit anywhere in the world, where would you go?

210. Take a stand and write about it: "A man should be able to have more than one wife."

211. Take a stand: "Old people should be put into rest homes."

212. Write a description of your family in the year 2000.

213. Write a marriage contract.

214. Take a stand: "Divorce should be illegal."

215. Take a stand: "Kids should be paid for babysitting for younger brothers and sisters."

216. Write about what makes you most proud of your family.

217. How many rooms would you like in your home? What would you use them for? Design an ideal house to scale model.[17]

218. What kinds of furniture would you want for your room or home? Would you choose all of it from one period or would you mix periods? Learn about periods such as Modern, Danish Modern, American Colonial, French Provincial, Victorian, etc. Identify their characteristics. Try to determine which period or periods reflect who you are or what you would try to say about yourself with your furnishings.

219. Learn about housing designs such as Modern, Victorian, Early American or Colonial, Western Ranch Style, Town Houses, Spanish, Cape Cod, Tudor, Gothic, Classical. Rank order the styles. Write a description of your number one choice and tell why you chose it.

220. What would you invest in if you made $250,000 a year?

221. Is there a difference between love and being in love? Explain.

222. What is a good marriage?

223. What should people know about each other before they get married?

224. Where would you spend your honeymoon? Plan a trip, including expenses and experiences.

225. How many children do you want? Why did you choose that number? How would you raise your children?

226. If you could change your religion, which would you choose? Why?

227. Design an ideal high school.

228. What would you do if you dropped out of school?

229. What would you do in school all day today if you had your choice?

230. What are the best positions to play in football, basketball, baseball, hockey, volleyball, soccer? Why?

231. What is the most boring sport to play? To watch? Why?

232. You are a flag. What do you stand for?

233. Be your own fortune teller—what will your life be like in five years? Suggest ways to make it happen.

234. "I prefer police brutality to riots." React to this statement.

235. Do you enjoy going to church or religious services? Why or why not?

236. What is the most important thing to do each day?

237. If you believed in reincarnation, who do you think you would have been in your last life? What kind of life would you have had?

238. How would your life be different if money was no worry? Is there any way you can move your life in this direction right now?

239. What would a day without electricity be like in your life? What would you miss the most?

240. The city is made up of many different types of people. There are people of different races, ethnic backgrounds, religions . . . the list goes on and on. Take a piece of paper and make up a list of qualities that reflect your personality (things that make you the person that you are). How do you think your list would differ from someone else in the room? From someone in your family? From your best friend? Suppose you were of a different race or religion, do you think your list would be different?

241. Write a brief essay on one problem that cities have (such as gangs, poor housing, lack of jobs, etc.). Then write about how you think that problem could be solved.

242. You are mayor of a city and you have just received a large sum of money from the state. What problem of the city would you direct your attention to? How exactly would you use the money to solve the problem?

243. If you had the power to do anything in the world to

change your neighborhood, what would you do? Why? How might you go about doing it?

244. "Women should get paid for doing housework for their families." React to this statement.[18]

245. "Mothers with young children should not work outside the home unless it is absolutely necessary." React to this statement.

246. Should our society have teenage correctional institutions? Why or why not? If yes, what kinds and where?

247. Write a story, using your imagination, entitled "If I Were a V-8 Piston."

248. If you had to rename the twelve months of the year, what would you name them and why?

249. If you found a credit card, what would you use it for or do with it?

250. List five major problems teenagers have and tell why each is a problem.

251. If you could choose, which would you prefer and why?
     1. To be an only child.
     2. To have one sister or brother.
     3. To have several sisters and brothers.

252. If you earned $5 million in one month, and you couldn't save or invest it, what would you do?

253. Do you think a person should have to use "proper English" in school? Why or why not?

254. Think back over your summer vacations—is there any

activity or event which occurred during a summer vacation that caused a change in your way of living? How? Why? When? Where?

255. What things have you done over the summer that you can't do during school term?

256. Movies:
    1. What was the funniest one you ever saw?
    2. Who were the stars?
    3. When or where did you see it?
    4. What made it so funny?
    5. What was the rating it had: G, PG, R, or X?

257. Who is your favorite actress? Why? What movie did you see her perform in? What was the rating it had?

258. What was the most exciting film you ever saw? What made it so exciting? Who were the stars? What was the rating it had?

259. Who is your favorite actor? Why? What movie did you see him perform in? What part did he play? What was the rating it had?

260. Plan a movie. Discuss your plan with the teacher, choose your sets and characters, write a script, and then film it. Show it to the class.

261. How do you think the words "responsibility" and "respect" relate to the word "marriage"?

262. What does religion mean to you? How important is it in your life?

263. What kind of people do you seek for your friends?

Why do you like this type of person? Are they like or unlike you?

264. When you have a problem, what kind of a person do you talk to and why?

265. Create a story about a bad scene with drugs.

266. Read any article from the newspaper on love or something you think shows love. Tell about it. Then cut out other articles that don't show love and tell why.

267. Are there jealousies in this room? Why? (Don't use names.) What might be done about them?

268. Write a story including all these elements: fighting, killing, suffering, dying, dirt, crying, starving.

269. How do you feel about reincarnation?

270. Girls only: What is a boyfriend? What kind of boy do you want for a boyfriend? What things would you do to show your boyfriend that he meant a lot to you?

271. How do you feel about drugs?

272. Write about your favorite parties: kinds, purposes, places, results.

273. What's your favorite Radio Station? Tell:
    1. Number on dial.
    2. Kind of music.
    3. Why it's your favorite.

274. Write some advice for a friend in a helpful rather than critical way. Don't use names.

275. Write about a date, real or made up: Where? Time you left? Things done? Time you came home? Problems?

276. Write a story on your perfect future.

277. Write about the Civil Rights Movement?
     1. What do you know about it?
     2. Who is involved?
     3. How are we involved?
     4. Why are they involved?
     5. What have you heard about it from friends or relatives?
     6. How do you feel about it?
     7. What do you do about it?

278. Do you feel television is helpful or harmful to our society—or both? Explain your answer.

279. How do you feel about being engaged for a long time before getting married? Do you feel it makes for a strong marriage? Why or why not?

280. Do you think the "generation gap" is real? If so, what do you think causes it? If not, why do you think there is no such gap?

281. How do you *show* love?

282. Do most parents trust their children? What do children do to make parents trust them?

283. What is the one place in the world you would most like to live for one year? Why?

284. What one thing do you most like to do? Write a short story about it.

285. What do you think about when you are alone with a date?

286. Write what you think about the pollution problem and how to solve it.

287. What would you do if you had a three-day suspension?

288. Should hitchhiking be outlawed? Why? Why not? Have you ever hitchhiked? Why? Why not?

289. "Money is all you need for happiness." React to this statement.

290. What are your feelings about divorce? Why do you feel like this?

291. Why are you in school? Do you think that school is helping you? Are you just going because you have to?

292. Pretend you are rich. Describe a typical day in your life. Would you change the way you live if you actually became rich?

293. You are a girl in high school, age 17, and you are pregnant. Describe your feelings, and the reactions of your friends, parents, relatives, boyfriend, and teachers.

294. What does the word "prejudice" mean to you? Do you feel you are prejudiced toward any race, religion, or ethnic group? Explain.

295. Describe your friends—what are they like? Don't use names.

296. Would you like to be married right now? Why or why not?

297. When new kids come to this school, how do you treat them? How do you act and feel when you are in a strange place and know no one?

298. If you could go to school in any foreign country, which one would it be? Why?

299. I hope my children won't have to. . . . Finish the sentence and explain.

300. If you had $100,000 and 100 acres of ground, what would you build?

301. In 1972, overall crime dropped for the first time in 17 years. Burglary, larceny and auto theft decreased. But murder, rape, assault, and robbery increased. Write why you feel these have increased. What can you do to help reduce crime?

302. Eighteen-year olds receive adult privileges in many states. What blessings, responsibilities, pitfalls, or dangers face these 18-year-olds?

303. Aerosol-spray sniffing can be fatal. Why do you feel teenagers risk death to get "high?"

304. Asian and African nations again face starvation this year. Should the U.S. get involved in this problem? What role should the U.S. play? Why?

305. What do you like best about your brother or sister? How can you let them know this?

306. How would you describe the United States to someone in another country?

307. If you were a writer, what kind of books would you write? Why?

308. Public opinion polls show that the favorite TV show of high school and college students is "Columbo." Explain why this is so, and what your own feelings about the show are.

309. What goals have you set for yourself to reach this week? How do you plan to reach these goals? Why have you set goals for yourself?

310. What would you like to happen to you when you get old?

311. What does morality mean? Are we experiencing a "new morality"? Is it good or bad? What are some consequences of it for *you*?

312. If you found that your boyfriend or girlfriend was on drugs, what would you do?

Putting a Value on Things [19]

PURPOSE

When we buy insurance, we are in reality placing a monetary value on certain things, such as a house, or jewelry. This strategy is designed to help students become aware of the relative values they assign to their personal possessions.

PROCEDURE

Have students make a list of their personal possessions; anything they own may be included on the list. When they finish, explain that each student is to pretend that he or she has $250 (or whatever sum you decide) with which to buy insurance for his or her possessions. Thus, if a student values one of his possessions at $50.00, it will leave him or her $200 with which to purchase insurance for other possessions.[20]

As a first step, have each student go down his or her list and try to place a monetary value on each item. Then, students are to allocate the amount of insurance they wish to place on various items until their $250 is spent. Inform students that when purchasing insurance, they do not need to insure an item for its full value.

Follow up the activity by having students share and compare their lists and allocations.

VARIATIONS

Personal possessions are not the only things that can be insured. Students might also explore the notion of insuring their personal attributes, talents, abilities, successes, friendships, goals, and so on. The idea here is considerably different from the reimbursement notion used with property or life insurance. What the student is pretending to buy is "assurance" that he or she will indeed reach his or goals, develop his or her talents, keep his or her friendships, and so on. (Of course, in reality, such assurance cannot be had.) A monetary value is assigned to the various goals, talents, friendships, etc., to show the relative value the student places on each.

Thus, you might have students make a list of their personal goals, for instance. Each student has $100 worth of insurance. The student's task, then, is to allocate his or her $100 to reflect the relative values that he or she places on each of his or her goals.

In Hawley and Hawley's activity "Lloyds of London," [21] students purchase various pretend insurance policies such as a health policy, friendship policy, joy of living policy, and so on. When the student decides upon a policy, he or she must write out what he or she wants the policy to insure. For example, a student purchasing a health policy might write that what he wants is assurance that he "will live to the age of ninety without a day of sickness or ill health." Students are then encouraged to think about how they might actually achieve at least a portion of their goal, e.g., by eating healthful foods, getting a regular medical checkup, keeping physically fit, and so on. The following are some insurance policies that students might wish to purchase.

1.   A Marriage Policy

2.   A Child Raising Policy

3.   A Love Policy

4.   A Self-Fulfillment Policy

5.   A Sexual Fulfillment Policy

6.   An Accident-Free-Life Policy

7.   A Longevity Policy

8.   A Wisdom of the Ages Policy

9. A Wealth Policy

10. A Peace and Tranquility Policy

11. A Beauty Policy or Good Looks Policy

12. A Friendship Policy

13. A Health Policy

14. A Joy of Living Policy

15. A Happiness Policy

16. A Charming Personality Policy

17. A Success Policy

18. A Popularity Policy

Paper Memorials

PURPOSE

The memorials we build to past and present heroes, events, and ideas are in reality statements of what we value. The purpose of this strategy is to give students a chance to build a paper structure as a memorial to something they value. It is also a good activity for building group rapport, examining decision-making processes, and observing various members' roles in a small group activity.

PROCEDURE

Divide the class into groups of five to seven members each. Explain that each group will be given a chance to build a paper structure as a memorial to someone or something they value or want to honor. First, however, they must do some preliminary groundwork.

The first task for each group is to decide who or what they wish to honor. Have each student select several alternatives privately. For example, one student might wish to build a structure to honor *peace, Martin Luther King,* and *love.* The group should then come together and compile a total listing of all the alternatives. From this group list, one alternative should be chosen by consensus. Every member of the group should agree and support the selection.

The second task the group faces is to make a plan for the construction of its structure. Each group will use newspapers and masking tape to construct its structure. Thus, during the planning phase, the group should experiment with different ways of rolling, folding, and taping the newspaper for construction purposes. The group is not to start building the structure, however. Members should also consider various construction forms which might be used to gain strength, stability, height, and so on. (The groups might be encouraged to do some research during this phase. In fact, the problem could provide the basis for a whole unit on architecture and/or building and bridge construction.) The groups should also be collecting plenty of newspaper during this time.

Finally, give the groups the task of building the structure. A time limit of fifteen to forty-five minutes can be set, or you can allow the groups to work on the structures for several days, depending upon your objectives and student interest in the activity.

When the groups finish, have them name their memorials and write a dedication statement. These should then be attached to the memorials.

Follow up the activity by having students discuss and share their thoughts and feelings about the experience with members of their own group, as well as with members from the other groups. Have them look at some of these questions:

1. What values does our memorial represent?

2. Are the values our group thought important very different from those of other groups? In what way?

3. How were decisions made in our group? Did everyone get a chance to express his or her feelings?

4. What role did each of the group members play in the process?

5. If we had it to do over again, what things would we do differently?

VARIATIONS

The whole activity can be compressed into a forty-five to sixty minute time period by allotting ten minutes for groundwork, ten minutes for planning, fifteen minutes for construction, and ten to twenty-five minutes for sharing and discussion.

Also, instead of memorials, the groups can build domes, temples, skyscrapers, bridges, houses, a thing of beauty, and so on.

A final activity can be added to the basic strategy to generate additional data for values analysis and discussion. Give the groups the task of rating each other's structures using a common set of agreed upon criteria—such as beauty, originality, height, appropriateness. For example, if there are three groups—A, B, and C—have Group A rate groups B and C by dividing 100 points between the two groups to represent A's assessment of the relative merits of the two structures. (The purpose here is not to generate competition for the sake of competition. Rather, the purpose is to generate data so that each individual can analyze how he or she responds to competitive situations—see the discussion questions on *186* and *188* which are used to examine the ratings.) The rating is to be done for each of the preselected and agreed upon criteria. For example, on originality Group A might give 60 points to Group B and 40 points to Group C. Group B rates Groups A and C in the same way, while Group C rates Groups A and B. No group rates itself. The points are then totaled; the group with the most points "wins." Use the grid on *page 187* to record the group ratings.

Follow up with a whole-class discussion. Use the following questions to stimulate discussion:

1. Did any groups assign points on some basis other than the criteria; for example, to underrate the closer competitor for "victory"?

2. Do you feel the ratings really reflect the true merits of the structure?

Criteria Grid

CRITERIA TO BE USED FOR RATING	RATING OF GROUP'S STRUCTURE							
	GROUP	A	B	C	D	E	F	G
BEAUTY	A							
	B							
	C							
	D							
	E							
	F							
	G							
ORIGINALITY	A							
	B							
	C							
	D							
	E							
	F							
	G							
HEIGHT	A							
	B							
	C							
	D							
	E							
	F							
	G							
APPROPRIATENESS (really gets the message across)	A							
	B							
	C							
	D							
	E							
	F							
	G							
TOTALS								

3. How did it feel to have others judge your work? Did you enjoy judging others' work?

4. In building your structure, was your primary motive *power* (to win), *affiliation* (for the fun of working with your group members), or *achievement* (to build a structure that satisfies your personal standards)?[22]

Values Fantasies

PURPOSE

Fantasy provides a safe but effective means of helping students become aware of and clarify their values-related thinking and feelings.

PROCEDURE

Ask students to write about a fantasy trip they would like to take. Have them use the following four items as guidelines for writing the story.

1. Give a brief description of where and when your visit takes place.

2. What do you see and do on the trip?

3. Who goes with you on the trip?

4. What do you like best about your trip? What do you like least?

Then, have students share their fantasies in small groups or by posting them around the room. Or, have students dramatize their fantasies.

If students have difficulty thinking of fantasy trips to take, suggest some of the following and let them choose.

1. Take a trip to Mars where you encounter a new civilization.

2. Take a trip in a time capsule into the future or the past.

3. Take a trip to an under-the-sea city in the year 2075.

4. Take a trip to a lost civilization in a primitive country.

5. Take a trip through your own body or brain.

6. Take a trip to a space city in the year 3000.

7. Take a trip into "adventure land."

8. Take a trip to the "land of success."

VARIATIONS

Have students write a fantasy in which they become a famous figure, fictional or historical. Or a fantasy about their ideal mate, friend, family, school, city, or world.

Values Sheets: A Cookbook Approach

PURPOSE

Values Sheets are one of the most useful classroom strategies for helping students clarify and affirm their values. However, because they are often difficult and time-consuming to develop, the busy teacher often passes over the strategy. This strategy is designed to provide a shortcut method of developing *Values Sheets*.[23] It is not intended to replace the values sheet which is tailor made by the teacher to fit the particular topic he has selected, but when the teacher just can't find the time to put together an original values sheet, this strategy will serve the students very well.

PROCEDURE

Step 1.   *Constructing the top of the values sheet.*   The top of a values sheet consists of an item which contains within it a values issue, problem, or dilemma. The item may be a clipping (newspaper headline or article), a cartoon, a poem, a picture, a painting or drawing, etc. Select an item and put it at the top of the values sheet.

Step 2.   *Selecting the questions for the bottom of the values sheet*. The bottom of a values sheet consists of a set of questions designed to help the student clarify his thinking about the top of the values sheet. Select one of the sets of questions from the *Values Sheet Bottoms* below. One of the sets should fit the top you have selected. If it does not, reword or adapt the questions until they do fit. Then, write the questions at the bottom of the values sheet, directly under the top you have selected. The questions should help the student (1) identify the value issue, problem or dilemma involved, (2) assess his feelings about the issue, (3) examine some alternatives for dealing with the issue, (4) examine the consequences involved, and (5) think of some action he or she can take in relation to the issue.

Step 3. *Using the Values Sheet.* The values sheet can be used in several ways.

A. The values sheet can be dittoed and given to students as an individual assignment to be completed in writing.

B. It can be given to a small group for use as a discussion starter and organizer.

C. Post the values sheet or sheets on a bulletin board or as part of a learning center. Write a set of self-instruction steps and let the students complete them at their own pace. *(See page 547.)*

D. Tie them into the subject matter you are teaching by using a poem, historical event, current event— whatever content is appropriate—as the top.

E. For early elementary students, post a picture at the top of a large sheet of paper. Print the questions below. Hold up the sheet and have the children respond to the questions orally.

Values Sheet Bottoms[24]

Bottom No. 1

1. What problem or problems are brought out or dramatized in this selection/picture? Which of these problems is of greatest concern to you?

2. Think of all the different possible ways that there are to solve or cope with this problem. List them.

3. Which of these alternatives do you think are the best solutions to the problem? Do your feelings support your thinking? If not, can you explain this?

4. Have you ever done anything about this problem in the past? Was it consistent with what you now think and feel is the best solution?

5. What were the consequences of what you did?

6. Can you think of anything you would want to do concerning this issue?

Bottom No. 2

1. How do you feel about the (choice, action, situation) faced by_____?

2. What other ways could _____(have acted/solved his problem)?

3. What would you have done?

4. Have you ever faced a similar problem?

5. What did you do?

6. What were the consequences of your action?

7. Would you act differently if faced with the same situation now?

Bottom No. 3

1. How do you feel about what took place?

2. Do you think such things happen often? Why?

3. What different attitudes do people have toward this problem?

4. What is your attitude?

5. Is there anything you can do about it? Is there anything you want to do?

6. What might happen if you did something?

Let's Build a City

PURPOSE

Few tasks are as revealing of our value system, our priorities, and our beliefs than the charge to design, build, and operate the ideal city. This strategy is well worth the effort put into it, both in terms of helping students develop a greater understanding of themselves and in increasing their understanding of the complex communities we live in and how they affect our lives.

PROCEDURE

The following steps are designed to be implemented over a period of a semester or longer. However, they can be shortened considerably. Also, the project need not run every day for long periods of time; small amounts of time can be devoted to the project periodically so that eventually the six steps outlined below are completed.

Step 1.   *Preparing the plan.*   Students are divided into groups of three to five members. Each group prepares a plan of its ideal city. The plan should include a variety of businesses and industries, residential areas, schools, social agencies, and recreational areas. Both a map and a written description of the city should be prepared. The written plan should include the proposed city's size, population, racial and ethnic makeup, kinds of businesses and industries, and a detailed description of the governmental structure, including the executive, legislative, and judicial elements. All this can, of course, be simplified for younger children.

Step 2.   *Agreeing on the plan.*   Each group is given a specific meeting location in the room. Each elects a chairman. The goal of each group during the negotiations phase is to get the other groups to agree to its plan, or to work out, through discussion, a city plan to which a majority of the class can agree. During the actual negotiating, the chairman must remain at his group's location at all times. He may receive representatives from other groups and send his own representatives out to other groups to get information and bargain, but he may not leave his station. Final agreement on the city plan need only be by a majority; however, students may want to consider the merits of agreeing to the plan by consensus.

Step 3. *Setting up the city government.* Once agreement is reached on a city plan, an interim committee composed of the group chairmen is given the responsibility to set up the governmental machinery and get government rolling. This means: setting up election procedures and dates, if there are to be elections: designating meeting areas and offices, such as the mayor's office, council meeting areas, etc.; and any other kinds of decisions that must be made to get the government in operation. Majority vote rules. The interim committee may hold either closed or open meetings.

Step 4. *Making the government work.* The elected and/or appointed government officials take over and begin making the government work. Many decisions will have to be made about such things as methods of land allocation, zoning, what laws to make, how to enforce the laws, what form of currency is to be used, how the currency will be distributed, how records will be kept, how the government will be financed, and so on. This, of course, will be an ongoing concern throughout the rest of the project.

Step 5. *Building the city.* Once some of the above decisions have been made, the city government can allocate the land to individuals or groups by giving it away, selling it, leasing it, or through some combination of these. Deeds of ownership or lease contracts are to be issued. Then, construction of the city begins by the individuals and/or groups who own or lease the land. A mini-city can actually be constructed out of light building materials—cardboard, paper, wood, plastic, styrofoam, etc.—or simply drawn on large sheets of paper and posted. Community groups and organizations can form to promote their interests, and can begin meeting with other groups and government officials to get better laws passed, solve problems facing them, etc. Businesses and industries can start producing goods and services, and can form organizations to promote their welfare and interests. For example, students who want to start a furniture factory might actually begin building tiny chairs and tables out of cardboard or some other suitable material. (Sounds like fun, doesn't it?)

Step 6. *Making the city work.* The mark of a good city is in how well it can handle crisis situations. After the city is built and things are running fairly smoothly, introduce a crisis situation. For example: a flood or some other natural disaster threatens and then hits the city; or, massive racial confrontations threaten to rip the city apart; or, several big industries come upon hard times and must lay off a third of their workers. Call a city meeting and outline in some detail the nature of the crisis situation. Have students think about some of the possible physical, social, and personal consequences of the crisis that might occur. Then, send the students back into their groups to work out alternative ways to meet the crisis. Don't forget to *examine process* periodically: call a city meeting and help students check on how well they are handling the crisis, what the consequences have been, and what alternative ways of organizing and solving the problems may have been overlooked.

ADDITIONAL SUGGESTIONS

The direction the city problem takes will depend to a large extent on what kind of help, organization, and structure the teacher provides. Your most critical task, however, is to help students learn more about their values and the valuing processes from the project. Hold frequent "town meetings" and raise the following kinds of questions when they are appropriate:

What are the consequences of the decisions we have made and the actions we have taken?

What are some alternative ways we could have handled that?

Are we making decisions and taking action that we want to take?

Are we proud of our actions?

Are we proud of our city?

Are we choosing freely?

What do our actions say about what we value?

Are our decisions and actions contradictory?

Is this really the kind of city we had in mind?

What are the problems we face?

What have we learned?

How do we feel about what is going on?

To begin a unit such as this, or to supplement the work throughout the project, "task cards" can be used very effectively. They can be made from construction paper and brightened by the use of pictures and illustrations. Place the cards in a box somewhere in the room and have them available for students to use whenever they have some free time. Try to display the students' completed work whenever possible.

Sample Task Cards[25]

1. Laws are rules for the community. One of the main duties of government is to make sure that people in the community obey the laws.

    A.   Name some groups with rules.

    B.   Does your family have any rules? Give some examples. Why do you have these rules?

    C.   Give some examples of rules in school. Do you think these are necessary? Why or why not?

    D.   What would happen if there were no rules for traffic?

2. Superman's super powers are:

    A.   Super speed.

    B.   Super strength.

    C.   Cannot be hurt in any way.

    D.   Super hearing.

    E.   Super vision.

How can each one of Superman's 5 super powers help him fight crime in the city? Is there anything you can do to help Superman in his fight against crime?

3. I'll bet there are a lot of things to do and see in your city! Will you write me a letter and let me know what you do for fun in your city? My name is Nancy.

4. What is this? (Picture of an orchestra pasted on paper.) Where could you find it in your city? What other types of music can you hear in the city? Where can you go to hear different kinds of music? Do you like music? What kinds?

5. One of these bicycles is yours (pictures of bicycles). You are going out to ride your bike after school today. Write a story about where you ride and what you see along the way.

6. Write the answers to these questions: What are these men doing (pictures of men playing football or baseball)? Do you like to do what they are doing? Where in the city can you play football (baseball)? Where can you play baseball (football), hockey, basketball, or go swimming? Who can you play with, and how would you get a team together?

7. What important things will you look for in the man you

choose to run the city government? On a piece of paper, answer this question and also:

    A.   What jobs does the mayor of the city have?

    B.   Would you give him any more jobs? Would you take away any of his jobs?

    C.   Do you know who the mayor of your city is? What is his name?

8. This is the mayor of our city (picture of mayor). What problems must he as mayor deal with? Do you think he is doing a good job? Why or why not? Would you vote for him if you could?

9. You are running for representative of your neighborhood. What would be your campaign slogan and why? Write your campaign slogan and explain why your friends should elect you. What are you going to do to help your neighborhood?

10. Get a newspaper from the back of the room. Find the section on city news (metropolitan news). Cut out an article and read it. Write a report about it and include your personal feelings about the article, such as how it relates to you.

11. Where is it legal to park in the city on the streets, and where is it illegal? How can you tell?

12. "Traffic flows as the city tows." So many people drive into the city that parking spaces are difficult to find.

Many people, instead of searching for a place to park, just park their car illegally. The police, to keep the traffic moving and uphold the parking rules, have started to tow away cars in certain areas marked "tow away zones." Once their cars have been towed, people must pay a $10 ticket and a $40 towing fee to get their car back.

What do you think of the city's towing policy? Is it fair or unfair? What else might the city do to keep people from parking illegally? What other forms of transportation might people use to get into the city?

13. You're moving in! Yes, you're moving to your new apartment. What will you need to live in your new apartment? Write a short story about moving into your very own apartment in the city.

14. Draw a picture of the street that you live on. Place your house on the street. Try to remember everything that you can about your street and house, and add it to your drawing. Use crayons and whatever else you need.

15. Can you draw an outline of the vertical appearance of the city (a sample skyline is provided)? It is called a skyline. On a piece of paper, draw a skyline. Include such shapes as a factory, a school, skyscrapers, stores, and apartment buildings. If you were going to build some new buildings, what would you build?

16. A map of the city can tell you where to go and how to get there. The language of maps can tell you how wide a

road is, where the road goes, if the road is straight, or crooked. (Sample maps may be drawn illustrating these things.) Can you draw a map? Draw a map showing how you would get from your house to the closest shopping area. Draw a map of your neighborhood and put stars next to your favorite places.

17. This is a picture of a flood victim (picture provided). If a bad flood happened in your city what would you do? Answer these questions:

    A. How would you prevent your house from being ruined?

    B. What five things (besides people) would you want to save from your house?

    C. Who would help your family? What would they do?

    D. Where would your family go while your house was under water?

    E. What would be your hardest jobs after the flood?

18. This is how the mail was brought from New York City to Philadelphia 200 years ago (picture of a stagecoach). What problems do you think a stagecoach might have in making the long trip? One example would be that the driver was at the mercy of rain and snow. He might be stopped for hours because of this. What forms of transportation are used today to carry the mail? Name at least three. List five people you write letters to and five people you like to get letters from.

19. Prices at the supermarket have risen drastically. Think of your refrigerator at home. How much would you pay for the food you see inside of it? Directions:

 A. Take out pieces of white paper.

 B. With crayons, draw a picture of each piece of food that you think is inside your refrigerator.

 C. Tonight when you go home, ask your mother how much the food you drew really cost. Was it more or less than you thought?

20. You are given $10.00 to spend in one day. What would you spend it on? Directions:

 A. From a magazine, cut out pictures of what you would like to buy with your $10.00.

 B. Paste the pictures on a piece of paper.

 C. Next to each picture, write how much you think that thing costs. Make sure all the things you have do not total more than $10.00.

21. There are many stores for our many needs. Can you think of some of the different stores you visit during the year?

 A. Take a piece of paper and draw as many different stores as you remember visiting.

 B. Make a list of these stores and the things you could buy in each store. How much would you guess these things cost?

    C. Talk with some of your friends about the prices you have listed. Do they think your cost estimates are correct? Check your answers by asking your parents, or by finding prices in the newspaper.

    D. If you had $100, which stores would you visit? What would you buy?

22. Air pollution is everywhere. What do you think makes our air unclean? Get a piece of paper and draw anything that you think makes our city air unclean. Is there anything you can do about air pollution? Explain.

23. What would happen if garbage piled up in a city? How would it affect the health of the people? Pretend you live in a tall apartment building. How do you depend upon the department of sanitation?

24. Many signs are placed up and down our city streets. This is a form of pollution. Draw your own city street the way you would like it to look. Do you have many signs? Are some signs more important than others? Explain.

25. Do you use more water taking a shower or a bath? Here's how you can find out.

    A. When you next take a bath, use a piece of adhesive tape to mark the height of the water in the tub.

    B. Let the tape remain in the tub. Next time,

take a shower. Be sure to put a stopper in the tub.

C.   When you are finished with your shower, use the tape to check the height of the water in the tub. Did you use more or less water than the time before?

D.   Is it important to save water? Why or why not?

On a separate piece of paper, finish the following sentences:

A.   I can save water when I brush my teeth by . . .

B.   I can save water when I sprinkle a lawn by . . .

C.   I can save water when I wash dishes by . . .

D.   I can save water when I get a drink by . . .

26. You and your friend just bought candy bars. You are walking from the store and your friend throws his candy wrapper into the street. What do you do?

27. Noise is also a form of pollution, and is all around us in the city. What sounds do you hear in the city? Write ten sounds that you hear when you are playing outside. Write down some other sounds you might hear if you were at a busy intersection downtown. Do any of these sounds bother you? Which ones? Can you do anything about them?

Values Sharing

PURPOSE

The *Values Sharing* group[26] consists of five to twelve student volunteers and the teacher. It is held in a corner of the room. Students and teacher pull their chairs into a circle. The teacher leads the group by asking questions and helping to direct communication flow; however, he also participates as an equal and full member of the group. The goal here is to encourage students to think about and begin to clarify their values in specifically designated areas. It also provides an opportunity for students to publicly affirm and share their values.

PROCEDURE

Identify a portion of the room where the *Values Sharing* group will always meet. If you prefer informality, carpet the area or have students bring in pillows so they can sit on the floor. If you choose the floor, make sure you join them. Use the *Values Sharing* group to build trust and explore students' values and concerns. Any of the values strategies described in this book, as well as the ones referred to in other sources, may be used in the group to promote personal inquiry and exploration.

It is a good idea to post the following rules in the area where the *Values Sharing* group regularly meets.

1. Only volunteers participate in a *Values Sharing* session.

2. You always have the right to pass or to leave the group.

3. You must listen to others in the group when they are speaking, and let them finish what they are saying before you begin.

4. You must respect the rights of other individuals in the group, and not attack them personally or make them feel "put down." You don't have to agree with what they say, but you should respect their right to say it.

In the choice-centered or individualized classroom, *Values Sharing* can become a regularly scheduled activity. Or, the teacher may agree to run a *Values Sharing* group whenever there is enough student interest to get five or more participants. In the conventional classroom, the teacher can give seat work to the rest of the class while he meets with the *Values Sharing* group.

VALUES SHARING CURRICULUM[27]

The sequence of topics on *pages 208-214* is designed to be used in the *Values Sharing* group. Although the topics can be used most appropriately with students of the middle grades—fourth through ninth—primary and high school teachers can use the topics by adapting or modifying them to fit the level of sophistication of their students.

The purpose of the sequence of topics it to help students clarify their values by exploring the three areas of *prizing, choosing*, and *acting*. Each topic is designed to encourage students to talk about what they prize, or how they make *value choices*, or how they *act upon* their values.

Set aside between twenty and forty minutes for each session. Introduce the topics with the words, "Today, I'd like you to tell us about. . . . " Remind students of the rules if necessary.

When four students have had their turn, ask others in the group if anyone can recall what has been said. Do not put anyone on the spot, but let students, one at a time, volunteer to try to recall what was said until all that has been said is recalled accurately. This lets students know they are being heard and helps students learn to listen to each other. Continue with the discussion until four more students have spoken and repeat the above process. Do this until the entire circle is completed. Be sure to take your turn and share your thoughts.

You may want to use the following sequence of topics as a starter. Adapt or modify them, or invent your own to fit the needs and level of your students.

Values Topics

SESSION	"TELL US ABOUT . . . "	AREA OF VALUE BEING EXPLORED
1.	Something you are proud of about your family.	Prizing

2. How you spend your free time
   (after school hours and weekends).   Acting

3. Something that you are proud of
   that you own.   Prizing

4. Something you can do now that you
   couldn't do a year ago.   Acting

5. A gift you have given and are proud of.   Prizing

6. How you helped someone once.   Acting

7. What you look for in choosing a friend.   Choosing

8. Something you are proud of that you have
   written, drawn, or made with your hands.   Prizing

9. Something good that has happened as a
   result of a choice you made.   Choosing

10. Something important that you
    are planning to do.   Acting

11. Whether you prefer to make choices
    yourself or have others make choices for you.   Choosing

12. Something you are proud of that
    you have worked hard for.   Prizing

13. Something good you have done that
    not many people know about.   Acting

14. A funny thing you did of which you are proud.   Prizing

15. A difficult choice you made recently.   Choosing

16. Something you did that took courage to do. Acting

17. Something important you decided in which you made the choice all by yourself.   Choosing

18. A goal that you have set of which you are proud.   Prizing

19. A belief or value you hold strongly and what you do about it.   Acting

20. Something difficult that you learned that you are proud of.   Prizing

21. A choice you made in which more than two alternatives were involved.   Choosing

22. Something that is an important pattern of behavior or a regular habit in your life.   Acting

23. A stand you have taken of which you are proud.   Prizing

24. Who you go to for advice when making important or difficult decisions.   Choosing

25. Something that you have done before that you would do differently today.   Acting

26. Something you are proud of that you have done today.   Prizing

27. A choice you made that did not work out the way you had hoped.   Choosing

28. Something that another person has done that you would like to do or do more of.   Acting

29. The most difficult choice you ever made.   Choosing

30. A change you would like to make in yourself.   Acting

ADDITIONAL VALUES TOPICS

Prizing Topics

1. What you are most proud of about your friends (school, family, neighborhood).

2. Your ideal friend (mate, school, world).

3. Your favorite food (TV program, movie, movie star, place to be alone, dress, song, possession, feeling, pastime, city, kind of party).

4. If you could have a wish come true what would you wish for?

5. A dream you have for the future.

6. Something you are proud of that only you can do.

7. Something you believe or value that you hope your children will also believe or value.

8. Where you would like to live someday (travel, spend a year, visit for a week, be in five years).

9. Something you want for yourself (others, your friends, your family).

10. Something you did last summer that you are proud of.

11. A belief or issue about which you have taken a public stand recently.

12. Something that you are proud of that you can do all by yourself.

13. A belief or conviction that you have shared with someone recently.

14.   Something you are proud of that you have done for another person.

15.   Something about one of the guiding principles in your life.

16.   Something you are proud of in your room.

Choosing Topics

1.   Some alternatives you considered in a difficult decision you once had to make.

2.   A choice you made that turned out well.

3.   A choice you had to make between two things you wanted very much.

4.   A choice you made that turned out badly.

5.   A choice you made that others thought was wrong but you made it anyway.

6.   When you make a decision, what you are most concerned about.

7.   A time that you refused to go along with the crowd.

8.   How you make difficult decisions.

9.   The last difficult decision you made, and what consequences you considered before making it.

10.   A decision you know you will have to make in the future and some alternatives you have been considering.

11.   Some advice others have given you about making decisions.

Acting Topics

1.   What you do when you're proud of something.

2.   Something you have done that you are proud of.

3.   What you do to make your wishes (dreams) come true.

4.   How you plan to get where you want to be professionally (teacher, doctor, farmer, etc.).

5.   The most exciting thing you have done recently.

6.   How you live by your values (convictions, beliefs).

7.   A pattern of behavior that you have that you like.

8.   Something you're going to do for someone before next week (tomorrow, month, year).

9.   Something you could do to start acting on your values.

10.   What you would do if you could do anything you wanted to do for one week.

11.   Something about an action you are going to take in the near future that you are looking forward to.

12.   Something you are planning to do after you leave home.

13.   Something you did that took real perseverance to do or complete.

14.   Something you do to live by your religion.

15.   Something you could do this week to act on a value you hold.

16.   Something you could do to make this a better world (school, city, neighborhood) to live in.

Values Negotiating[28]

PURPOSE

This strategy gives students a chance to publicly affirm a stand on a particular issue and to share their ideas about the issue with others. It also serves to point out to students that there are many different ways to view and think about any given problem or issue.

PROCEDURE

Divide students into groups of about ten. Ask them to place in a straight row as many chairs as there are persons in the group. Then present the groups with an issue on which there is a full range of possible positions and opinions—for example, "Should school attendance be voluntary or compulsory?" This issue could be placed on a continuum with totally voluntary attendance for all ages at one end, and compulsory school attendance through graduate school at the other.

You can draw the continuum on the board and ask

students where they think they would be on it. A few students might volunteer to write their names above their positions. Then explain that the row of chairs represents the same continuum. Ask students to place themselves in the chairs according to how they feel about the issue.

After they sit down, they should discuss with the people on either side of them how they feel about the issue to be sure they are in the right place. If they then feel that they should be further up or down on the continuum, they must negotiate for the chair they want by talking with the person in it and the people on either side of it. If some students are sure they are in the right chair immediately, encourage them to listen in on some of the discussions up and down the continuum to double check on how others feel relative to how they feel.

The negotiating can continue until everyone is satisfied with his or her position (this can take from 20 minutes to two hours) or you can cut the discussion off. A third alternative is to set a time limit for the negotiation phase.

The negotiation phase can be followed up in several ways. One, the teacher can play "devil's advocate" to see if people are really clear about their positions relative to others in the group. Two, students can meet with persons who occupied the same chair in the other groups and compare their respective positions. Three, each member can write and post a brief statement of his position, allowing for intra-group and inter-group comparisons.

Facing Bench[29]

PURPOSE

A Quaker Friends Meeting is a time and place to speak with one's neighbors about the issues, problems, and concerns of the day. As anyone who has attended a Quaker meeting on a regular basis can tell you, it is an excellent forum for clarifying one's own beliefs and values. This strategy is designed to implement some of the ideas behind the Friends Meeting in the classroom on a continuing basis. The purpose is to give students a forum for speaking their minds and clarifying their values. It also serves to build a sense of community in the classroom.

PROCEDURE

Introduce students to the strategy by talking about the nature and purpose of a Quaker Friends Meeting. (You might have students do some reading and investigation on the subject, or perhaps several students would like to take on the investigation as a project and report to the class when they are finished. Better yet, have students attend a Friends Meeting.) Indicate that you would like to try a similar type of meeting in class on a regular basis, perhaps once a week for a period of forty-five minutes.

Just prior to the meeting, students arrange their chairs or desks in a large semi-circle so that everyone is part of the semi-circle or horseshoe. A bench, or several chairs placed together to form a bench, is placed in the front of the room facing the semi-circle. The bench, although part of the circle,

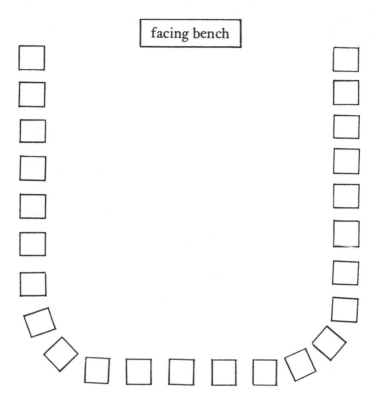

is to be set off from the circle by leaving some space at either end *(see diagram above)*. The bench is called a "facing bench." As the meeting begins, anyone who has an issue or topic of concern to discuss during the meeting comes forward and sits on the facing bench. Even if no one comes forward, the meeting continues; sit out the silence, someone will come forth.

The meeting is conducted according to the following rules. Read and discuss them, making sure everyone understands them. Post them near the facing bench as a reminder.

1. Only a person sitting on the facing bench may raise an issue, topic, or problem for discussion. He does so by *standing* and speaking his piece when it is his turn. As long as he is at the facing bench, discussion is to stay on the subject he has raised. When he is satisfied that the topic has been thoroughly discussed, he leaves the facing bench and the next person may take her turn raising the issue she wants to discuss.

2. Others sitting in the circle or at the facing bench may speak to the subject under discussion by *standing* and speaking their thoughts and feelings. When finished, sit down.

3. Any subject of personal or general concern may be discussed in the meeting.

4. Anyone may come forth to the facing bench at any time to await his turn to raise an issue as long as there is a vacant seat on the facing bench.

5. All have an equal voice during the discussion, including the teacher.

6. Everyone's right to speak and state his or her position must be respected. You must accept a person's right to believe and feel as he or she

does even though you may disagree with his or her statements.

Plan to hold the meeting at a regularly scheduled time each week for a set amount of time. Then stick to it. Students will come to look forward to the time.

When you speak, don't impose your status as the teacher (or older adult) upon the discussion. It is important that you share your thoughts, feelings, and perhaps your wisdom, but in ways which clearly say, "here's what I think and this is what led me to think it—take it for what it is worth."

Values Forum

PURPOSE

The purpose of this strategy, like the previous one, is to provide an ongoing forum for students to share and publicly affirm their values and strongly held beliefs. It also provides students with an opportunity to explore the values systems of others who may believe and value differently than they do.

PROCEDURE

To create the *Values Forum*, simply set aside an amount of time and some space in the classroom where students can, on a regularly scheduled basis, speak their own minds or invite others to share their ideas and values. There are two rules. One, the person on the soap box (at the podium, with the mike, etc.) controls the forum; he decides what the topic is and who will speak besides himself. Rule two, participants should respect the speaker's right to be heard even though they may disagree with his views.

One teacher we know started a values forum in his classroom which, within weeks, became a school-wide function. He started by giving the responsibility for organizing and running the forum to a student planning committee. The committee decided that two days a week, guest speakers from the community would be invited in to speak at the forum. The speakers were so successful that the values forum was expanded to all-day sessions, five days per week. This was possible because the school day was organized on a flexible modular schedule which freed students for independent study and activity for 50 percent of the school day. Thus, a large instructional area accommodating about 100 persons was given over to the forum. It was filled to overflowing as students listened to community speakers and took their turns speaking out. Topics ranged from civil rights to religion; community speakers represented such organizations as Planned Parenthood, The John Birch Society, The U.S. Army, and some 60 other local civic groups, organizations, or individuals. On a number of occasions, the forum had to be scheduled in the auditorium to accommodate the massive turnout of students, teachers, and parents.

Your forum need not be so elaborate, but watch it if you don't want it to grow out of hand!!!

A LIST OF POTENTIAL FORUM SPEAKERS

Business leaders in the community.

Representatives from corporations located in the community.

Individuals from the professions: doctor, dentist, lawyer.

Religious leaders from the community.

Planned Parenthood.

Pro- and anti-abortion groups.

Police, firemen.

Tradesmen: carpenters, machinists, etc.

Individuals with unusual hobbies.

Sportsmen.

Artists, dancers, actors, etc.

County agricultural agent.

Political party leaders.

Airport officials.

Drug prevention and rehabilitation workers.

Marriage counselors.

Sanitation men.

Childbirth education groups.

Factory workers.

Self-employed businessmen.

Farmer, farm implement dealer, etc.

Government officials, representatives, etc.

School administrators, board of education members.

Banking officials.

Used-car and new-car salesmen.

U.S. Army, Navy, etc.

Local rock groups, band leaders, singers, etc.

Civil rights leaders.

Women's lib leaders.

College and university representatives.

Hospital officials, nurses, etc.

Union officials.

Bus drivers, airplane pilots, stewardesses.

Have the students brainstorm additions to the list, or the entire list itself.

Talk Show [30]

PURPOSE

TV and radio talk shows have become big entertainment. This strategy is an adaptation of the TV talk show to the classroom. It is intended to help students gain insights into the values and behavior of other people, helping them to better understand and appreciate others. It also gives students a chance to publicly affirm their own beliefs and values.

PROCEDURE

This strategy was developed by a teacher who could seem to find no way of getting one of his students interested in doing anything constructive in the classroom. When the student was not sleeping in class, he was in trouble. The only thing he seemed interested in was the Johnny Carson's *Tonight* show. Finally, completely frustrated and grasping for straws, the teacher armed the student with a tape recorder and gave him the assignment of interviewing people on the street much like Johnny Carson interviews his guests on TV. The student turned on to the idea, and was soon conducting his own talk show in the classroom.

Introduce the strategy by explaining how talk shows can help people learn more about themselves and each other. Then, give the students a homework assignment to watch several afternoon or evening talk shows and keep a record of the kinds of questions that were asked and discussed. Use this record to help students learn the difference between simply entertaining questions and those questions which both entertain and help promote insight and understanding of a person's values. Then have students submit questions which they think will be both entertaining and useful for values inquiry.[31]

Finally, set up and conduct a talk show. Perhaps the first few times you will want to act as host, but encourage students to assume the role. The guests can be student volunteers or persons from outside the classroom. Both can promote personal inquiry since outside guests can be selected for the new or different ways of thinking and valuing they will introduce to the students. Either way, the *Talk Show* is likely to become one of the favorite activities in the classroom.

Petitions

PURPOSE

Petitions are a useful means of building and mobilizing support for an issue in which we believe. This strategy provides students with an opportunity to identify some of the things they feel strongly enough about to either initiate or sign a circulating petition. It is a means of helping students publicly affirm their values.

PROCEDURE

Introduce the strategy by circulating a petition among the members of the class. Write your own or choose one from the list below. Students are to sign it if they support it, or refuse to sign it if they do not.

Then, ask the students each to write his or her own petition. They should start with the words, "We, the undersigned. . . . " The petitions should be specific.

When students finish their petitions, each student should carry his own petition around the room and try to get other students to sign it. Students should be encouraged to sign only those petitions which they really believe in, and not feel pressured to sign every petition they read.

Sample Petitions

1. We, the undersigned, believe that billboards should be removed from all roadsides.

2. We, the undersigned, believe that strict anti-pollution laws should be passed and enforced, regardless of cost to manufacturer or consumer.

3. We, the undersigned, believe that *all* people are entitled to as *much* free education as they want.

4. We, the undersigned, believe that there should be bicycle paths constructed throughout cities as an alternate means of transportation.

5. We, the undersigned, believe that people who leave their trash after picnicking should not be allowed to use public parks and facilities.

6. We, the undersigned, believe that the merit of sports and recreational programs is greatly underestimated and that more social agencies and educational programs should be funded to provide such programs.

7. We, the undersigned, petition our representatives in government to sponsor and actively support legislation to develop safe, cost-competitive solar power within ten years or less, and phase out the operation of nuclear plants as quickly as possible.

FOLLOW-UP

If students feel particularly strong about a certain petition, encourage them to take further action. For example, they might start a drive to gain as many signatures in the community as possible, and then forward the petition to the appropriate governmental, community, organizational, or industrial representatives.

Notes

1. Two examples of *Values Lists* may be found in *Values Clarification*. These are strategies Number 1, "Twenty Things You Love to Do," and Number 38, "Who Comes to Your House?"

2. Suggested by Jim and Janet Wilson.

3. Our thanks to Virginia Leopold for the idea behind this strategy.

4. For a detailed explanation of this option and the ones below, see Howard Kirschenbaum, Sidney B. Simon, and Rodney W. Napier, *Wadjaget: The Grading Game*, New York, Hart, 1966.

5. The research on this item suggests that there is little if any correlation between academic and on-the-job performance. See *Wadjaget* for a discussion of this research.

6. Marie Oehler.

7. Adapted from a survey in Daniel Yankelovich, Inc., *The Changing Values on Campus*, New York, Washington Square Press, 1972.

8. Our thanks to Doris Ferleger and Winnie Schwartz for the idea behind this strategy.

9. In group-dynamics circles, the four cells are known as the Jo-Hari Window.

10. Items 1-123 were developed by Bob Muschlitz and students at Solanco High School, Quarryville, Pa.

11. Items 124-150 were developed by Jackie Goldberg, Cathy Lutz, and John DeGorio.

12. Items 151-159 were developed by Rowena Sobel and Tina Gordon.

13. Items 160-171 were developed by Susan Swartz.

14. Items 172-181 are from the work of Doris Ferleger and Winnie Schwartz.

15. Items 182-198 were developed by Thomas Kerr.

16. Items 199-216 were developed by Liz Bard, Cappy Knight, Dave Holstein, and Phyllis Kamanshine.

17. Items 217-243 were developed by Irene Bender.

18. Items 244-312 were developed by Robert Muschlitz, David M. Pretulak, and Mary Martha Howe.

19. The idea for this strategy comes from an activity called "Lloyds of London" in Robert C. Hawley and Isabel L. Hawley, *Human Values in the Classroom*, New York, Hart, 1975.

20. The concept of insurance is a difficult one for some students, thus some further explanation may be needed here.

21. In *Human Values in the Classroom*.

22. For more on *power, affiliation,* and *achievement motives*, see Alschuler et al., *Teaching Achievement Motivation*, Middletown, Conn., Educational Ventures, 1971.

23. A detailed discussion of how to construct and use values sheets plus many examples may be found in *Values and Teaching*.

24. Developed by Saville Sax, Mary Martha Whitworth (Howe), Wanda Penny, Gerald Montgomery, and Philip Sheldon, Nextep Fellowship Program, Southern Illinois University, Edwardsville, Ill.

25. Developed by Amy Barmat, Liz Moult, and Sharyn Rubin.

26. A similar but much more extensive technique for elementary age children called the *Magic Circle* has been developed by Bessell and Palomares. It has also been used successfully with older children. We *highly* recommend it and the training that goes with it.

27. Our thanks to Ed Betof for his input on this curriculum.

28. Developed by Edward Betof.

29. The idea for this strategy was suggested by Edward Betof.

30. Our thanks to Bob Muschlitz for this strategy.

31. Many questions for this strategy can be found in *Values Clarification*.

8. Helping Students Choose Their Values Freely, from Alternatives, After Weighing the Consequences

"I Prefer..." Statements[1]

PURPOSE

For some of us, the act of choosing is a difficult process. We are so conditioned by the advertising media, and influenced by the reward/punishment system of the schools, businesses, and conventional child rearing, that making a choice based upon *our own preferences* can be an anxiety-provoking experience. This strategy, simple in nature, helps us start to make choices based upon our own preferences.

PROCEDURE

Explain the purpose of the strategy to students. Then, introduce the strategy with the following, "I'm going to ask each of you to write several 'I prefer . . . ' statements. For example, these are some of mine: I prefer living in the country to living in the city; I prefer cooked spinach to cooked carrots; I prefer living close to the earth to living luxuriously. You can make your own 'I prefer . . . ' statements about anything—food, clothing, cars, brand names, TV programs, friendship traits, personal traits, values, music, and so on. See how many 'I prefer . . . ' statements you can get on paper in the next five minutes."

At the end of five minutes, try one of the following, depending upon your preference. Whip quickly around the group with each student reading one of his or her statements. Or, call upon several volunteers to read their lists and perhaps discuss some of their reasons. In either case, help students see that people prefer different things and that diversity of thought is to be respected. Or, have students form into small groups to share and discuss their lists with each other.

VARIATIONS

Ask students to go on a treasure hunt around the school or at home and find things to make "I prefer . . . " statements about. Objects can actually be brought into the classroom and put on display or used for discussion. Students can also draw "I prefer . . . " pictures or cut pictures out of magazines to show their preferences. These can be used as a basis for values discussions. For example, two different pictures can be cut from a magazine. One might be of a small family of a construction engineer, all wearing hardhats, seated on the tailgate of a new station wagon, with oil derricks in the background. The other might be of a farmer's large family, with long hair, beards, faded overalls, and long skirts, in an old Ford pickup truck. The two contrasting pictures can be used to raise such issues as preference of life styles, what is happiness, what is progress, the population crisis, and so forth.

ADDITIONAL SUGGESTIONS

Ask students to file their preference lists, and in six months look at them again to see if their preferences have changed. Also, encourage students to examine their "I prefer . . . " statements by asking the question, "How did I come by this preference? Is it something I really prefer or is it something that I prefer mostly because others seem to prefer it?"

A way to get students started writing "I prefer . . . " statements might be to list ten or fifteen different categories on the board and ask them to write a statement for five or six of the categories. For example, books, houses, sports, hobbies, cities, types of friends, etc.

Priority Lists

PURPOSE

Learning to choose and set priorities is an important part of the valuing process. Much of the values conflict we face in our lives may stem from the fact that we have not learned, or taken the time, to set priorities for our decisions and actions. This strategy provides students with an opportunity to practice setting priorities.

PROCEDURE

Introduce the strategy. Then, have students make a list of fifteen things they would like to do in the next several weeks/months. If students are having difficulty thinking of items to put on their lists, have several students read one or two of the items on their lists, or put a list on the chalkboard as students brainstorm some things that might be placed on their lists.

When students have completed their lists, ask them to narrow the lists to eight things they would most like to do, by putting a line through those seven items that are less appealing than the others. Then, explain that they are to develop a priority list of things they would like to do by placing the number one beside the item they would most like to do, the number two beside the item they would like to do almost as much, and so on down the list.

Follow up the activity by having students share and compare their priority lists in groups of four to six. In several weeks, the students can get together again in the same groups and look over these lists to see if they really acted in accordance with their lists of priorities.

VARIATIONS

Priority lists can be done on any number of things, from decisions that need to be made to letters that need writing. The following are some suggested variations:

1.   Things I want to accomplish this summer (this year, before I die, before I retire, etc.).

2.   Personal decisions that I need to make.

3. Actions that need to be taken.

4. Jobs that need doing.

5. Places I'd like to visit.

6. Things I'd like to buy.

7. Things I want to take with me on a trip.

8. Friends I'd like to invite to a party (trip to the shore, dinner, etc.).

9. Things I want to improve about myself (my relationships).

10. Letters that need writing.

The Disposable Computer[2]

PURPOSE

This strategy is a fun and novel way of learning to set priorities in the difficult, but often necessary, group setting. It also gives people in the group a chance to compare their thinking and priorities to those of the other group members, and requires that each group member publicly affirm and defend his or her choices during the decision-making process.

PROCEDURE

Before introducing the strategy, find a box and paint it black, or cover it with black construction paper. Or, better yet, get several creative students to make a "disposable computer" from paper or cardboard. The day you are going to use the strategy, bring the black box to class and set it on a table or chair in front of the class. You may divide the class into groups of five to ten, or larger.

Introduce the strategy with a brief statement of purpose. Tell the groups that you have been lucky enough to secure one of the first disposable computers to come on the market. The particular computer that sits in front of them is capable of answering any question or solving any problem put to it, no matter how simple or difficult. But it will answer *only one question or problem* and then must be disposed of. As a result, each group will have to decide upon one question or problem that it would like to ask the computer. Stress that coming up with the most important question possible may require considerable time, and that each member of the group should have this thinking reflected in the question or problem that is to be put to the computer.

Indicate that students can work on the activity in any way they want, but that each *must have a say* and all *must agree unanimously* to the final question or problem to be asked. Suggest that one way to proceed might be for each group member to write down privately several questions and problems he or she thinks to be important enough to ask the computer. Then, each group member has a turn to share his questions and problems and defend them. Another way is for the entire class to brainstorm a list of important questions and problems, and later discuss the merits of each until one is chosen.

Set a time limit. We suggest twenty to thirty minutes, but you may wish to make it more or less depending upon how involved your students get.

ADDITIONAL SUGGESTIONS

This strategy was used by a physics teacher who was searching for a way to get his students to explore values-related science issues on their own, in a group setting. The strategy is adaptable to other content areas as well. For example, a world history teacher might have students role play members of the ancient Greek Senate and arrive at the question they would have thought most important in their day. A business teacher might have students focus on the most important economic question today, and so on.

Of course, the computer won't be able to answer questions or solve the problems that students raise. But what is important is the process of asking the questions and defining the problems and sorting out the consequences. (You may need to help students look at the consequences of the questions they are asking if they are not doing so.) However, students could be given the task of attempting to answer the question(s) and solve the problem(s) raised. This can stimulate some interesting group or independent study projects.

The strategy itself raises a number of values issues such as:

Can a computer be programed to answer moral or values issues?

Should it be used in such a way?

What would be the consequences?

Who controls the computer?

Who should control it?

Who should it serve?

How can we insure that computers are not misused?

Are computers just an extension of man's mind as the car is an extension of his feet?

Does the computer alter the nature of what it means to be human?

Is this good?

Raise some of the above questions after the activity is over and let students discuss them.

If students have trouble thinking of some questions and problems, give them these to consider as a starter:

1. What is the cure for cancer?

2. Find a way to increase the life span of each individual 30 years.

3. Develop a way to harness the sun as a clean, low-cost energy source.

4. Discover a chemical substance that when put in drinking water greatly reduces the aggression in human beings. (Has no side effects.)

5. How can we solve the poverty problem?

6. What should we do about overpopulation?

Values Auction[3]

PURPOSE
This strategy is designed to help students get in touch with their value priorities and practice making decisions by consensus in a group setting.

PROCEDURE

Divide the class into groups of six. Ask students to pretend that they will soon be taking a trip to a new planet which is almost identical to Earth; once there, each group will be given a large portion of the land mass to start a new civilization. Explain that the major role each group is to play is to pass on the most important values of Earth to the new civilization. The difficulty is that only fourteen different values can be transmitted, and no two civilizations may have the same values. The problem of dividing up the values is to be solved by holding a values auction, with each of the fourteen values being sold to the highest bidder. Each group will be given 1,000 points to be used in purchasing the values. During the auction, each group tries to buy as many values as it can until its points are gone, at which time the group is forced to withdraw from the auction.

Provide each group with a list of the fourteen values in Worksheet No. 1, and give the groups fifteen to twenty minutes to plan a strategy for the auction.

To start the auction, the teacher chooses one of the values and, in his or her best auctioneer's voice, proceeds with, "Who will give me ten points? I've got ten, now who will give me twenty?" And so on until the bidding stops; then close out the action with a "sold!" Go on to a second value and a third until all the values are sold, or the groups have run out of points.

Then, give the groups time to discuss how successful they feel they were in obtaining their goals, what values they ended up with, how they made decisions, and what type of civilization they think they will have with the values they bought. Finally, the total class could discuss the activity.

The strategy could lead nicely into a more involved project, such as designing this new civilization or planning a new city.

VARIATION

Instead of choosing general values for the whole civilization, groups might be asked to choose character traits they would like the individual members of the civilization to have. In this case, they would be given Worksheet No. 2.

Worksheet No. 1: A List of Fourteen Values

Which values do you want to be most important in your civilization? Rank them from most important to least important.

    ____ Wealth

    ____ Equality

_____ Family

_____ Progress

_____ Tradition

_____ Freedom

_____ Love

_____ Health

_____ Peace

_____ Justice

_____ Beauty

_____ Wisdom

_____ Power

_____ Happiness

Worksheet No. 2:
A List of Twenty Character Traits

1. Honest

2. Playful

3. Self-confident

4. Orderly

5. Aggressive

6. Courageous

7. Cooperative

8. Competitive

9. Creative

10. Loyal

11. Responsible

12. Caring

13. Self-directing

14. Independent

15. Rational

16. Curious

17. Spontaneous

18. Friendly

19. Flexible

20. Openminded

Who's Coming to Dinner?[4]

PURPOSE

This is both a values strategy and a group decision-making exercise. It gives students a chance to decide on some values priorities for themselves and then to share these with others. It helps students see that others often have very different priorities from their own. It is also a good strategy for building trusting and supportive relationships in a small group.

PROCEDURE

Have each student privately write down the names of five persons they would like to invite to a special dinner. The dinner is special because anyone living or dead, real or fictitious, can be invited.

Then, form the students into groups of six. Each person should share with his group his list and his reasons for including each name. The six members of the group are then to pool their names, making a total list of thirty potential guests. From this list, the group is to agree upon ten persons whom they, as a group, would like to invite to dinner.

When the groups finish, have them share their selections with the class.

FOLLOW-UP

Have students discuss in their groups any or all of the following questions:

1. What kind of a menu would you plan for your guests?

2. What would the seating arrangement be?

3. If it were a pot-luck dinner, what would you have each guest bring?

4. If the guests were to bring gifts, what would you hope each would bring?

5. How do you think the guests will get along with each other?

Time Capsule[5]

PURPOSE

This strategy serves to build rapport in a small group and helps students learn more about the value priorities of others in the group. It also gives individuals a chance to think about what things they value about our society and how to symbolize these things.

PROCEDURE

Divide the students into groups of five to eight. Explain that each group is to decide what it would like to put in a time capsule that, when opened in 2,000 years, would let the future know what our present society is like.

Each group should first brainstorm for five minutes a list

of all the possible things they might put in. Remind them that there should be no evaluation or discussion of the items at this time.

When the groups finish brainstorming their lists, they are then to select (as a group) ten items from the list which they wish to place in the time capsule. These should be items on which everyone in the group can agree.

When the groups finish, have the students form new groups of five to eight members and share their lists. They can then look for similarities and differences in the different groups' lists, and discuss some of their reasons for including various items.

Kidney Machine[6]

PURPOSE

This strategy and the three variations which follow are exercises in group problem solving; as such, they generate a good deal of dialogue between group members concerning the ordering of values they place on things. Also, they raise the issue of making life and death decisions and thus involve participants deeply.

PROCEDURE

Divide students into groups of five to nine. Provide them with a copy of the worksheet(s) on *pages 244-251*. Make sure the instructions are clear and understood by all. Follow up the activity by having the group share their rankings. Then, discuss some of the problems they encountered in making their decisions. Make a list on the chalkboard of the values that were raised by the activity. Which values came out on top? Which were on the bottom?

Introduce the students to the strategy by saying:

"The Kidney Machine saves the lives of people suffering from kidney malfunction by hooking them up to the machine one day a week. Many people seek the service of the machine, but only a few can be served. You are on a volunteer committee to decide who should receive the machine's services. The decision must be made on other than medical criteria, since the list of candidates from which you must choose has been screened by doctors and all of the candidates can benefit equally. There is no cost to the patients for the use of the machine.

"As a committee, you are to discuss, and then determine by consensus, a final ranking of how these people should be assigned to the vacancies on the machine. Then, as a group, prepare a list of criteria that you used in arriving at your final ranking. List the criteria in order from most important to least important."

Worksheet

1. *Glenn*—filmmaker; no family; 33 years of age; is thought by some to be one of the best upcoming filmmakers in the business.

2. *Rodrigues*—migrant worker; wife and three-month-old child; 21 years old; wife is crippled.

3. *Arch*—dentist; wife and three children; 40 years old; very active in his community.

4. *Williams*—black activist organizer; husband and two children; age 28.

5. *Brown*—self-employed plumber; wife and twelve children; 43 years old; oldest child is 16.

6. *Schwartz*—secretary in a law firm; single; 22 years old; women's rights organizer.

7. *Batt*—student at Harvard; single; 21 years old; plans to study medicine; will achieve B.S. with honors.

8. *Greene*—garage mechanic; wife and four children; 29 years of age; very involved in church work.

9. *Allen*—housewife; husband and six children; 37 years old; husband is on welfare and drinks heavily.

10. *Levin*—president of a large business corporation; wife and two children; age 45.

Job Openings:
A Variation on the Kidney Machine[7]

Instructions: You are in a position of placing people who need jobs. You have nine applications for one job opening. All of these people want and need the job. You must decide who should get the job by rank ordering the following list of candidates.

1. An ex-convict trying to go straight. He has been out of prison for over a year and has stayed out of trouble. He has held several jobs during this time, but was fired each time when his bosses found out he spent time in prison. He is becoming frustrated, discouraged, and angry.

2. A 24-year-old Vietnam veteran who was awarded several medals for bravery. He has a low-paying part-time job now, but is highly qualified for this job.

3. A woman whose husband recently died. She has four young children, ages one to six, whom she now must support. She will be getting $200 a month from insurance, but this is not enough to live on.

4. A 60-year-old man who needs this as a second job. His wife has been in the hospital for several months. To continue her treatments, which are expected to continue for seven more months, he needs this job.

5. A former dope addict who has kept away from drugs for eleven months. He is a very serious young man who is determined to do well. He has had trouble finding jobs because of his former addiction, and his psychologist and priest say there is a strong possibility he will return to drugs if he is not employed soon.

6. A highly intelligent Negro who lives in a slum. He needs the job to continue his college education and to help support his brothers and sisters. He wants to become a doctor and help the poor in his neighborhood.

7. A young woman who left her parent's home to try to make it on her own. She has a strong interest in this type of work, and is the best qualified of all the applicants.

8. A recent immigrant to this country who is the father of four. His knowledge of English is poor, and this will probably slow him down on the job at first. But he is a clever and confident person who learns quickly.

9. A physically handicapped person who is looking for a chance to prove himself. He possesses a great deal of determination and courage. His handicap will hurt his performance on the job somewhat.

Life Raft [8]

Instructions: You are the survivors of a jumbo jet which has gone down in the Atlantic Ocean. There is only one life raft. It will hold ten people. You must decide by consensus who will be saved from the following passenger list. You have about fifteen minutes before the plane sinks and takes all of you down with it. The passengers are:

1. *Salesman*—56; married; five children ages nine to 17; going to Israel to help with industrial development; a leader in his community.

2. *Black Panther Leader*—25; single; en route to England to organize Black Panther contingents among oppressed

British blacks, and to train cadre for leadership positions in revolution.

3. *Doctor*—63; married; three children over 21; gave up lucrative practice because he believes he has discovered a possible cure for leukemia.

4. *Women's Liberation Leader*—34; single; going to France to address international meeting of advocates of her cause.

5. *Stewardess*—22; single; former Miss America.

6. *Roustabout*—47; single; gambler; former ship captain; excellent knowledge of the sea.

7. *Musician*—41; black; blind; en route to Europe for concert tour.

8. *Nun*—28; single; specializes in teaching mentally retarded children.

9. *Farmer*—43; married; on his way to Africa to work with A.I.D.; excellent hunter and fisherman; former Marine with survival training; suffered heart attack two years ago.

10. *Student*—22; single; going to Sweden to evade draft; is in third year of medical school, planning to practice medicine in ghetto community.

11. *Peace Corps Member*—24; married; returning to her post and husband after visiting a sick parent; married three months.

12. *Nurse*—29; single; has entered new profession during the

last two years as it seems to be more profitable; four months pregnant.

13. *CIA Agent*—36; married; two children ages one and two; about to leave government work; has memorized vital information concerning a government overthrow in Algeria.

14. *Fugitive*—34; single; former Ivy League college professor; escaped from prison where he was serving sentence for sale of dangerous drugs; seeks asylum in foreign country where he will renounce U.S. citizenship.

15. *Minister*—43; married, no children; a prominent civil rights leader who is going to Europe to receive an award.

16. *Teacher*—26; single; leave of absence to study in Paris; great writing potential; leader in innovative education projects.

17. *Interior Decorator*—40; homosexual; reputation as being the best decorator in America.

18. *Girl*—11; flying to boarding school in France; very wealthy family; crippled from birth.

19. *Banker*—43; six children, ages 10 to 21; leading John Birch Society member.

20. *Widow*—73; en route to Italy to fulfill promise to husband that she would visit their old home once more. Trip cost her her life's savings.

Club Members[9]

Instructions: Below is a list of twenty "types" that could belong to your club or gang. Your task is to arrange them in order of their desirability within your club or gang. Number them starting with one as the most valuable, two as the next most valuable, etc.

RANK   TYPE

_____   Bully.

_____   Shoplifter who never gets caught.

_____   Competitive, always wants to be first.

_____   Daydreamer.

_____   Debater, can start arguments over anything.

_____   Constantly questioning authority.

_____   Mediator or peacemaker; two-faced.

_____   Follows all directions, never questions why.

_____   Track star.

_____   Big mouth.

_____   Graffiti writer.

_____   Genius, but boring.

_____   Militant about his race, religion, etc.

_____   Gossipy.

_____	"Action man" who never stops to think.
_____	Radical.
_____	Cheater.
_____	Public and peer pleaser.
_____	Drug pusher.
_____	Fighter, with anything but his hands.

Divide into small groups; compare answers and discuss your reasons.

Value Dilemmas

PURPOSE

The really tough part of making values decisions is when two or more values we hold come into conflict—when we must choose between *honesty* and *loyalty*, for example. This strategy is designed to help students learn to deal more effectively with value dilemmas and identify their current value priorities.

PROCEDURE

Explain to the class the purpose of the strategy. Select one of the value dilemmas on *pages 254-279,* or make up one of your own, and present it to the students. The strategy can be followed up in a number of ways:

1. Break students into groups of four to five and let them discuss how each would resolve the dilemma.

2. Hold a large group discussion, with students discussing what action they would take to resolve the dilemma.

3. Give as an individual assignment. Students must write about what action they would take.

4. Have the students write individual solutions to the dilemma first, then share in a small group.

5. Post two or more of the dilemmas on the bulletin board. Let students choose which one they want to write about.

The worksheet below may help facilitate discussion and the clarifying of values for some dilemmas.

Worksheet

1. What decision would you make and/or action would you take concerning this dilemma.

2. What might be the consequences of making this decision and/or taking this action? Who would be affected? How would they be affected?

3. Are there any alternative ways of handling this dilemma. List them. What might be the consequences of some of these alternatives?

4. How do you feel about the decision you made and/or action you took? Do you feel good about it? Do you have misgivings? Explain.

5. Have you ever found yourself in a situation similar to the one in the dilemma? What did you do? What were the consequences?

VARIATIONS

Instead of using the suggested procedures for the values dilemmas, try one of the following:

Have students dramatize or role play the endings of the dilemma.

Have students write dilemmas based on their own experiences.

Use a dilemma as the agenda for a community meeting in order to work on a group concern.

Give the task of reaching a group consensus (groups of five or six) based on dilemmas. This exercise could be combined with the rules of *Active Listening (see page 70), The Positive Focus Game (see page 56), or Conflict Resolution (see page 75).*

Encourage students to respond to dilemmas in ways that reflect their *own* values. Responses such as "I would . . . ", "I believe . . . ", "If I were Johnny", as opposed to "he (she) should . . . " or "Johnny should . . . ", encourage deeper participation in the action phase of the valuing process.

Value Dilemmas[10]

1. *Shoplifting*

Sharon, a 16-year-old, has just been hired as a salesgirl in a record store in her neighborhood. She had been trying to get a job for several months in order to add to the income at home. Her mother has been struggling financially since Sharon's father died.

The store's owner stresses over and over again how important it is for Sharon to keep her eyes open for shoplifters. He keeps a meticulous count on the inventory and cash register receipts. In fact, Sharon had a chance at the job because the owner had fired her predecessor for insufficient vigilance.

During the second week on the job, Sharon's best friend Lucy comes into the store. Sharon watches as Lucy slips two records under her coat. Lucy then approaches Sharon at the cash register in order to pay for yet another record. Sharon whispers to Lucy that she ought to return the records. Lucy's response is a wink and a snicker.

- Should Sharon tell the owner and risk a friendship as well as sure arrest of Lucy? Why?

- Should Sharon charge Lucy for the one visible record and risk the same thing happening again, as well as risking an eventual loss of her job? Why?

2. Drug Dilemma

A policeman discovers that his 15-year-old son is using downers. Upon further questioning, the son reveals that he has been selling drugs to several of his classmates since last summer.

The father is utterly confused. He loves his son and feels a need to protect him. But he also realizes that he has a responsibility as a citizen and as a police officer to report his information to his superiors. In addition, he is deeply concerned about the other boys and their parents. In the state this family lives in, the first offense for "use" is probation. The first offense for the sale of drugs is a mandatory sentence of at least a year, even for minors.

- What should the father do? Why?

- After coming to a decision, change the situation by removing the father's role as a policeman. Does this change your decision? Why or why not?

3. Venereal Disease

Bob and Linda are high school seniors who have been going steady for some time. Recently, Linda has secretly been dating Bob's best friend, John. John knows that Linda and Bob are going steady.

Today, John finds out from his doctor that he has contracted syphilis. Since he and Linda engaged in sexual intercourse two weeks ago, she almost certainly will develop the primary signs within a few weeks. John tells Linda.

Linda and Bob have also been sexually intimate. She realizes that although her symptoms have not yet developed, they probably will. She also knows that she probably has transmitted the disease to Bob. Bob has the reputation of being very tough and easily "flying off the handle."

- Should Linda say nothing to Bob, thus risking his health? Why?

- Should Linda tell Bob, thereby risking their relationship (not to mention possible injury from Bob's wrath)?

- Rank order the characters on the basis of most moral to least moral.

4.   *Car Accident*

Jamie is 16 and has just gotten her driver's license. She has invited Jill to go for a ride the first time she takes her father's car by herself. The girls are so busy talking and laughing that Jamie goes through a red light and hits a woman. The woman is banged up pretty badly. Jamie is so scared that, when the police arrive on the scene, she makes up a story about another car forcing her through the light.

Jamie is charged with reckless driving. Jill knows that she will have to testify in court when the case comes to trial. There are no other witnesses.

- Should Jill tell the truth in court and risk Jamie getting a record? Why?

- Should she lie to protect her friend? Why?

5. *Football and Drugs*

A high school football coach sees one of his football players passing a very small plastic bag containing white powder to another player in the locker room. The two do not see the coach. Suddenly, the words of a student who had not made the football squad came to his mind. "Coach, you would be surprised to know who is on drugs in this school." He had dismissed the comment from his mind. Now, he wondered if the boy had meant to warn him about some of his players.

The boy passing the envelope is the star quarterback; the recipient is the fullback and captain of the team. The championship game is to be played in one week. The whole town and school is crazy with football fever. The hopes of the team winning rest squarely on the quarterback and the fullback; without them, there is no hope of gaining the championship.

There is a rule at the school that anyone caught using, selling, or possessing any form of illegal drug will be suspended. The coach has always gone by the rules and has encouraged his players to follow his example.

- What should he do? Report the incident? Confront the boys and find out what they are passing? Ignore it with the knowledge that he will be protecting the championship?

6. *Paralyzed Man*

A 28-year old man is injured critically in an automobile accident. His spinal cord is severed, and he is paralyzed from the chest down. Only round-the-clock medical attention is keeping him alive. The doctors tell him that he has no chance of ever being able to use his arms or legs. Additionally, he has suffered severe head injuries and has unbearable pain that drugs can only partially alleviate. Because of the pain and the bleak diagnosis, the man asks his doctor to allow him to die by discontinuing his treatment.

- Should the doctor grant the man's request and allow him a quick and natural death? Why?

- Should the doctor feel obligated to use all of his skill and knowledge in order to keep him alive? Why?

Let's say that the doctor decides he must do everything he can to keep the injured man alive. He tells his patient of this decision. The injured man's closest relative is a 25-year-old brother. He pleads with his brother to take him out of misery. His younger brother loves the injured man dearly and is distraught because of his condition. He has a dozen sleeping pills at home. This quantity would be enough to end his misery.

- Should the brother do anything that would aid in ending the injured man's life? Why?

7. *Missing in Action*

Barbara is 31 years old. Nine years ago, she married Lou, her childhood sweetheart. After being married for little over a year, Lou was drafted into the Army. Subsequently, he was sent to Vietnam, where his batallion was attacked. Barbara received a letter from Lou that same day, not two years since their marriage. That was the last time Barbara heard from him. Lou's name has never appeared on a P.O.W. or casualty list.

For seven and a half years, Barbara has prayed and hoped that her husband is alive. She has always taken pride in her fidelity to her husband. Barbara has recently turned down a number of dates with men she would have dated had she not been married. She can legally declare herself free of marriage. However, she continues to feel that her husband is still alive somewhere. Her dilemma is:

- Should she continue to wait for a definite answer about her husband (which likely will never come)? Why?

- Should she begin dating again with the notion of eventually marrying and beginning a family, which has been her lifelong dream? Why?

8. *Taxes—Cheating*

Although he has often been tempted, Leonard Williams has never cheated on his income tax return. He has always felt that he has an obligation as an American citizen to pay the proper amount of federal income tax. He thinks he is being patriotic; his wife calls him old-fashioned.

Mr. Williams views a television news special that focuses

on tax "loopholes" that citizens who are in the upper tax brackets can take advantage of. Several cases are cited where multi-millionaires paid no taxes at all. It is also pointed out how several politicians were able to avoid paying taxes by selling personal artifacts and papers relating to their positions. Disgusted, Mr. Williams angrily reflects to his wife on how he makes only $11,000 a year but ends up paying a couple of thousand bucks to Uncle Sam.

·For the first time, he seriously considers falsifying some figures on his tax return.

- What should he do? Why?

- Are there times when cheating is justified? Why or why not?

9. Sorority Dilemma

Sandra is the treasurer of her sorority and is the only one who knows how much money the house has. They have been saving up for a dance to be held in one week, and Sandra has assured them that they have enough money to pay for the band and the food. However, from time to time Sandra has used the sorority money to buy herself things that she has wanted, always meaning to repay the sorority with her allowance money.

Now, one week before the dance, Sandra checks the cashbox and realizes that she has used almost half of the group's money. There won't be enough to pay for the band and the food.

- Should Sandra tell her parents what she did to see if they will lend her the extra money? Why?

- Should she lie to her sorority sisters about how much money they have accumulated so that they will cancel the dance? Why?

- Is there any other alternative?

10. *Camp Dilemma*

At summer camp, many of the teens smoke without their parents' knowledge, even though the camp forbids smoking. One day, three girls are sitting behind their cabin while the rest of the girls are inside resting. Susan, a very shy girl, sits with the other two because she really likes the girls, and wants very much to be liked by them. The other girls start smoking, and offer Susan a cigarette. Susan has never smoked before. She doesn't like to break camp rules, and she also feels that smoking is harmful to one's health, but she knows these girls will reject her and even laugh at her if she refuses to smoke.

- What should she do?

11. *Basketball Coach*

As the varsity basketball coach of the Warren County Public High School, Donald Hoak has a well-deserved reputation as a builder of character. He is respected by practically everyone who knows him. His players view the rules that he sets for the team as strict but realistic. For example, at the beginning of the season all of the players on his team agreed that it was good to have a 10:30 curfew the night before any game and that a one-game suspension would result if any player broke curfew. This has occurred once this season and twice last season.

Mr. Hoak is also proud of the number of college contacts that he has been able to develop over the years. He is usually able to help his players gain admission to college, many with scholarships.

Billy Wilson has played on Mr. Hoak's team for three years. He has always abided by the rules of the team and has worked very hard to improve his skills. Mr. Hoak has been trying to arrange for a college coach to come and look at Billy play, in the hope that a scholarship would result. Coming from a family with very little money, Billy realizes that a scholarship is the only possible way that he will be able to attend college. Mr. Hoak has been able to interest only one coach in Billy. The coach has rearranged a very busy schedule to come and watch Billy play on Saturday night.

On Saturday, Coach Hoak's daughter tells him that she was at a party Friday night that Billy also attended; the party, she says, did not end until one o'clock. Mr. Hoak calls Billy at home and asks him if this is true. Billy says yes.

The game that night is scheduled for 8:00. Mr. Hoak asks Billy to come to his house at 5:30 in order to discuss his breaking of the training rule.

Mr. Hoak's dilemma is this:

If he allows Billy to play, he will have to explain to the team why the rules are good for some but not for others. This is contrary to everything that he stands for. He feels strongly that rules are good only when enforced consistently.

On the other hand, if he suspends Billy there is practically no chance that this, or any other, college coach will be able to see him play again, since this is the next to last game of the season. A suspension would just about end any chance for a scholarship for Billy.

• What should Mr. Hoak do? Why?

12.   *Cheating—School*

Ronnie is taking a final exam in her English class. She has prepared diligently for the test. When she turns to the second page of the exam she realizes that she has studied the wrong material. Knowing that she needs a "B" in the final to get a "B" in the course, she becomes very flustered. Her grade is very important because it can qualify her for a summer music scholarship that a local bank is sponsoring.

Ronnie has always been against cheating and has never cheated, although it is common knowledge that cheating occurs as a daily practice in her class.

Going through her mind now is the knowledge that she can get the required information from her boyfriend, who is sitting next to her. Her teacher has left the room because he feels that students should be trusted during tests.

Ronnie likes the idea of being trusted, but also likes the idea of the music scholarship.

• Should she cheat just this once or not? Why?

• Are there times when cheating (anywhere, not just in school) is justified? Why or why not?

13. *Environment*

John and Joan Billingham have been married for twenty-two years and have remained deeply in love with one another. John is the owner of a large industrial chemical firm that he founded and developed with years of hard and dedicated work. His company is the largest employer in the "factory town" of Bridgeton. As a result of his business's growth, the town's population has increased threefold over the last fifteen years. John has provided his employees with good pay as well as excellent benefits. Joan has dedicated herself to community service, particularly in the area of environmental protection. Both of the Billinghams are greatly respected in the community.

The problem of air pollution has been increasing in Bridgeton over the last six or seven years. In the past year, the area has been cited twice for exceeding the "air management limit" for pollution. This is causing a serious health threat to the community.

During the past year, John's business has suffered several severe financial setbacks. Reluctantly, John has had to order several personnel reductions. He is presently contemplating the laying off of an additional 100 men. If his company's financial picture does not change soon, there is the chance that the business may fold, thus causing financial havoc for Bridgeton.

Joan has recently been designated Director of Environmental Protection. She has headed an investigation to determine the major causes of the pollution problem in the Bridgeton area.

To her amazement, she has discovered that John's company has been secretly (and with his knowledge) pouring hazardous pollutants into the air at night. As darkness arrives the chimneys are opened, thereby making detection very difficult.

Joan's dilemma is:

> Should she make this knowledge public? If she does, she risks her husband's reputation as well as the threat of heavy fines which are mandatory. These fines would further jeopardize the tenuous financial condition of the company. If she doesn't act, she is threatening her reputation as well as deliberately acting against her sworn responsibilities as a public official. She is also contributing to the serious health threat the polluted air causes for the community.

• What should she do? Why? Keep in mind that in their state, as in most states, a wife does not have to testify against her husband in a court of law.

14. *Runaway*

Jo Anne is 16 and is in the eleventh grade at the Thomas Dewey High School. She lives with her brother, mother, and stepfather. She and her mom have been hassling a good deal lately, and in the last two weeks it has become unbearable. Jo Anne's mother dislikes her boyfriend and has refused to let Jo Anne see him.

With all of the trouble at home, Jo Anne has depended more and more on her friendship with Mrs. Riley, a teacher at school. Jo Anne has finally had enough and runs away to a friend's house. Being confused, she calls Mrs. Riley to talk with her and tells her where she is. Mrs. Riley promises not to call Jo Anne's mother to tell her where she is. A day later, Jo Anne's mother calls Mrs. Riley because she knows of their friendship. She insists that Mrs. Riley tell her where Jo Anne is.

- Should Mrs. Riley tell Jo Anne's mother where she is and break a confidence? Why or why not?

15. *College Dilemma*

Tom went to college right after high school and flunked out. It wasn't that he couldn't do the work; there were too many extracurricular activities like parties, girls, drinking. . . . Tom took a year off to work, and through this found out how much he wanted his college education.

Now 20, Tom's decided to reapply to a local school and live at home. The application asks if he has ever attended another college. Tom knows that if he sends his first year college records he will not be accepted because his grades were too low.

- Should Tom answer truthfully on the application and risk not being accepted? Why?

- Should Tom lie and maybe risk being expelled if caught later? Why? Or should he take some other course of action?

16. *Dating*

Joyce is a pretty 16-year-old who is in her junior year at East Falls High School. Her prom is just two weeks away and Joyce is dying to go. Larry asks her to go, and she accepts even though she doesn't like him. She really wants to go with David, but is afraid he wouldn't ask her.

The next day, David calls and asks her to go. She is excited, but doesn't know what to say. She tells David she will call him back in an hour.

- Should she go with Larry because he asked her first? Why?

- Should she go with David whom she really likes? Why?

17. *Guitar*

Jean is a 13-year-old who has been wanting to take guitar lessons very much. Jean's parents promise her that they would pay for weekly guitar lessons if Jean were able to save enough money to buy the guitar. The guitar that she has in mind costs $50.

Jean saves one dollar per week from her allowance and three to five dollars a week from babysitting. After several months, she has the $50. However, just as Jean reaches her $50 goal, her parents are faced with several unexpected medical bills. Her parents do not believe in taking out bank loans, although they have a good credit rating. They tell Jean that they expect her to contribute her money to help with the bills and they will pay her back at the rate of five dollars per month. Jean doesn't want to give up her money.

- Should Jean refuse to contribute her money to help with the family bills? Why? Why not?

Variation

Jean lied to her parents and said that she contributed the

money to the United Fund at school. Actually, she hid the money at home. She told her brother Steve about the lie.

● Should Steve tell his parents? Why? Why not?

18. *Dying Woman*

A woman is suffering from a rare form of cancer. A druggist has just discovered a drug that will cure her. However, the druggist wants $2,000 for a small dose. The woman's husband tries to borrow the money but can only raise half the amount needed. He then goes to the druggist and begs him to give his wife the drug. The druggist refuses, saying that he worked hard to discover it, and that he won't dispense it unless he is paid the full $2,000.

● Should the husband break into the druggist's shop and steal the drug, with the intention of repaying the druggist when he can? Why? Why not?

Let's say the husband does steal the drug. He gives it to his doctor, who administers it to the woman, but reports the situation to the police. The husband is put in jail for stealing the drug.

However, he escapes after a year and goes to another city where he uses another name. He works hard to earn the money to repay the druggist from whom he had stolen the drug. Another worker, also from his home town, recognizes him as the escaped thief.

● Should the doctor have reported him to the police?

- Should the worker report him to the police?

- What should the police do?

19.   *Unexpected Pregnancy*

Judy is 17 and a high school senior. She is a very talented artist and has a scholarship to one of the finest art colleges in the country. She has been going steady with David for three years and they are very much in love. David is a sophomore in college, on a scholarship, studying to be a doctor. They often talk and dream of the happy marriage and family they will have someday.

Right after Christmas, Judy discovers she is two months pregnant. Neither she nor David is ready to get married, but they both love children. What should she do?

20.   *Friendships*

Don lives in a very conservative, all-white suburban community and goes to a high school where there are no blacks and only a few students from other minority groups. Most of his friends and their parents are openly prejudiced and love to tell jokes about other races and ethnic groups.

During the past summer, Don spent a month visiting his aunt in a big city and became very good friends with Jim, a black boy his age. Don's ideas about other races changed radically and he wishes to show his school friends what a great guy Jim is.

Soon after school starts, one of Don's best friends invites him to a big party at his house on Saturday night. Don is very excited about the party because a new girl he is very interested in will also be there. A few hours before the party, Jim calls Don to say he is in town unexpectedly and would love to see him that evening.

- Should Don invite him to come to the party with him, knowing how his friends feel about other races?

- Should Don tell Jim he is busy and maybe hurt his feelings, as well as miss a chance to see his good friend?

- Should Don stay home from the party, visit with Jim, and keep his friendship with Jim a secret?

21. *Living Together*[11]

Joe and Mary have been living together (not married) for almost six years now and have no children. They both have well-paying jobs, live in an apartment that is tastefully furnished and decorated, and both drive their own cars. While they are by no means rich, they do live comfortably and are just now starting to acquire many of the things they've always wanted but could not afford.

Now that Mary is beginning to feel very secure in her relationship with Joe, she wants to get married, buy a home, and have children. Joe, however, announces to Mary that he is leaving her. While he still "cares" about her and doesn't want to hurt her, he says he no longer loves her, does not desire her any more, and is in love with another girl. Mary, on the other hand, is still very much in love with Joe, feels that their relationship really has a lot going for it, and argues that even though they were not formally married they still made a commitment to spend a lifetime together. Mary says she needs Joe and he should honor his commitment. Joe says his first commitment is to himself and to his own happiness and that he can only be happy with his new love.

1. How do you feel about two people living together who have not been married legally?
    a. Do you feel they are living in sin?

2. Do you feel this kind of living arrangement should be as morally binding as a marriage contract?
    a. How about legally binding? Do you think the courts should force alimony, property settlements, etc?

3. Do you think it's all right for Joe to leave Mary if he no longer loves her or desires her and cannot be happy?

4. How would you feel about the situation if Mary were not able to support herself afterwards?

5. How would you feel about the situation if there were any children involved?

6. Do you think it's ever okay for one person to leave a mate who is still in love with and emotionally dependent upon that person?

7. Do you feel that a person should ever sacrifice his own happiness for the happiness of someone else?

8. Do you think Mary should give Joe up, thereby sacrificing her own happiness for Joe to be happy?

22. *Working Mother*

Bill and Yvonne have been married for two years and have an 18-month-old baby boy. Bill works twelve hours a day as a garage mechanic but doesn't make very much money. In fact, he makes just about enough to pay the rent on their small three-room apartment, buy the groceries, put enough gas in his old, battered Chevy to get him to work and back, and put a little money aside in case of an emergency. There is never any money left at the end of the month for a dinner out or even a movie, not to mention a babysitter.

Since Bill and Yvonne were married right out of high school and Yvonne was pregnant at the time of their marriage, she has never worked at any type of a job and has no marketable skills. Still, Yvonne wants to find some kind of a job so there can be a little extra money around to buy a few things for the baby, maybe some new clothes for herself, and some new furnishings for the apartment. She has even found a woman down the street who will watch the baby while Yvonne's at work and not charge very much money.

Bill says absolutely not. While he recognizes his own limited earning potential and hates to see his family have so little, he firmly believes that Yvonne should remain at home to raise their child. He argues that since he never knew his real mother or father and spent most of his childhood and adolescent years being pushed from one foster home to another, he wants his son to grow up having his mother close by him.

1. Do you think Bill is doing the right thing? Why?

2. Do you think Bill's attitude towards the idea of a

working wife and mother, as the result of his own childhood, is justified? Why?

3. Do you think Bill is selfish for depriving his wife and child of the things a few extra dollars could buy?

4. Which way do you think the child will suffer more—by not having his mother around as much in his early years or by growing up deprived of things his parents could not afford?

5. If a child has a babysitter who is mature and responsible while his mother is at work, is it the same as having his mother around when he needs her? Explain.

6. Would you feel differently about this whole situation if Yvonne had some special skills which would add *very* substantially to their income? Explain.

7. *Girls:* Would you want to work if you had a young child?

    Boys: Would you want your wife to work if you had a young child?

23. *Prom Night*

Betty and Ray are going to their senior prom together and want to do something afterwards to make it a really special night. The prom and dinner will probably break up around 2:00 a.m. and they're leaving for the shore with another couple at 7:00 a.m. They could just cruise around for five hours but there's nothing special about spending five hours riding around. They could go to one of the house parties where most of the other kids are going, but they prefer to spend this evening alone, not with a crowd of "kids." They finally decide to take a motel room and spend the night together and make the evening something really special.

Betty has to tell her mother where she is going to be after the prom. Betty's afraid that if she just says she is not quite sure what they're going to do her mother will make her come home. She hates having to lie to her mother but this is her high school prom and it only comes once in a lifetime. Betty tells her mother that she and Ray will be going to one of the parties, at Paul's house, and that Paul's parents will be in attendance.

1. Do you feel that Betty and Ray have the right idea about what to do to make their prom night special? Why?

2. What are some other things they might have done?

3. Does an event which comes only "once in a lifetime" justify doing something you wouldn't normally do? Why?

4. Which would be an easier thing for you to accept:
    a. Knowing you are doing something wrong but doing it anyway because you're enjoying it?
    b. Not doing something you think you'd enjoy and feeling afterwards that maybe you'd missed a good thing?

5. Do you think Betty should have told her mother the truth?

6. Which would you have done:
   a. Told the truth and hassled over it with your mother trying to get her approval?
   b. Lied as Betty did?

24. *Abortion*

Sue is 18, a senior in high school, four months from graduation, and nine weeks pregnant. So far, there are only two other people who know—her doctor and her older sister. No one else knows: neither her mother nor her boyfriend, Jay.

She could have the baby and keep it, but this would mean not going to college, which she had counted on doing. Another option is to have the child and place it up for adoption. But then how would it be to have a child and never see it again? She'd always be wondering where her "baby" was, who the parents were, and what kind of a life they were giving her child. No, she decides, her only alternative is to have an abortion. That's it, her decision is made. Tomorrow she will call the clinic and make the arrangements; and her sister, the only other person she can trust, will accompany her. No one would ever know, and at her graduation she won't have to walk down the aisle pregnant!

1. Do you think Sue made the right decision in view of her situation?

2. What decision do you think you might have made?

3. How do you feel about her not having discussed it with Jay? Do you think they should have made a decision together?

4. Do you think Sue should have at least told her mother?

5. Do you consider having an abortion taking a human life?
   a. Is it ever all right to take a human life?

25. *Dating and Drinking*

Georgia and Pearl have just turned 16 and are now allowed to go out on dates. They have been asked out by two older boys, both 19, whom they met at a dance. The girls expect that they will go to a movie and afterwards for a pizza and Coke. But, after the movie, one of the guys suggests going to a party at a friend's house where, the boy mentions, there will be wine and beer. Both Georgia and Pearl were strictly warned by their mother to stay away from drinking and to demand that the boys bring them home if drinking is suggested. Not wanting to appear babyish, however, and ruin their chances for another date, the girls agree to go.

Once at the party, Georgia and Pearl find that they are really enjoying themselves. They start to drink and soon lose the fear of their mother finding out. Upon leaving the party, the boys are quite drunk. Pearl's date is driving and begins to play games with other vehicles—passing carelessly and following too closely. Suddenly, headlights appear directly in front of them and it's too late to react, even if they were sober. They smash the car and, although no one is seriously hurt, they of course must now tell their mother.

1. Do you think Georgia and Pearl made the right decision about going to the party with the boys (knowing that beer and wine would be served)?
   a. Do you think their decision would have been alright if they did not know that beer and wine would be served?

2. Do you think there is any danger in 16-year-olds dating boys who are older and of legal drinking age? Why or why not?

3. Would you have chosen to disobey your parents and go drinking with the boys, or not go and risk the chance of not getting another date?

4. If your date were not in a condition to drive, would you have demanded that someone else drive you home? Why or why not?

5. At what age do you feel that it is right for girls to begin dating? At what age will you allow your daughter to begin dating?

6. At what age do you feel it is permissible for girls to date boys who drive their own cars?

7. If you were Georgia and Pearl's mother, would you prohibit your daughters from going on another date because of this incident?
   a. If so, for how long?

8. Do you feel it is necessary for Georgia and Pearl to be punished because of their decision? Why or why not?

26. *Drug Search*

Henry and John have been best friends since elementary school. If you wanted to fight with one of them, you'd better be prepared to take on the other one too. Both Henry and John have been experimenting with a lot of drugs, but in the past year Henry has become a heavy user and has been "busted" several times. Once more and he will be sent to jail for at least ten years. Henry knows a narc when he sees one, and one day as Henry and John are walking home from the recreation center Henry spots a narc approaching them from across the street. The narcs also know Henry pretty well, and they're sure to search him whenever they see him. There's also been a rumor that lately quite a bit of heroin has been passed around at school.

Today's the worst possible day, thought Henry. A new shipment just came in and he's loaded with it. If he gets searched, he's had it. They'd never suspect John. He's never been in trouble. In less than a minute they'll be face to face with the narc. Henry asks John to quickly take his stuff and hold it until they are safely home.

John, valuing his longtime friendship with Henry, hates to refuse. If, by chance, they should both be searched it would mean trouble for him. While John values his friendship with Henry, he also values his freedom and his clean record. John refuses to become involved in any way in this entanglement with the law.

1. Did John make the right decision in refusing to hold Henry's stuff? Why or why not?

2. What would you have done in the same situation?

3. Do you feel that it was a fair request for Henry to ask this of John? Why or why not?

4. Do you think it is possible to have so strong a friendship that one person would do anything at all for the other, regardless of the cost or consequences? Explain.

5. Would you ever not only help a friend, but also put yourself in a wrongful or blameful position, rather than allow him or her to get into trouble?

6. Would you want a friend who would lie or put himself or herself out for you? Under what circumstances?

7. Would you want a friend who would get himself or herself into trouble with the law for you?

8. What other things might John have done?

"Dear Abby"

PURPOSE

This strategy can be used to help students to develop an awareness of and clarify their values as well as to gather alternative ways of solving personal problems they and others may face.

PROCEDURE

You can use this strategy in a number of ways and for a number of different purposes. One way to use it is simply to open the newspaper to the personal advice column in which people write to "Abby," "Ann," etc. Select one or two of the problems and read them to the students, or have them reproduced and distributed. Follow up with large or small group discussions, or have students write an answer telling the letter writer what they would recommend. Then read the advice of Abby (or whoever) and have students compare their answers with hers. Be sure to state that each answer only reflects one person's views and we all have a right to our own opinions. Abby's opinions are not necessarily any more "correct" than the students'!

A second way to use the strategy is to have students write *"Dear Abby"* questions on 3 x 5 cards and post them on a bulletin board or in a "Dear Abby" Center. Other students may then write their advice to these questions on 3 x 5 cards and post their answers beside the questions. This serves to raise issues and concerns, to identify alternative ways of handling a problem, and to give students who seek it feedback about how others would handle the problem. We have made up some examples you might use to get things started *(see pages 281-289).*

A third way is to build a *"Dear Abby"* box with a slit in the top in which students place personal problems or questions they would like advice on. The teacher then, from time to time, reads the class the personal problems *anonymously*, and encourages students to give their opinions as to the best method for dealing with the problem. Thus, the student who has raised the problem can hear what others say without revealing any distress.

If you let students generate the problems, don't expect them all to be tame. Be careful not to expose the writers or let students expose themselves, unless they want to. Don't try to be their psychologist or solve their problems for them. Instead, let their peers give them feedback. They will raise new alternatives, bring up consequences, and probably help the student much more than would the simple giving of advice.

"Dear Abby's"[12]

1. Dear Abby:
    My boyfriend handed me ten dollars on my birthday and told me he was too busy to go out and buy something for me. He does things like this often. I love him very much but this kind of thing hurts. What should I do?

    —HEARTSICK

2. Dear Abby:
    Whenever I go out with my girlfriend to a party, she always winds up getting into a fight over something. She will make a wild and foolish statement and then vehemently attack the other person for disagreeing with her. Then she expects me to come to her defense. Rather than make a scene, I suggest that we leave the party. The rest of the evening is spoiled. I love her, but I love to go to parties. What can I do?

    —VERY UPSET

3. Dear Abby:

    My problem is that my face is always breaking out in pimples. I am 14 years old and boys won't even look at me. I have gone to the doctor but he tells me that it is something that I will have to outgrow. He has given me some drugs and tells me to watch what I eat but it doesn't help. What should I do?

    —PIMPLED AND PERPLEXED

4. Dear Abby:

    I am an attractive 12-year-old girl. I love a boy who is 14. My mother tells me that I don't love him, but I really do. She also says that he is too old. He goes to my school and I see him all the time. He asked me to go to the movies but my mother won't let me.

    How can I convince my mother to let me date him.

    —TWELVE AND IN LOVE

5. Dear Abby:

    I am a junior in high school. My problem is that no girls will go out with me. I don't think that I am bad looking, although I am rather thin. I am 5' 10" and weigh 130 pounds. I like to talk to the girls and they like to talk to me. We talk, and talk, and talk. But when I ask them out, they are always busy. I won't ask anybody out who my friends think isn't good looking. I would like to, but I'm afraid of what my friends will say. What do you suggest?

    —DATELESS

6. Dear Abby:

    My boyfriend and I are both 16. We have been dating for about a year. My problem is that whenever we are at my home my mother never leaves us alone. She always stays around us, either in the room or in the next room. When I ask her about it she always has a reason. My mother and I get along well but we can't agree on this. Do you think that this is right?

    −JOAN

7. Dear Abby:

    My wife and I have three children whom we love very much. We are having a problem with our middle child. He is 13 years old and physically active. He simply will not help with the chores around the house. My two daughters are always willing to help. They resent his laziness and are always fighting with him. He is a good kid but he is lazy. What do you think is the best way to handle the situation?

    −PARENTS OF A LAZY BOY

8. Dear Abby:

    My husband and I have been married for ten years. Since last year, I have been working to add money for the household. My husband never has helped clean up around the house much. But now that I am working, I think that he ought to help. His pat answer is "that's woman's work." Then he sits down in front of the T.V. with his beer. I love him but he won't help me.

    −TIRED OF WOMAN'S WORK

9. Dear Abby:
    I've got a monster on my hands. My wife and I have been married for two years. All of a sudden she and her best friend have become women's libbers. She expects me to help out around the house all the time. When I come home from work I'm tired. She doesn't work. Except for this problem, we get along fine.

    —LIBBER'S HUSBAND

10. Dear Abby:
    I have a different kind of problem. I am an attractive 16-year-old girl. I like a boy who happens to have a deformed leg. He was born that way. He is very nice and we have fun together. My father is very old fashioned. He says a girl should do the best she can when she picks her boyfriends. I want to continue seeing my friend but my father says that I can do better. My mother is no help. She just goes along with Father.

    —CONFUSED

11. Dear Abby:
    Please tell me what to do. I have several good friends who think it's cool to shoplift. They are both 15 years old. They haven't been caught but I'm sure that they will be. I like them but don't want to get involved. I also want to convince them that they shouldn't shoplift.

    —WENDY

12. Dear Abby:
    I live in a real bad neighborhood. I'm nine years old. There are gangs all around. Everybody is always

fighting. My mother tells me that I am just looking for trouble if I join a gang. Everybody is always beating on me because I don't belong to a gang.

—WAYNE

13. Dear Abby:
How do you know when you are going too far with a boy? Boys are really different. You say something to one boy and he reacts one way. Say the same thing to another and he gets all kinds of ideas. I am a virgin and want to stay that way. I do like to make out, but only so far. What is the best way to understand boys and what is too far?

—SUE

14. Dear Abby:
My best friend is a drug user. He usually takes uppers and downers. I smoke grass but that's all. I don't think that he should be using pills. What do you think I ought to do to get him to stop?

—STEVE S.

15. Dear Abby:
My husband is a constant spendthrift. He spends more money than we are both making. We are constantly in debt trying to keep up with his spending. I've talked to him and he promises to do better but never does.

—WORRIED

16. Dear Abby:
My son has always been a good boy but recently he has

stopped listening to his father and me. He started dating a new girl right before this. If we tell him to stop dating this girl, we're afraid that he'll rebel even more. Should we insist on his not seeing this girl?

—WORRIED MOTHER

17. Dear Abby:
I am 10 years old and am writing to you in desperation. My mom will not let me pick out my own clothes for school. She says that I'm too young. All of my friends pick out their clothes for school. If you tell my mom it's all right, she'll let me.

—SANDY

18. Dear Abby:
Our daughter is using speed on weekends. She says that she likes the feeling it gives her. We promised her a new car for her birthday. She promises to stop using speed, if we get her the car. What do you think?

—WORRIED PARENTS

19. Dear Abby:
I am 14 and my boyfriend has asked me to go steady. My parents said that I should wait because there will be lots of boys. I want to go steady now. How can I convince my parents?

—GOING STEADY

20. Dear Abby:
I am divorced and have custody of my children. Their mother left us and didn't want to take care of the

children. I need to hire a woman to take care of the children. What should I look for in such a woman?

—LONELY FATHER

21. Dear Abby:

My son is 15 and is a diabetic. He knows that he has to watch his diet or get sick. He's had to be hospitalized three times in the last four months because he says that he forgets to take his insulin. How can I get him to take his insulin regularly, or should I give it to him?

—MRS. JONES

22. Dear Abby:

I have raised my grandchildren since they were babies. My daughter left them with me and took off. Now she is remarried and wants to take the children back with her and her new husband. It has been five years since they've seen their mother. Do I have any right to keep them?

—GRANDMA

23. Dear Abby:

My daughter is allergic to dogs. My son brought home a stray puppy and wants to keep the pup. He keeps crying that it's not fair to make him give up the dog because of his sister. What should I do?

—CONFUSED MOTHER

24. Dear Abby:

Ever since I had my first baby, my mother tells me how to take care of my children and interferes with everything that I do with them. I love my mother, but I want to raise my own children. How can I tell her without hurting her feelings?

—WANTING TO BE A MOTHER

25.   Dear Abby:
      I have tried to stop smoking no less than ten times. How can I stop and really not start again?

—SMOKER

26.   Dear Abby:
      I am only seven years old and my mother is writing this to you. I like a girl in my class, but she won't play with me. The more I try to be nice to her, the less she likes me. What can I do to get her to like me?

—LAURIE S.

27.   Dear Abby:
      Every day I have to tell my kids to pick up their clothes, brush their teeth, and put their books away. You would think by now they would know, but they don't. I have tried yelling, giving stares, and ignoring them. How can I get them to do what they're supposed to?

—ANGRY MOTHER

28.   Dear Abby:
      I have been finding strange new clothes in my daughter's closet and trinkets hidden in her drawers. I think that she may be shoplifting. How can I find out without seeming to accuse her?

—SKL

29. Dear Abby:

    My daughter is 15 and has asked for birth control information. We had no idea that she was even interested. If we give her this information, aren't we giving her permission to have sex?

    —OLD FASHIONED PARENT

30. Dear Abby:

    I have one sister who is pretty and one who is very smart. I have a third sister who is so witty that people laugh the minute she opens her mouth. People look at me as if I've got nothing. I'm beginning to think they are right. I feel dumb, ugly, and sour most of the time. What can I do about myself? Please hurry with your answer. I need your help.

    —MISS "NOBODY"

Ways to Spend Free Time

PURPOSE

The quality of our lives is determined in part by how we spend the time we have available. We may not be able to control large portions of our time that relate to schooling, work, and other obligations, but we can control what we do with our free time. Even if this is but a small part of each week, how we spend it can have a real effect on how much satisfaction we derive from living. This strategy can be used to gain some insight into what we really prefer to do with our free time and also generate some new alternatives for free time.

PROCEDURE

Divide the class into groups of five or six. Have one student in each group volunteer to be secretary. Ask students to brainstorm in the next ten minutes as many ways as they can think of to spend a free Saturday or Sunday. Have them follow these rules during the brainstorming:

1. Quantity of ideas is important, not quality.

2. Don't discuss, debate, or evaluate the ideas.

3. Any idea goes, even the way-out ones.

4. Write down *every* idea.

While the group is brainstorming, the secretary makes a list of all the ideas.

You may want to write a few ideas on the blackboard to get them started:

Learn to play a guitar.	Cook a gourmet meal.
Weave a rug.	Take a whitewater canoe trip.
Take a plane ride.	Go mountain climbing.
Learn to sky dive.	Visit a television show.
Take a child to the zoo.	See a ballet.
Try waterskiing.	Learn to macramé.
Make a movie.	Build a piece of furniture.

Go on an archeology dig.   Plant a garden.

Go sailing.
                             Go on a three-day survival trip
Practice yoga.   with just a knife and matches.

When ten minutes is up, each group makes a copy of its list on large newsprint and posts it. (Or, they may turn them in so the teacher can compile and ditto them for everyone.) The students then circulate among the posted lists and make a personal list of twenty to thirty of the items that they think sound interesting and/or things they currently do. Each student can then code his list in the following manner:

1. Place the letter (R) beside any item that you currently do on a regular basis.

2. Place the symbol (*) beside any item that you would like to do more of.

3. Place an exclamation mark (!) beside any item that you would like to do or try.

4. Place the letter (T) beside any item that you are really tired of but you do because your friends or family do it.

5. Place the letter (X) beside any item that you do just because it's there or because it's simple to arrange, not because you get a lot of satisfaction from doing it.

Follow up the activity by having students complete several times and share in their group the sentence stem, "I learned that I. . . . "

Additional codings you may want to use are:

1. Place a check beside the items which you have at one time done or participated in.

2. Place a (−) beside all those items that you do not like to do or would not like to try.

3. Identify your ten favorite items and rank them by placing the numbers 1 through 10 to indicate the order of your preference.

4. Place a heart beside each item that, if a loved one were to code this list, you would want him or her to put a (*) beside.

5. Place the letter (M) beside those items that you think your mother might have liked to do when she was your age.

6. Place the letter (F) beside those items that you think your father might have liked to do when he was your age.

7. Place a question mark (?) beside those items that you do but you don't know why you do them.

8. Place an (R) beside those items you might like to try, but are too risky for you.

VARIATION

Teacher makes up a list of 50 to 100 ideas before beginning the strategy. He or she dittoes the list for each student. Have the students first add any of their own ideas to the list, then do the coding.

Consequences of My Actions

PURPOSE

This strategy helps students begin to take note of the consequences of their actions. This is an important part of the valuing process, and one that is frequently difficult for students to deal with.

PROCEDURE

Ask each student to decide on a change that he would like to make in his behavior. Then have him do one thing to try out his new behavior each day during the forthcoming week. For example, a student might like to start being nicer to his brothers and sisters: on Monday he might read them a story; on Tuesday bring them a candy bar; etc. Students are to record the consequences of their new behavior on both themselves *and* others involved in the situation. Have them use the form provided on *page 294.*

   At the end of the week, bring students together to share and compare their findings. This can be done as a whole class or in small groups. As a follow-up, have students write about the experience.

The assignment can be repeated as many times as you and your students find useful.

The Consequences of My Actions

DATE:	ACTION:	POSITIVE CONSEQUENCES:	NEGATIVE CONSEQUENCES:

Feelings Checklist[13]

PURPOSE

Psychologist Carl Rogers believes that in making important decisions about our values and behavior, we must not only weigh the consequences of our decisions, we must also get in touch with our feelings to determine if the decision *feels good or right*. Our internal evidence, he says, should be just as important a consideration in making a decision as the external evidence we collect. Only when we have examined both kinds of evidence can we say that the resulting choice is a free one.

The purpose of this strategy is to help students learn to identify and examine their feelings when making decisions in small group settings.

PROCEDURE

Use this strategy in conjunction with any small-group decision-making activity. Either during the decision making or right after a decision has been made, ask the group recorder to list on a grid *(see page 296)* all of the feelings group members have at the present moment.

Then, the grid is to be passed in turn to each member. The member is to write his or her name in one of the blank spaces at the top of the grid and check the appropriate box in the column under his name for each feeling that he has at the present moment.

When everyone in the group has had a turn, the group examines the grid for patterns. Are there more negative than

positive feelings checked? Are some feelings checked more
frequently than others?

The group discusses the patterns and what these might
mean in terms of the decisions the group is about to make or
has already made. The central question to be focused on is,
"Do our decisions feel good or right?"

	NAMES									
FEELINGS										
1.										
2.										
3.										
4.										
5.										
6.										
7.										
8.										
9.										
10.										
11.										
12.										
etc.										

Origin/Pawn[14]

PURPOSE

People who feel they are in control of their own lives may be thought of as "origins." Origins are usually very happy people who are getting the most out of life on their own terms. People who feel that they do not determine their own fates, but that others or circumstances are "pushing them around," may be thought of as "pawns." Pawns are usually not very happy or satisfied. The quesiton is: Are we origins or are we pawns? Which would we like to be? How can we become what we want to be? This strategy is designed to help students explore whether they are origins or pawns, and how to move toward being more of an origin, if this is what they want.

PROCEDURE

Introduce students to the concept of being an origin or a pawn. Ask the students which they are more like. Have them make a list of the kinds of people who are likely to be origins, and a list of people who are likely to be pawns. Discuss and compare the lists until the students have the concepts well established in their minds.

Now, ask students to draw the rating scales below, or reproduce them yourself and distribute in the form of a worksheet. The students are to place four marks on each rating scale to indicate: (1) where they are now, (2) where they were two years ago, (3) where they would like to be two years from now, and (4) where they think they will actually be two years into the future.

Follow up by asking students to list some of the ways they might become more of an origin. Have them share and discuss.

Worksheet No. 1

Instructions: First, place an (X) on each of the following scales to indicate where you are on the scale *now*. Second, place a (-) on the scales to indicate where you were two years ago. Third, place a (*) on the scales to indicate where you would like to be in two years. Finally, place a (√) on the scales to indicate where you think you will really be in two years.

ORIGIN   1   2   3   4   5   6   7   8   9   PAWN

I do things because
I decide I want to
do them.

I do things because
others tell me what
to do.

ORIGIN   1   2   3   4   5   6   7   8   9   PAWN

I plan out my actions
and prepare for what
might get in the way.

I depend upon luck
to help me act.

ORIGIN   1   2   3   4   5   6   7   8   9   PAWN

I work hard at an   I give up before
objective until I'm satisfied   I finish.
that I have done my best.

ORIGIN   1   2   3   4   5   6   7   8   9   PAWN

I do things I want to   I always consider
do, no matter what others   what others will think
may think of me.   of mc before I do things.

Now list some of the ways that you might become more of
an origin:

1.

2.

3.

4.

Etc.

FOLLOW-UP

Outside forces can block students from becoming origins.
The following worksheet helps them to see that others can
prevent them from being self-directing. Have students share
and discuss their ratings.

Worksheet No. 2

Instructions: Place the following symbols on the scale below to indicate where you think:

  T = your teacher likes you best.

  P = your parents like you best.

  F = your friends like you best.

  Y = you like you best.

ORIGIN	1	2	3	4	5	6	7	8	9	PAWN

I do things for myself.
I make my own decisions
about what I am going
to do.

I wait for others
to do things for me.
I wait to be told what
to do before I act.

ADDITIONAL FOLLOW-UP

Hand out Worksheet No. 3 to students and have them complete it. Have students divide into pairs, trios, or small groups to share what they found out about themselves.

Worksheet No. 3: Part I [15]

Instructions: Place an (X) on each of the scales below to indicate how you see yourself. Then place a (√) to indicate how you think others see you. Finally, place a (*) to indicate how you would like to be.

1.   How self-reliant am I?

|————————————————————————————————|

VERY   LACKING SELF-
SELF-RELIANT   RELIANCE

2.   How self-confident am I?

|————————————————————————————————|

VERY   LACKING
SELF-CONFIDENT   SELF-CONFIDENCE

3.   How aggressive am I?

|————————————————————————————————|

VERY AGGRESSIVE   NON-AGGRESSIVE

4.   How self-centered or other-centered am I?

|————————————————————————————————|

VERY SELF-   VERY OTHER-
CENTERED   CENTERED

5. How self-disciplined am I?

|——|

VERY SELF-   LACKING SELF-
DISCIPLINED   DISCIPLINE

6. How willing am I to risk (to try new things and behavior)?

|——|

VERY WILLING   UNWILLING
TO RISK   TO RISK

7. How creative am I?

|——|

VERY   LACKING
CREATIVE   CREATIVITY

8. How flexible am I?

|——|

VERY   VERY IN-
FLEXIBLE   FLEXIBLE

9. How open-minded am I?

|——|

VERY OPEN-   VERY CLOSED-
MINDED   MINDED

10. How willing am I to stand up for my beliefs?

|———————————————————————————————|

GREAT DEAL   LACKING
OF COURAGE   COURAGE

11. How influential am I?

|———————————————————————————————|

VERY   LACKING
INFLUENTIAL   INFLUENCE

12. How responsible and dependable am I?

|———————————————————————————————|

VERY   IRRESPONSIBLE
RESPONSIBLE

Worksheet No. 3: Part II

Instructions: Below is the series of scales you used to rate yourself. Rank the scales according to their importance in contributing to an individual's being an origin or pawn. Give a rank of 1 to the most important item, a 2 to the next most important, and so on through rank 12.

RANK   SCALES

———   self-reliant/lacking self-reliance

———   self-confident/lacking self-confidence

_____	aggressive/non-aggressive
_____	self-centered/other-centered
_____	self-disciplined/lacking self-discipline
_____	willing to risk/unwilling to risk
_____	creative/lacking creativity
_____	flexible/inflexible
_____	openminded/closedminded
_____	courage/lacking courage
_____	influential/lacking influence
_____	responsible/irresponsible

Critical Turning Points[16]

PURPOSE

Charting the critical turning points in our life can help us understand how we got to be where we are. The crucial question is, were we in charge or did it all happen by chance? Did we direct our own lives or were we simply pawns? Were we choosing freely? This strategy helps students gather data concerning this issue.

PROCEDURE

Have students draw a line on their papers. At one end of the line they are to write the word "birth" and at the other end, the word "present." They are to start at the present, and go backward through their lives to identify the turning points or critical past events that have helped determine who they are at present. A critical turning point may be defined as any event in the person's life which, had it not occurred, the person would have been different today.

Each time students identify a turning point or critical past event, they are to indicate it on the line by marking the year it occurred and noting with a key word or two what the point or event was. When they have finished, ask them to go back over each point or event on the time line and indicate whether they were an "origin" or "pawn" with regard to the event or point, by placing an (O) for origin or a (P) for pawn (see previous strategy). Percentages can be allocated to indicate to what degree the student was acting as an origin and to what degree he was acting as a pawn in any given situation.

Follow up the activity by having students share what they found out about the critical turning points and past events in their lives. They might also answer some of the following questions privately and then, if they wish, share them with a partner.

1. Am I happy with what I found out about who has controlled the critical turning points in my life? Why or why not?

2. Who or what is controlling my decision making now? Is there anything I want to change about this? What are some things I might do to change?

3. How might my life be different right now if I were more of an origin? More of a pawn?

4. What are three important decisions I will have to make in the near future that may influence my life? For each decision, list some things you might begin to do now to prepare yourself to be more of an origin at decision time.

Board of Directors[17]

PURPOSE

The idea behind this strategy is that each of us has a personal board of directors just as each business corporation has a board of directors. This board is composed of the people who are most influential in our decision making. They are the people we consult either physically or psychologically when we are faced with making an important decision.

Anyone can sit on our board of directors: some we have chosen freely; others sit because they are our boss, teacher, father, or some other figure of authority. We may have few or many people on our board, depending upon our needs and circumstances. And, it is possible for someone whom we have never met to sit on our personal board of directors. (For example, Carl Rogers sits on one author's board of directors even though the author has only read Rogers' books.) The purpose of this strategy is to have students inquire into their decision making to explore the question of who influences their decision making, and how, when, and why they do so.

PROCEDURE

Introduce the strategy, and have each student draw either a rectangular or a round table. Around the table, he is to place several chairs. The exact number depends on how many people sit on his personal board of directors. In each of the chairs, he is to place the name of the person who sits on his board and who is currently influential in his decision making. At the head of the table, he is to place the name of the person who is chairman of the board, or his own name if he sits as chairman. When the students finish, have them place the following symbols beside each of the names around the table to which they apply:

1. Place a (Phy) beside anyone whom you actually consult physically, in person, when you make a decision.

2. Place a (Psy) beside anyone who has a psychological influence on your decision making. (Students may reflect the ratio of physical to psychological influence by placing a percentage beside the symbols, i.e., (Phy) 50 percent, (Psy) 50 percent.)

3. Place an (X) beside anyone whom you would like to remove from your board. As above, you may choose to indicate a percentage, i.e., 25 percent of my husband's influence.

4. Rank the board members in order of how frequently you consult them: 1 = most frequent, 2 = next most frequent, and so on.

5. Rank them in terms of their order of influence in your decision making.

6. Place an (F) beside anyone who is a member of your family.

7. Place an (A) beside anyone who is an authority figure such as a teacher, minister, policeman, boss, etc.

8. Place an (FC) beside anyone who is freely chosen by you to sit on the board.

9. Place a (√) beside anyone who, if they felt strongly one way and you felt strongly another way, you would do what you thought best despite what they might think, feel, or do.

10. Place an (M) beside the males and an (F) beside the females.

When students have completed coding their boards, have them reflect on their codings to see if they can discover any patterns and learn something new about themselves. The following questions might be helpful:

Did you draw a round table or a rectangular table?

If you drew a round one, does this mean or imply that all the members sit equally on the board?

Is there a pattern as to who sits on your board?

Are the members who are most influential the ones you have freely chosen?

Follow up the activity by having student volunteers share some of the things they discovered about themselves.

ADDITIONAL SUGGESTIONS

Students can describe a second board of directors, with seven chairs labeled A to G. They are to place in the corresponding chair the name of an influential person in their life who:

A. Has been a family member.

B. Has been a personal friend.

C. Has been a threat.

D. Was at one time a trusted friend but no longer is held in esteem.

E. They wish could occupy a chair.

F. Had the most positive influence.

G. Had the most negative influence.

Chairs can also be placed around the table and labeled by specific area or kind of decision. For example, students can place the name of an influential person when it comes to making decisions about:

A.   Clothes.

B.   Love and sex.

C.   Money.

D.   Religion and morals.

E.   Politics.

F.   Music.

Another possibility is to have students write a rationale or justification for each of the freely chosen people who sit on their boards of directors. Don't force this one; it can be sticky. However, it can be meaningful for the student who wants to do it.

Growing Up with Values[18]

PURPOSE

This strategy helps students identify some of the values they have acquired while growing up. Students can also begin to recognize the people who have been influential in forming their values. The sharing and discussion part of the strategy is a powerful exercise for helping students to understand how people come to develop different sets of values.

PROCEDURE

Have each student draw a three-column grid on his paper *(see model on page 313)*. Draw a large grid on the blackboard or a sheet of posted newsprint. In column 1, list ten areas in which you think your students have formed some values. The following are some suggested areas:

1. Money.
2. Time.
3. Love/Sex/Marriage.
4. Education.
5. Religion.
6. Politics.
7. Health.
8. War/Peace.
9. Leisure time.
10. Work.
11. Habits.
12. Race.
13. Drugs.
14. Friends.

In the first column of their grids, students are to write one important thing they learned about each topic as they were growing up. For example, under "Education," a student might write that he or she learned that it was essential to go not only to college, but also to professional school to be successful. Under "Love," another student might write that he or she learned that premarital sex is immoral. Give the students plenty of time to fill in this column.

Divide the students into groups of six and ask them to share some of the things they wrote in the first column with their groups, and to discuss any ideas, similarities, or differences that come up. When they have finished this discussion (you may want to set a time limit), ask each student to fill in Column 2 by writing the name of the person who taught them the information in Column 1. This might include mother, father, other family members, teacher, minister, friend, etc. In some cases, the student might have learned the value on his own, perhaps through experience, and he can write "EXP" to indicate this.

In Column 3, the student should write the extent to which he now agrees with the statement he made in Column 1 by using one of the following codes:

(SA)   Strongly agree.

(PA)   Partially agree.

(N)   Neutral (or don't know).

(PD)   Partially disagree.

(SD)   Strongly disagree.

Then ask the students to examine their grids and see if they notice any patterns (for example, "Most of what I strongly believe, I learned from my father"). Have each student summarize his or her findings by writing several "I Learned . . . " statements. Then have the small groups get together again and share these statements, the patterns they discovered, and anything else they found out from the activity.

VARIATION

We have found this variation of the strategy to be extremely useful in working with school faculties, parent groups, and other adults to help people get in touch with the methods that were used by others to transmit values to them. Follow the above directions until the first two columns are com-

Growing Up with Values Grid

COLUMN 1 (TOPIC/WHAT YOU LEARNED)	COLUMN 2	COLUMN 3
Money—"Get as much as you can as quickly as you can."	father	PA
Education—		
Friends—		
Sex—		
Etc.		

pleted. Then, in Column 3, have each person attempt to identify the method through which he acquired the information or value in Column 1. Describe the four ways of transmitting values below, and then have each person fill in Column 3 with the following letters.

(I) *Imposition.*   Someone moralized to you about the issue or imposed his or her beliefs on you.

(L-F) *Laissez-faire.*   You came to this or discovered it on your own.

(M) *Modeling.* Someone personified and thus modeled the value or belief by the way he or she lived his or her life.

(VC) *Values Clarification.* You hold this of your own free choice as a result of examining all of the alternatives and weighing the consequences of each.

Each person then adds a fourth column to the grid, in which he puts the information about the degree of agreement or disagreement. "I Learned . . ." statements and/or small group discussion can follow the exercise.

Notes

1. The authors learned this strategy from Elliott Seif.

2. The authors learned this strategy from Val Mulgrew, who attributed its development to John Shivers. A similar activity is also reported in Postman and Weingartner, *Teaching As a Subversive Activity*, New York, Dell, 1969.

3. This is an adaptation of a game developed by Virginia Allison called "Life Auction" which appears in *Human Values in the Classroom* by Hawley and Hawley.

4. We learned this strategy from Sam Barnett, who adapted it from a writing technique used by Bo Dixon, a teacher at the Haverford School, Haverford, Pa.

5. We learned this strategy from Sam Barnett.

6. Adapted from unpublished materials in a resource manual for teachers, author unknown.

7. Author unknown.

8. Our thanks to Gordon Hart for the passenger list.

9. Developed by J. R. Palaia.

10. Value dilemmas 1-17 were developed and written by Edward and Nila Betof for use in this book.

44 additional values dilemmas for use in grades four through nine may be found in a small booklet published by the NEA titled *Unfinished Stories for Use in the Classroom*. Send 75¢ to: NEA Publications, Sales Section, 1201 Sixteenth Street N.W., Washington, D.C. 20036.

Several 8mm and 16mm films based on unfinished stories are also available from Doubleday and Co., Inc., Education Services Division, Garden City, N.Y. 11530.

11. Dilemmas 21-26 were developed by Carole A. Cipriano and follow the form of Values Sheets, as outlined in *Values and Teaching*.

12. Developed by Edward and Nila Betof.

13. We thank Howard Kirschenbaum for the kernel idea behind this strategy.

14. Adapted from materials developed by R. DeCharms.

15. Adapted from unpublished materials, author unknown.

16. The idea for this strategy was suggested by Elliott Seif.

17. We learned this strategy from Howard Kirschenbaum, who attributed it to Sidney Simon.

18. Our thanks to Chip Landis for the idea behind this strategy.

9. Helping Students Learn to Set Goals and Take Action on Their Values

Taking Action on My Values

PURPOSE

Acting upon one's values is an important dimension of the valuing process, and it is this area in which many of us are weak. We may feel strongly about our values, but we often fail to act upon them.

This strategy is designed to help students get in touch with some of the things they do about their values, and to help them plan to take more action.

PROCEDURE

Provide students with the worksheet below. They are to select three values which they feel strongly about, and write these in Column 1. In Column 2, they are to write at least one thing that they do on a regular basis to take action on each of the three values. In the third column, they are to write one additional thing which they do not do now, but which they could do on a regular basis to take action on each of the values.

Then, have students form groups of five or six persons and share and compare their worksheets. As a final task, students should decide whether they want to do any of the things they have written in Column 3.

Worksheet

Some values you may feel strongly about:

1. A prosperous life.
2. Making a contribution to the world.
3. A peaceful world.
4. Cleanliness.
5. Helping others.
6. Creativeness.
7. Equal opportunity for all.
8. National security.
9. A world of beauty.
10. Ecology.
11. A healthy body.
12. Social recognition.
13. Others_____

VALUE	HOW I ACT ON IT	HOW I COULD ACT ON IT
Example: Ecology.	Take glass bottles to a recycling center weekly.	Ride my bike to school instead of mom or dad driving me.
1.		
2.		
3.		

VARIATION

Have students find something in a newspaper or magazine they feel strongly about that is values related. Then they are to write about at least one action they have taken in the past that is directly related to the issue, and one action that they could take in the future.

My Personal Goals Inventory

PURPOSE

Our goals are a reflection of how we intend to act upon our values. The purpose of the personal goals inventory is to help students begin to look at their life goals in a systematic way. For students who do not set goals, it will serve to raise the question of whether or not it would be useful for them to do so.

PROCEDURE

Once students have become clear about what they value in life, what is worth having and living for, the personal goals inventory can help them set some goals to *achieve* the kind of life they want to live. Provide students with a copy of the personal goals inventory worksheet below. Have them discuss some of the reasons why it might be useful for them to set and work toward some specific personal goals. Then, they are to fill in as much of the goals inventory as they can, and keep it up to date as they add to or change their goals.

Worksheet

Instructions: This is a personal goals inventory in the areas of *school, family, leisure time, friends, personal development, job and career,* and *life goals.* For each of these areas, think of the specific goals you have for yourself or which you might like to set and work toward. List these goals in the spaces provided. Then, check the boxes to the right of the goals you have written if they apply. For example, if the goal is very important to you, check the first box, and so on. Keep this inventory handy so that any time you wish to add to or change your goals, you can do so.

I. *My School and Academic Goals*

Do I want to:

Get better grades?
Prepare for a vocation?
Get into college?
Learn specific skills?
Get along better with my teachers?
Other ————

My specific goals are:

1. ———————————————————————————————
2. ———————————————————————————————
3. ———————————————————————————————
Etc. ———————————————————————————————

II. *My Family Goals*

Do I want to:

Get along better with my family?
Meet the right future mate?
Do something for my family?
Other ————

A.	*This goal is very important to me.*						
B.	*I am proud that it is a goal of mine.*						
C.	*It is realistic in that I have a good chance of achieving the goal.*						
D.	*I have chosen this goal because I want to work toward it, not just because others want me to do it.*						
E.	*There are risks or possible negative consequences involved in achieving this goal.*						
F.	*I have weighed the risks involved and still think the goal is worth it.*						
G.	*This goal is consistent with the other goals I have set for myself.*						
H.	*I am going to make a plan of action to achieve this goal.*						

My specific goals are:

1. _____

2. _____

3. _____

Etc. _____

III. *My Friendship and Personal
Relationship Goals*

Do I want to:

Improve my relationships with others?
Have more friends?
Have different kinds of friends?
Have more influence on others?
Other _____

			A.	B.	C.	D.	E.	F.	G.	H.
			This goal is very important to me.	*I am proud that it is a goal of mine.*	*It is realistic in that I have a good chance of achieving the goal.*	*I have chosen this goal because I want to work toward it, not just because others want me to do it.*	*There are risks or possible negative consequences involved in achieving this goal.*	*I have weighed the risks involved and still think the goal is worth it.*	*This goal is consistent with the other goals I have set for myself.*	*I am going to make a plan of action to achieve this goal.*

My specific goals are:

1. _____

2. _____

3. _____

Etc. _____

IV. *My Leisure Time Goals*

Do I want to:

Spend my leisure time more productively?
Have more leisure time?
Get more satisfaction from my leisure time activities?
Learn a new hobby?
Other _____

	A.	B.	C.	D.	E.	F.	G.	H.
	This goal is very important to me.	*I am proud that it is a goal of mine.*	*It is realistic in that I have a good chance of achieving the goal.*	*I have chosen this goal because I want to work toward it, not just because others want me to do it.*	*There are risks or possible negative consequences involved in achieving this goal.*	*I have weighed the risks involved and still think the goal is worth it.*	*This goal is consistent with the other goals I have set for myself.*	*I am going to make a plan of action to achieve this goal.*

My specific goals are:

1. _____

2. _____

3. _____

Etc. _____

V. *My Personal Development Goals*

Do I want to:

Change something about myself?
Improve my physical image?
Get in better physical condition?
Act more mature?
Be more joyful and spontaneous?
Act upon a value I hold?
Other _____

A. This goal is very important to me.	B. I am proud that it is a goal of mine.	C. It is realistic in that I have a good chance of achieving the goal.	D. I have chosen this goal because I want to work toward it, not just because others want me to do it.	E. There are risks or possible negative consequences involved in achieving this goal.	F. I have weighed the risks involved and still think the goal is worth it.	G. This goal is consistent with the other goals I have set for myself.	H. I am going to make a plan of action to achieve this goal.

My specific goals are:

1. _____

2. _____

3. _____

Etc. _____

VI. *My Job and Career Goals*

Do I want to:

    Find a job?
    Get a different job?
    Have a higher paying job?
    Test out a career to see if it is suited to me?
    Other _____

A. This goal is very important to me.

B. I am proud that it is a goal of mine.

C. It is realistic in that I have a good chance of achieving the goal.

D. I have chosen this goal because I want to work toward it, not just because others want me to do it.

E. There are risks or possible negative consequences involved in achieving this goal.

F. I have weighed the risks involved and still think the goal is worth it.

G. This goal is consistent with the other goals I have set for myself.

H. I am going to make a plan of action to achieve this goal.

My specific goals are:

1. _____

2. _____

3. _____

Etc. _____

VII. *My Long Range Life Goals*

Do I want to:

Have a certain kind of life style?
Accomplish something important?
Devote my life to something?
Other _____

			A.	*This goal is very important to me.*
			B.	*I am proud that it is a goal of mine.*
			C.	*It is realistic in that I have a good chance of achieving the goal.*
			D.	*I have chosen this goal because I want to work toward it, not just because others want me to do it.*
			E.	*There are risks or possible negative consequences involved in achieving this goal.*
			F.	*I have weighed the risks involved and still think the goal is worth it.*
			G.	*This goal is consistent with the other goals I have set for myself.*
			H.	*I am going to make a plan of action to achieve this goal.*

My long range goals are:

1. _____

2. _____

3. _____

Etc. _____

VIII.   *Other Goals I Have*

My specific goals are:

1. _____

2. _____

3. _____

Etc. _____

	A.	B.	C.	D.	E.	F.	G.	H.
	This goal is very important to me.	*I am proud that it is a goal of mine.*	*It is realistic in that I have a good chance of achieving the goal.*	*I have chosen this goal because I want to work toward it, not just because others want me to do it.*	*There are risks or possible negative consequences involved in achieving this goal.*	*I have weighed the risks involved and still think the goal is worth it.*	*This goal is consistent with the other goals I have set for myself.*	*I am going to make a plan of action to achieve this goal.*

From Here to There

PURPOSE

Bringing about change in our personal lives is often a difficult and complex undertaking. There are often many constraints and risks which stand in the way and must be removed before we can achieve our personal goals. This strategy is designed to help students get in touch with some of the things they would like to change about themselves, what the new goals might be, and some of the risks, constraints, and consequences that are involved.

PROCEDURE

Introduce the strategy. Have students draw a window with nine panes (see below).

	FROM HERE $\longrightarrow$	TO THERE	CONSTRAINTS/ RISKS/ CONSEQUENCES
PERSONAL LEVEL	A.	B.	C.
INTERPERSONAL LEVEL	D.	E.	F.
PERSONAL ENVIRONMENT	G.	H.	I.

Each student is to privately fill in the windows with pictures or symbols by doing the following steps:

1. In window (A), draw a picture of something you would like to change about yourself. In (B), draw a picture of what you would be like after the change, if you could make it. In (C), draw a picture of a barrier or constraint which might stand in your way and/or a risk which might be involved if you actually tried to make the change. *(See diagram on page 336 for model.)*

2. Draw a picture in window (D) to represent something you would like to change in your relationship with others. In (E), represent what you would like your relationship to be like after the change. In (F), represent a constraint or risk involved.

3. In window (G), draw a picture of a change you would like to make in your personal environment (at home, school, etc.) which, if it could be made, would help you be the kind of person you want to be or have the kind of relationship with others that you want. In (H), draw what you would like the new environment to look like. In (I), draw a constraint or risk involved in trying to change your personal environment.

When students complete their windows, have them divide into pairs or trios to share and compare notes. Encourage students to decide whether they really want to make some of the changes they have drawn. If they do, suggest that they do a *Plan of Action (see page 342).*

The figure on 336 is an example of a completed grid. (For an explanation of the drawings, see the following figure.)

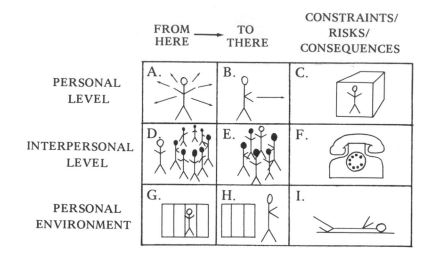

VARIATION

Have students write in each of the windows instead of using pictures, symbols, drawings.

	FROM HERE ────────▶ TO THERE			CONSTRAINTS/RISKS/ CONSEQUENCES
PER-SONAL LEVEL	A. I am disorganized, trying to go too many directions all at one time.	B. I want to try to set and accomplish one goal at a time.	C. I'll feel cut off and out of touch with things, like I'm in a box.
INTER-PER-SONAL LEVEL	D. I am often not a part of the group.	E. I want to have more friends and be included in group activities.	F. Friends can call me at any time with their problems.
PER-SONAL ENVIRON-MENT	G. In this school, I feel like I am in jail.	H. I want to have more freedom and responsibility.	I. I might not be able to handle the freedom and responsibility and fall flat on my face.

Origami [1]

PURPOSE

We have included this game for several reasons. One, it is an excellent Values Clarification strategy. It helps students examine several of their motives and the values that lay behind them. Second, it is designed to help students explore their goal setting behavior and learn to set more realistic goals. Third, it will serve as an introduction to the Achievement Motivation Approach which Alschuler, Tabor, and McIntyre have developed to personalize and humanize classrooms and schools. [2]

PROCEDURE

Introduce the strategy by telling students that you want them to examine their goal setting ability by playing a paper-folding game called *Origami*. Their task will be to see how many pieces of paper they can fold in five minutes. Explain that the game will be played in several rounds and that you will give the instructions for each round.

Round One

Provide students with scrap paper of a uniform size. The first round is a trial round in which they will be given thirty seconds to see how many pieces of paper each student can fold by himself. Each piece of paper is to be folded twice. The first fold should make the piece half its size; the second fold should make it half again its size. *See figures on 338.*

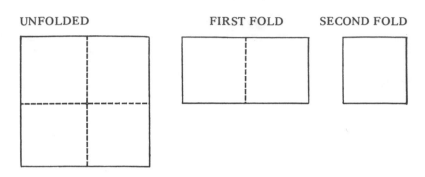

UNFOLDED   FIRST FOLD   SECOND FOLD

For each round, including the trial round, the following rules apply.

1. Start the round with the paper in a uniform stack.

2. Fold each sheet individually.

3. Each sheet must be folded so that no more than one quarter of an inch overlaps on any side. If so, the sheet will be discarded and will not count.

4. At the signal for the end of the round, everyone must stop immediately. Partly folded sheets do not count.

Start the round and stop it after thirty seconds. Have students total the number of sheets they folded according to the rules. Find out what the high and low numbers were. Put these on a chalkboard with all the numbers in between. Then, get a show of hands for each number and write the number of students who completed that number of sheets beside it.

Round Two

Before beginning this round, explain the scoring procedures. Each student is to make a bid or estimate of how many sheets he or she can complete in five minutes. If the student actually completes what he bids, he gets that number of points. Anything over his bid is not counted. If the student does not make his points, he gets zero points.

Students are to place their estimates on a sheet of paper with their name and turn it in to you. Then, they are to select the number of sheets of paper that they bid, plus a few extras in case they wish to discard some misfolded sheets during the round.

Start the round and stop it exactly five minutes later. Students are then to pair up and count each other's folded sheets, discarding any that do not meet the specifications. Each student should then compare his total number folded with his bid to get his score. He should record his score himself. *This is his own private information and doesn't have to be shared unless he wants to.* Then have students report to you the actual number they folded. Again, find out the low and high numbers and place these and all the numbers in between on the chalkboard. Get a show of hands for each and record it as in Round One.

Before starting the next round, have students form trios or small groups and process the round by discussing the following questions:

1. Based on the previous round, did you set a goal which was:

   _____ a. So low you were sure to make it?

_____ b. Somewhat lower than what you thought you could make?

_____ c. Exactly what you thought you could make?

_____ d. Just enough higher to provide a challenge?

_____ e. Considerably higher than you thought you could make?

2. Did other people's scores affect the number that you bid? If so, in what ways?

3. What were your feelings during each round? What do you feel now?

4. If you had to rank your motives during this round, what would your ranking be?

_____ a. I was doing it for the fun of the game.

_____ b. I was doing it to win (beat others).

_____ c. I was doing it to see if I could achieve my goal.

_____ d. Other _____

Round Three

Have students complete this round using the same procedures as in the second round. However, during the processing phase, add the following questions:

1. Did you set a more realistic goal for this round than for the previous round?

2. Is your goal setting behavior in this game characteristic of your goal setting behavior in general? In what ways is it the same? In what ways is it different? What could you do to become more effective at goal setting?

Round Four

Have students form teams of five to seven members each. Each team is to make a bid as to how many sheets they think they can fold collectively, as a team, in five minutes. The same rules and procedures as in previous rounds apply. During the processing phase, use the following questions:

1. How did the team arrive at its goal? Majority vote? Consensus? Group average? Other?

2. What was the team motive during this round?

    —— a. To have fun together.

    —— b. To win (beat the other teams).

    —— c. To achieve the team goal.

3. What happened during the bidding and playing? Who did what? Who were the leaders? What things helped the group? What things hindered the group?

4. How do the group members feel about the team's results?

My Personal Plan of Action

PURPOSE

Personal goal achievement is no easy task, especially if the goal we have set for ourselves involves a moderate-to-high degree of risk. Planning is often required if we are to succeed. This strategy teaches students the steps and skills involved in action planning and goal achievement.

PROCEDURE

Introduce the strategy by discussing with students some of the things that can keep people from reaching their goals. Use a concrete example which students can relate to. Then explain that you want to teach them how to plan so that they will avoid such pitfalls.

Give students a copy of Worksheet No. 1. Their task is to complete the worksheet either in class or as homework. Explain that the goal they set should be something they really want to achieve. It can be personal, school-related, family-related, or job-related, but it should be something that they can hope to accomplish in the reasonably near future. If students have already completed *My Personal Goals Inventory (see page 318),* have them select one of the goals from this.

When they have completed the worksheet, divide them into pairs or trios and have them share and try to strengthen each other's action plans. Following this, the worksheet should be placed in the students' work folders.

Worksheet No. 2 should be given out as students who have implemented their plans of action either achieve or fail to achieve their goals.

Worksheet No. 1

1.   I want to achieve the following goals:_____

_____

2.   What could keep me from reaching this goal?

_____ I don't really have the skills, ability
         and/or knowledge needed.

_____ I don't want it badly enough
         to really work for it.

_____ I'm afraid that I might fail.

_____ I'm afraid of what others might think.

_____ Others don't want me to reach this goal.

_____ The goal is really too difficult
         to ever accomplish.

Some other reasons might be:_____

_____

3.   What are some things I could do so

the above things don't prevent
me from reaching my goal?

_____

_____

4.   Who can help me?

Name: Kind of help:

_____   _____

_____   _____

5.   What are my chances for success?

_____ Very Good.   Why do I feel this way?

_____ Good.   _____

_____ Fair.   _____

_____ Poor.   _____

_____ Very Poor.   _____

6.   What are some of the good things that
     might happen if I reach this goal?

_____

_____

7.   What are some of the bad things that
     might happen if I reach this goal?

_____

_____

_____

8. What are the chances that the bad things
   would happen if I reached the goal?

   ___ Very High.   What could be done to
                         reduce the odds?
   ___ High.

   ___ 50/50.   _____

   ___ Low.   _____

   ___ Very Low.   _____

9. Do I still want to try to reach this goal?

   ___ Yes.

   ___ No.

   ___ Still Undecided.

10. What are some first steps I could take
    to reach this goal?

    _____

11. What else must I do if I am really to succeed?

    _____

    _____

12. Am I going to take the above steps?

    ___ Yes.

    ___ No.

    ___ Still Undecided.

13. If my answer to No. 12 is Yes, I make
the following self-contract:

SELF-CONTRACT

I,_____, have decided to try to
achieve the goal of_____. The first step I
will take to reach this goal will be to_____
by_____. My target date for reaching the goal
is_____.

DATE_____ SIGNED_____
(WITNESSED BY)_____

Worksheet No. 2

1. My plan of action:

_____ Worked very well, since I reached my goal.

_____ Worked somewhat, since I nearly or partially reached my goal.

_____ Did not work, since I failed to achieve my goal.

2. How do I feel about succeeding/failing?
_____
_____

3. I think the following thing(s) contributed to my success/failure:
_____
_____

4. If I were to do it again, I would do the following things differently:

I Wish I Could/I Knew I Could

PURPOSE

This strategy is designed to help younger students to identify some of the things they wish they could do, and then to develop a plan of action to do them.

PROCEDURE

Provide students with a dittoed copy of Figure 1 on *page 348.* In the first column, titled "I Wish I Could . . ." ask them to list three goals that they wish they could achieve in the near future. Then, they are to study the three goals and, for any goal that they think they might be able to achieve or that they would like to try to achieve, they are to move the goal to Column 2, titled "I Think I Can. . . . "

The next step is to have the students draw up a plan of action for achieving any one of the goals in Column 2. The plan should include (1) listing the steps they are going to take to achieve the goal, (2) what some of the difficulties might be, and (3) what could be done to remove or deal with these difficulties *(see Figure 2 on page 350).* When students have developed their plans and are convinced that they should start putting these plans into action, have them move the goals to Column 3, titled "I Know I Can. . . . " When they finally accomplish the goal, it is moved into Column 4, titled

"I Knew I Could. . . . " Encourage students to add new "I Wish I Could's" to their lists at any time and then follow through until the goal is finally moved to Column 4.

Figure 1

I WISH I COULD . . .	I THINK I CAN . . .	I KNOW I CAN . . .	I KNEW I COULD . . .
1.			
2.			
3.			
4.			
5.			

Writing My Own PBO's

PURPOSE

Writing personal behavioral objectives is another way of helping students learn to set goals and systematically move toward goal achievement.

PROCEDURE

Writing personal behavioral objectives (PBO's) is not difficult once you get the hang of it. Before trying to help students learn to write them, write some for yourself. They should start with the following words: "By_____(date)_____ I will...." Fill in the date you expect to complete the objective, and then finish the sentence with a specific statement of what you are going to do and how you will do it. The following are several examples:

By_____(date)_____ I will:

- Lose fifteen pounds by cutting out all sweets from my diet.

- Be able to summarize in writing the author's major points in Chapter 4 of *The History of America.*

- Have invited three friends to dinner whom I have not seen in several months.

- Save $45.00 in three weeks by taking $15.00

Figure 2

*Goal I Want to Achieve:*_____

STEPS I MUST TAKE	DIFFICULTIES I MIGHT FACE WITH EACH STEP
1.	
2.	
3.	
4.	
5.	
6.	

HOW I CAN HANDLE THE DIFFICULTY	WHO CAN HELP ME WITH IT	DATE I HOPE TO ACCOMPLISH STEP

from my weekly paycheck and putting it into my savings account.

- Write two letters—one to my parents and the other to my sister—instead of playing tennis Sunday afternoon.

To teach the strategy, ask the class or small group to generate a list of things they would like to do in the next week. Write the list on the chalkboard. Post or give them a sheet of paper with several examples of PBO's on it. Explain that you want to teach them how to write their own PBO's. Start by having them select one of the items from the list on the chalkboard. By calling out, they are to tell you how to write it in the PBO style. Write out their words on the chalkboard.

Now ask them if the statement could be made any more specific. Make any changes they suggest, and then ask them the same question again. Continue until the PBO is as specific as possible. You may wish to make some suggestions during the process.

Do several more items from the list on the chalkboard until they seem to have the hang of it. Then ask each student to privately write out three PBO's of his own. If they have problems, give them some help. When they finish, they can review the PBO's in small groups, if they wish; or, those who want to can hand theirs in for you to review.

Finally, ask students to write at least one PBO each week and hand it in to you or put it in their values inquiry folder. Stress that they should write PBO's *only* for those things which they really intend to do. Periodically, have students look back over their PBO's to see how many they have actually accomplished. If some students are not accomplishing their personal objectives, help them find out why.

ADDITIONAL SUGGESTION

If the PBO is a difficult one to achieve, such as losing weight, the student may want to set up a token reinforcement schedule to help himself reach his goal (see below). Suggest this as a possibility to any student who is having difficulty achieving his stated personal objective. If he responds to the idea, help him set it up. Don't force it on him, however.

For tokens, you may use poker chips worth so many points per color, or dittoed slips of paper with the number of points and a place for the student's name and your signature. Each time the student loses a pound of weight, he gets 100 points. Each time he gains a pound, he pays you 100 points. The points can then be turned in for things the student finds reinforcing—for some students, collecting the points and seeing the number get higher and higher is in itself reinforcing. Before the token system is put into operation, help the student (1) prepare a list of things that could serve as reinforcers and (2) place point values on them. Some things should be easy to buy because they will be worth much fewer points than other, more difficult things. The following is a sample list:

1. Listening to music through a headset while reading. *100 pts.*

2. Playing a game of checkers or chess with a friend as a break from the regular schoolwork. *500 pts.*

3. Having a small class party for 15 minutes to celebrate your success so far.   *1,000 pts.*

4. Tickets to the movies.   *2,000 pts.*

Am I a Risk Taker?

PURPOSE

Taking action or trying out new behavior often involves risk. For some, doing anything new is too risky; thus, they never grow. For others, nothing is too risky; they are always in trouble. This strategy is designed to help students get in touch with their risk-taking pattern of behavior and decide whether they wish to alter it or not.

PROCEDURE

Introduce the strategy by having the students talk about taking risks and what is involved. Then give out the worksheet below. When students have completed it, form them into groups of four or five and have them share and compare worksheets. Follow up the activity by having students complete the following sentence stem, "I learned that I. . . . " These can be shared in the small group or with the whole class.

Worksheet

Instructions: Code your lists with the following symbols. Place a:

(Phys.) beside any item on the list
that involves physical risk.

(Psy.) beside any item that involves psychological risk.

(Soc.) beside any item that involves social risk.

($) beside any item that involves financial risk.

1. List and code ten things that you would consider risky if you were to do them.

2. List and code five of the most risky things you have ever done. What were the consequences of each?

3. List and code five things you would never do because of the risks involved.

4. List and code five risks you would take or might like to

take if the odds could be bettered and/or the stakes increased.

5. List several times when you did not do something because it was too risky and you were sorry afterward.

6. List several times when you did not do something because it was too risky and you were happy afterward.

7. Look over your lists and codings above. Do you see any patterns? Describe.

8. Are you pleased with what you see? Would you like to make any changes? Describe.

Personal Problem-Solving

PURPOSE

In living by their values, students often encounter value dilemmas, conflicts, and problems. This strategy teaches them a systematic way to deal with these dilemmas or problems.

PROCEDURE

Introduce the strategy by asking students to write a short outline of a personal value problem, dilemma, or conflict they have faced in the past. The outline should deal with the following questions:

1. What was the nature of the problem, dilemma, or conflict?

2. What alternative solutions did you consider in dealing with the problem?

3. What were some of the consequences involved? To you? To others?

4. Who, if anyone, did you go to to discuss the problem, seek advice, or get help? What kind of help did you receive?

5. What did you finally do? What was the outcome? Was it favorable to you? To others?

6. If you had it to do again, what would you do differently?

If there is enough trust in the group, and a desire among students to do so, let them share and discuss their outlines in pairs or small groups of their own choosing.

Follow up by distributing the worksheet below. Indicate that the problem that students select can be a small one, like deciding what to wear in the morning, or something larger and more complex; all you are interested in is helping students learn a method for arriving at a solution. Later on, they can then use the method whenever they face an important problem. When students have completed the worksheet, let them share it with another student or a small group if they volunteer to do so.

Worksheet

Instructions: Please answer each of the following questions by writing your responses in the appropriate space. Use additional paper, if needed.

1. What are some of the personal values problems, dilemmas, or conflicts that you are currently facing?

2. Select one of the problems, dilemmas, or conflicts above that you would like to work on. Explain in some detail the nature of the problem.

3. What do you see as some of the possible solutions to the problem? (List as many as you can think of.)

4. For *each* of the above solutions, make a grid, and list the positive and negative consequences that might result.

SOLUTION	POSITIVE CONSEQUENCES	NEGATIVE CONSEQUENCES

5. Which solution do you consider the one most worth trying?

6. What might be some of the barriers you would encounter in implementing the solution? What steps would need to be taken to remove or deal with these barriers? List on the grid below.

SOLUTION	BARRIERS	CORRECTIVE ACTION NEEDED

7. Do you want to try implementing the solution? If yes, make a plan of action with the steps you will take and dates that these steps will be taken.

8. What was the outcome of your efforts?

Taking a Consistency Check

PURPOSE

Acting repeatedly and consistently is a basic element of the valuing process. This strategy is designed to help students examine the action they take on their values and to assess whether or not it forms a consistent pattern. The purpose is to help them take more consistent action on their values.

PROCEDURE

Introduce the strategy and ask students to identify a value that they hold strongly: one that they do something about, that they take repeated action on, e.g. ecology. Instruct them to make a list of all the ways that they have acted upon this strongly held value. Also, they are to list, or make a note of, anything that they have done which is inconsistent with the value held. For example, a student might recycle his newspapers, avoid buying soft drinks in no-return bottles, etc., but then go on a picnic with disposable paper plates and cups, and plastic silverware. This might be considered inconsistent with his belief in ecology.

Finally, each student is to pair off with someone in the class who knows him or her well. Each shares his list with the other. Then, each partner is to give feedback to the other about any behavior he or she has noted which is inconsistent with the value held. Follow up the activity by having students complete and share "I learned that I . . . " statements.

Notes

1. Origami is the Japanese art of paper folding. This strategy is adapted from the *Origami Game* developed by Alfred Alschuler and available from Educational Ventures, Middletown, Conn. Other games and classroom materials which teach achievement motivation are also available.

2. See *Teaching Achievement Motivation*.

PART III

PERSONALIZING THE CURRICULUM

10. Introduction to Part III

In a personalized classroom, the curriculum should serve the needs and goals of students. This means that the curriculum must be open and flexible, preferably one that grows out of the actual needs, concerns, interests, and goals of the students it is to serve. In the first section of this third part of the book, we have detailed a curriculum development process designed to be used by teachers and students to cooperatively build a curriculum which truly serves students. We have also included a sample unit which was developed using this model.

However, many teachers do not find themselves in a situation where they can start from scratch and build their own curriculum. Rather, they are saddled with curriculum requirements which prevent or curtail this kind of organic development. In section two of this third part, we have included three strategies which can be used by the teacher to adapt his subject matter so that it is at least related to student concerns and interests, even if it is not tailor-made.

11. Developing Curriculum from Student Concerns[1]

Most curriculums are developed without any involvement of the students they are intended to serve. Thus, unless the curriculum developer is extremely sensitive to the population his work is designed to serve, he more than likely will produce a closed curriculum, one that fails to deal with the real concerns[2] that students bring to the classroom. A skillful and sensitive teacher working *with* his or her students is much more likely to produce a creative, open learning program in which knowledge and cognitive skills serve student purposes, goals and values.

The procedure which follows is designed to help the teacher develop a unit of study with the participation of his or her students. (However, the procedure may also be used without involving students in the process, if this proves difficult, impossible, or inappropriate. In fact, we suggest doing a unit by yourself, using the process, before trying it with your students.) These procedures may be used with a large group or a small group, or with an individual student as the basis for an independent study project.

Step 1.   *Brainstorming a List of Topics.*   Ask students to call out any topics, themes, or problems which interest or concern them, and which they would like to study. List these on a piece of newsprint or the chalkboard in the exact words they use; don't try to rephrase. Add to the list until students run out of ideas. Also, add your own ideas.

Step 2.   *Selecting the Topic.*   Help students develop a list of criteria for selecting the topic to be used for the unit of study (or provide them with your own criteria). Here is a sample list, not meant to be all-inclusive.

1. Is the topic a "burning issue"? Is it something that really concerns or interests us?

2. Will the topic help us develop better insights about ourselves, our values, purposes, goals? Will it help to make us better persons?

3. Will the topic help us develop a better understanding of the world we live in? Will it help us live in it more effectively?

4. Will the topic help us develop our skills in thinking, problem solving, writing, reading?

5. Can we get enough information about the topic to make the study worthwhile?

Help students select the topic using the criteria developed. If you are working with small groups, each group may wish to select its own topic. The remaining topics can be posted and used for future units.

Step 3. *Developing a Flow Chart.* The next step is to have students develop a flow chart to break down the main topic into manageable sub-topics. Ask students to write the topic in the center of a piece of paper. Then, they are to draw several lines out from the topic and list anything related to the main topic that can be studied; this is repeated with the new sub-topics, thus creating a web of inter-related sub-topics *(see figure on page 367).* We suggest that you do public flow chart the first time, using a piece of newsprint. The newsprint can be posted for future reference by the students.

Step 4. *Doing a Question Census.* Depending upon the purpose and length of the unit, the question census can be general, to include the whole flow chart, or specifically limited to one or two sub-topics. To conduct a question census, ask students to make a list of all the questions that they think would be important and useful in studying the unit; this is best done in pairs or trios. Then, the questions are compiled into one large list and posted. Include your questions in the list, too. Check the list to make sure there is a balance of fact, concept, and values level questions. (*See pages 395-400* for a description of these three levels.) If the list is weak in one area, help strengthen it by including additional questions of the type needed.

Step 5. *Identifying the Available Resources for the Unit.*[3] Post five large sheets of newsprint around the room. On each, place the heading from the list on *page 368.*

A Money Flow Chart

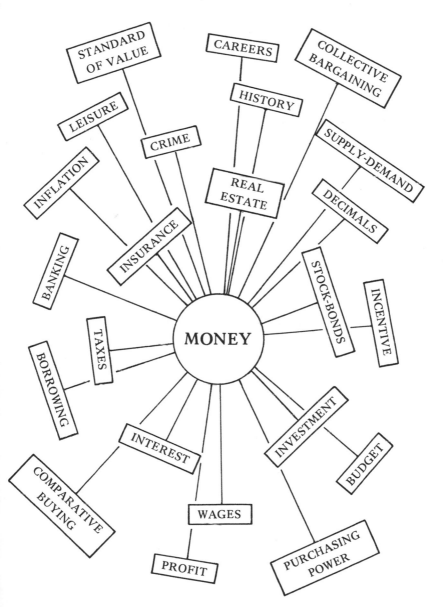

1. *Readings:*   includes books, magazine articles, essays, newspaper articles, poems, etc.

2. *Audio-visuals:*   includes movies, filmstrips, TV programs, video tapes, audio tapes, records, etc.

3. *Field Trips:*   includes trips to museums, libraries, organizations, business firms, parks, etc.

4. *People:*   includes parents, community leaders, businessmen, other teachers and students, etc.

5. *Manipulative   Devices:*   includes   learning games, science apparatus, plants, animals, measuring tools, art supplies, "junk," etc.

Appoint five recorders, one per sheet of newsprint, and provide them with magic markers. Then, ask the class or group to look over the five headings and think of any related resources or items that might be used in the unit. For example, you might ask, "What are all the really good readings that we can think of related to our topic?" Or, "Who are all of the really interesting and exciting people we can think of who might be willing to serve as guest speakers, provide us with information, or lead us in an activity?"

As students think of ideas, resources, places, people, and. things, the recorders are to list them on the sheets under the appropriate headings. Include your own ideas and suggestions in the listings.

Step 6. *Developing Activities from the Question Census.* The next step is to develop activities which help students gather data and seek answers to the questions posed. We suggest that you start by dividing students into pairs. Ask each pair to select a question from the question census which they would like to work on. Make sure that the pairs do not all choose the same questions; however, don't force students to work on questions that do not interest them.

The task of each pair is to develop an activity or project which is related to the question, and which would serve to move them closer to an answer or solution. The activities and projects should involve more than just reading and writing skills. They should also be active, and experiential.

The activity or project is to be written up in either a leader-directed format or a self-instructional format. (For a discussion of how to write self-instructional task cards, *see page 471.*) When the pairs finish writing up their activities, have them take turns reading them in a whole-class session. The activities should be viewed and strengthened.

This step can be repeated several times until the unit is complete or fleshed out to both your and your students' satisfaction.

Step 7. *Purposing the Unit.* The next step is to determine, jointly with your students, what purpose(s) the activities serve. (Some teachers feel it is inappropriate to involve students in this step of the process. For very young children we can concede the point, but for older students, especially at the secondary level, we think it is important that they develop this understanding *and* that they have a voice in determining the objectives of any given unit of study.) On a grid *(see page 392 for model)*, list the names and/or numbers of the activities of the unit along the top. Along the vertical axis of the grid, list the important *valuing, cognitive skill*, and *knowledge* objectives that you (and your students, if appropriate) think the students should master. Then, examine each activity in the unit to determine what *valuing, cognitive skill*, and *knowledge* objectives that activity serves to promote, and check the appropriate boxes.

Step 8. *Making Curriculum Revisions.*   Examine the grid for patterns. For example, the grid might reflect a heavy emphasis on some objectives and a lighter emphasis on other objectives. Perhaps this is as it should be; on the other hand, it might be a weakness of the unit. Assess the weaknesses of the unit and make the needed curriculum revisions.

Step 9. *Structuring the Unit to Facilitate Teaching and Learning.*   This step is designed to help you gain input from students so that you can better plan a structure that will facilitate the teaching and learning of the unit. Raise the following questions to gather student ideas and suggestions. Then, do the initial planning and final formulation yourself, unless you are already skillful—or as you become more skillful—in helping students formulate an instructional plan. We suggest that you get input from your students on the following questions:

1. What classroom organization and structure will best facilitate the teaching and learning of this unit? (Some options might include learning

centers, individual study areas, group areas, conventional seating, room dividers, project areas, storage areas, etc.)

2. What requirements should we have for the unit? Which activities, if any, should be required of all students? Which activities, if any, should be required of some students? Which students should these be?

3. What methods of evaluation will best facilitate the teaching and learning of this unit? (Some options might include learning contracts, student self-evaluation, evaluation by other students, teacher-student conferences, using feedback forms and rating scales, conventional grades, pass/fail or credit/no credit options.)

When you have formulated your instructional plan, share it with the class to get their final suggestions and criticism before implementation.

Step 10. *Implementing and Teaching the Unit.* Use the teaching strategies and methods suggested in this book and/or your own methods to implement and teach the unit. Make any needed revisions as you proceed.

ADDITIONAL SUGGESTIONS

Students must be rather sophisticated if they are to be involved at every step of the above curriculum development process. Yet by modifying the steps and involving students in only those steps which are appropriate, the joint planning process can be used even with very young children. For example, a kindergarten teacher we know adapted the process to develop a unit on pets with his pupils. He used the flow chart to help children identify different kinds of pets—i.e., large and small pets, house and farm pets, etc. He then helped the children identify some of the questions they wished to have answered about pets, and who might help them find some answers—i.e., pet owners, pet shop keepers, zoo keepers, etc. Children asked if they could bring in pets to the classroom; the teacher agreed, and much of the next several weeks were devoted to helping children learn about, love, and care for the pets.

A SAMPLE UNIT

We have adapted the following interdisciplinary unit from a unit developed by Ruby Bratcher for use in her fifth-sixth grade reading center at the Rhodes Middle School in Philadelphia. It is a good example of what can be produced using the above ten-step curriculum development process. The activities, written in a self-instructional format, were placed on 4 x 6 index cards and posted for students' use. The unit was an outgrowth of a TV program, *The Rookies:* "The Authentic Death of Billy Stomper," the script of which was used as the basis for a unique, new reading approach called the Language Arts Television Reading Program. The program was developed by Michael J. McAndrew and Bernard Solomon. A brief synopsis of the script follows on *page 374.*

A FLOW CHART FOR A UNIT
ON CRIME AND LAW ENFORCEMENT

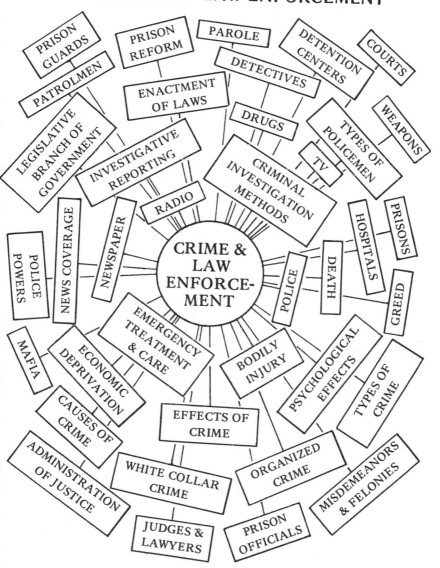

While walking her dog through the park one evening, Pamela Hines, a university student in Jamaica, witnesses the shooting of Billy Stomper, a dope pusher, who later dies. Terry Webster, a police officer who arrives on the scene with two other officers minutes after the shooting, befriends Pamela and they fall in love.

Junior, Billy Stomper's murderer, learns where Pamela lives from a masseuse who identified Pamela's parking sticker. Junior goes to Pamela's apartment building and shoots her. Pamela dies in the hospital emergency room. Terry vows to get Pamela's killer.

The two suspects are observed by Terry, who radios to the other two rookies. They pick up the chase which leads to the park. Terry shoots and kills Pam's murderer. The other suspect is wounded and taken in custody.

A QUESTION CENSUS FOR A UNIT
ON CRIME AND LAW ENFORCEMENT

1. What is freedom? What is justice?

2. What does the phrase "law and order" mean to you?

3. What does "freedom and justice" mean to you?

4. Can we have law and order and freedom and justice at the same time?

5. Have you ever been arrested?

6. Do you know someone who has been arrested?

7. Do you think policemen give fair treatment to people they arrest?

8. Why do you think many people do not like the police?

9. What are some things the police have to do?

10. What is a crime?

11. What is "organized crime"?

12. Do you think organized crime is doing well in our city and our country? Why?

13. How do you think organized crime can be prevented?

14. What is a victim? Have you ever been a victim?

15. Who are the victims of crimes?

16. What is a victimless crime (crime without a victim)?

17. What victimless crimes are harmless to people?

18. What victimless crimes bring harm to people?

19. Does the media encourage certain kinds of crimes by publicizing them?

20. How much time or space does the media devote to crime?

21. Do you think prisons can be improved?

22. If you could improve prisons, what improvements would you make?

23. What do you think should be done to improve the way the police, courts, and judges deal with young people who are arrested?

24. What do you think should be done to improve the treatment young people receive from prison officials and law officers?

25. What laws would you change if you were able to do so?

26. What laws do you think need to be enacted?

27. What laws are needed now that were not needed 100 years ago?

28. Are there any laws that we do not have now that you think will be needed 25 years from now?

29. Would you enact any laws to improve your neighborhood if you could?

30. What do you think would help your block be a better place?

ACTIVITY CARDS

1. I am on my way to the corner store. I see a man on the sidewalk, bleeding. I . . .
   a. Try to help him.
   b. Try to get someone else to help him.
   c. Leave him alone and act as though I hadn't seen him.

   Write a TV script about it. Get several of your friends to help you produce the story and play the parts. See me when you are ready to tape it.

2. It's near dinnertime. I am going home from the

playground. A man is pacing back and forth as though he is waiting for someone. A car with two men in it speeds by. I hear four gunshots. I see the man fall to the ground. As the car approaches me, it stops and I see both men very clearly before the car starts up again and speeds away. Three policemen appear and call for an ambulance. They do not see me. I . . .

    a. Run home and tell no one.

    b. Go to the policemen and tell what I saw.

    c. Tell my parents what I saw.

Write a short play about it. Then, get some friends to play the parts and put it on for the class.

3. I have witnessed a murder. I have told the police on the scene what I saw. My friends now tell me that I should mind my own business. When I go to the police station to give my statement, I . . .

    a. Tell them I could not see very well or I don't remember.

    b. Tell exactly what I saw.

    c. Tell them I do not want to be involved.

If you had a son and he was in the same situation, what would you want him to do? Write a letter to your son explaining your position.

4. I am a doctor. A dope pusher I hate has been injured seriously but I am sure I can save him. I . . .

    a. Pretend to do my best but let him die.

    b. Make no attempt to help him.

    c. Do everything in my power to save him.

Write a dialogue about your thinking in this situation. For example, one voice in your head might say "You must save him; he's a human being!" The other voice might say, "Let him die; he's no good!" Share this dialogue with a partner. Each of you pretend you are one of the voices.

5. I am a police officer. A dope pusher who is hated by the entire police force has been murdered. I . . .
   a. Try to find his murderer.
   b. Pretend to investigate the murder.
   c. Do nothing about the murder since I feel he deserved to die.

   Rank order these three answers. Then find two other people who ranked them differently from you. Share your ideas by playing the *Positive Focus Game (see page 56)*.

6. You are on your way home from school with a friend. Someone commits a crime right in front of you. You and your friend see everything. When the police arrive, you tell them that you saw what happened and you want them to catch the guilty people.
   Make a list of the things you would tell the interrogator in order to help the police capture the suspects.

7. You are an interrogator on the police force. A crime has been committed and you want to be sure the police force can find the suspects.
   Make a list of the questions you would ask

someone who said he had seen the whole thing (an eye witness). Be sure to ask questions that would help find the suspects. Try out your questions by role playing the scene with a partner.

8. Talk to some of the people you know in your neighborhood. Find out if they have ever been victims of a crime. Find out what happened, if the person was caught by the police, and how the victim felt about what happened. Write it up as a newspaper story. Type it up, print a headline for it, and post it for others to read.

9. Go to a travel office. Ask them for all the information they can give you on Jamaica. Visit the IMC[4] and look at filmstrips, pictures, and films on Jamaica. Listen to Jamaican music on records or tapes. Prepare a fifteen-minute travelogue on Jamaica and present it to a small group of students.

10. What is your opinion?
    A *fact* is something which can be *proved* or is *known* to be true. An *opinion* is what someone *thinks* or *believes* to be true but cannot be proved. The following statements are *opinions*.

    If you believe the statement is *true*, put a *T* in front of it.
    If you believe the statement is *false*, put an *F* in front of it.
    If you are *undecided* about the statement, put a *U* in front of it.

_____ Most policemen are honest.

_____ Detectives are smarter than patrolmen.

_____ The police do a good job of stopping crime.

_____ The police deserve a raise in salary.

_____ When you call the police in an emergency, they get to you as quickly as they can.

_____ A policeman has an easy job.

_____ Police give fair treatment to all people they arrest.

_____ Policemen should not be called "Pigs."

_____ There are some crimes that hurt no one.

_____ It is all right to commit a crime that hurts no one.

Get together a group of four or five students who have filled in this exercise. Discuss your answers. Try to *really* listen to what each person has to say, and remember that each person has a right to his opinion, even if it differs from yours.

Follow-Up Activity: Invite a patrolman to come to your class and share some of his experiences. Ask him to answer some of the questions you have about policemen. The next day, get your discussion group together again and see if anyone has changed his or her ideas.

11. If you are a police officer and you stop a driver you

suspect to be drunk, what do you do with him?
If he offers you ten dollars, do you let him go?
How much does he have to offer for you to let him go?
Write a short paper answering these questions and
explaining your answers. Share your paper with a
partner and ask him to react to it.

12.   If you are driving your car and a police officer stops you
      and accuses you of driving through a red light, do you
      accept the tickct he writes for you? Do you pay for the
      ticket?

         Try to find out what happens when you don't pay
      a ticket. Also, call the police station and ask what you
      can do if you get a ticket and you don't think you did
      anything wrong. Write up this information and post it
      for others to read.

13.   You are a police officer and receive a call from Dispatch
      that a burglary is in progress. You drive into the area,
      get out of your squad car and, with your service revolver
      drawn, go into an alley behind the building. Suddenly a
      person runs toward you with something pointed toward
      you. What would you do? What would happen next?
      What else could you have done? What would have
      happened if you had done that? Write your answers and
      share them with a partner.

14.   You are on the police force and working on a special
      case. A suspect thinks you are getting too close for
      comfort. He kills someone you love. You know who is
      guilty but you cannot prove it.

Get together with two other students. Together, make a list of all the things you might do. Next to each thing, list some of the possible consequences of doing that thing. Then, as a group, try to decide which thing would be best to do.

15. *Cause and Effect:* The reason something happens is called the *Cause*. The thing that happens is called its *Effect*. Match these causes with their effects by drawing a line from the cause to its effect.

CAUSES	EFFECTS
A. Pamela Hines witnesses the murder of Billy Stomper.	A. The police do not like Billy Stomper.
B. Billy Stomper pushes dope to kids.	B. Pamela gives the police a misleading statement.
C. Billy kicks people who owe him money.	C. People call him Billy Stomper.
D. The masseuse identifies Pamela's parking sticker.	D. Junior shoots Pamela Hines.
E. Pamela's friends tell her not to become involved.	E. Junior knows where to find Pamela.

16. The following are *effects*. Write a short story or paragraph giving the cause of one or more effect.

. . . so our house fell in.

. . . so everyone looked up at the sky.

. . . therefore, we never went there again.

. . . so I bought a blue one instead.

. . . so everyone ran into the street.

. . . so I closed my eyes and went to sleep.

. . . so we picked up the pieces and put them back together.

17. The following are *causes*. Write a short story or paragraph giving the effect of one or more of the causes.

   a. The sky grew dark and cloudy.
   b. I was only trying to straighten the picture on the wall.
   c. As we got to the station, we saw our train departing.
   d. Our star basketball player sprained his ankle in the first five minutes of the game.
   e. Just as I thought, I got an E in math on my report card.

18. Write your own version of "The Billy Stomper Story." In your story, find *three* causes and their effects. Write them on your paper in a cause-effect statement. Example:

$$\overset{C}{Because\ it\ rained,} \overset{E}{the\ picnic\ was\ called\ off.}$$

or

$$\overset{E}{The\ picnic\ was\ called\ off} \overset{C}{because\ it\ rained.}$$

Then think of something that happens in the script which causes an effect and that effect becomes a cause which leads to another effect. Write those causes and effects on your paper in a cause-effect statement. Example:

C   E—C
Because it rained, the picnic was called off,

E
so we went to the movies.

If you would like to produce your story, see me for further details.

19. Pretend you have witnessed a serious crime. Write a paragraph telling the effects this might have on your life (how your life could be changed).

20. If you lived in Jamaica, there are some things you would do differently from the way you do them in Philadelphia. Write a paragraph telling some of these differences. Tell the cause of each difference.

    You may need to read about Jamaica before you begin.

21. Sometimes a person is shot once and dies. Sometimes a person is shot four or more times and lives.

    Write a paragraph telling some of the causes of why a person may live or die after he has been shot.

    Draw a diagram of the body showing the places where a person can be shot once and die.

22. Use the Almanac to find out how many crimes were committed in Philadelphia last year. What percentage were personal crimes and what percentage were property crimes? List the various classifications of crime and how many crimes were committed in each classification. Make a graph of these.

23. In the IMC, find some information about instruments and machines that doctors and nurses use, and how the use of these instruments and machines can help in saving lives. Tell what kinds of things or injuries cause doctors and nurses to decide to use particular instruments.
    Follow-up: Invite a doctor or nurse to visit your class. Share your research with him or her and ask him or her to tell you more about instruments and perhaps show you some.

24. When a patient is taken to the emergency room of a hospital, the staff does many things to try to save a life. Write a list of the things the staff did and used to try to save Billy's life and then Pamela's life.

25. Find out how blood pressure (B.P.) is read and what each number means. What effect does a very high B.P. or a very low B.P. reading have for a person?

26. What is the average temperature for a human being? What is the pulse rate? What causes these to go up or down? Using the thermometer, put it under your arm and wait several minutes. What does it read? Take your

pulse rate by counting the number of heart beats for fifteen seconds. Then, multiply this number by four. It is your pulse rate. Find your pulse by placing your fingers on your throat under your adam's apple.

27. Take the pulse rate and temperature of ten friends using the procedures in Activity 26. Make a graph to display your findings. Figure out the average temperature and pulse rate.

28. If you were a bullet shot from a pistol, where would you enter the body if you wanted only to injure and not kill the person? What things inside the body would you see as you traveled through? What would you be sure to avoid? What would be the effect if you hit some of those parts inside the body? Write a story telling about it.

29. Complete the following statements. You may use one word or many words.

   a. Because I am on the police force, my friends . . .

   b. My children think I am . . . since I am a policeman.

   c. I am on the police force; therefore my most important responsibility is to. . . .

   d. Although I am on the police force, people who know me expect me to . . .

   e. Since I am on the police force, my friends expect me to . . .

   f. If I were not on the police force, I would be able to . . .

   g. Since I am a policeman, I can . . .

30. Find out if a policeman walks a beat in your neighborhood. If so, find out his route and go meet him. Ask if you could talk with him when he has a minute to spare. Find out about his job, what he does, and how he likes it. Write up your findings and share them with someone.

31. What are the beginning and maximum yearly salaries for a Philadelphia policeman? Where can you find out?

   How much money do you think you should make weekly if you were on the police force? Tell how you would spend your money if you had a family of four. Include the following expenses: food, clothing, shelter, medical expenses, education, recreation.

32. If you could pick your shift as a policeman, which shift would you prefer to work? Write a paragraph about it.

   In which section of town would you prefer to work? Write about it. Share your answers in a small group. Why do different people in the group have different answers?

33. What types of policeman are there (patrolman, detective, etc.)? What does each do? Which type of policeman

would you prefer to be? Why did you make that choice? Write about it.

34. Visit a courtroom. See me for details. Keep a record of what you see and hear. Share your experience with several friends or write about it.

35. List the things that make a policeman's job hard and then list the things that make it easy. Are there any things you can do to make his job easier? Talk about this with your friends. Then make a poster about the policeman's job.

36. Read each situation carefully. Decide upon a way to solve each problem. Write the solution on your paper. All problems refer to your *beginning salary.*

   a.   You are a beginning policeman in Philadelphia. What is your weekly salary? (Refer to the "Bulletin Almanac.")

   b.   Overtime hours are hours that people work *above* a normal *day* or work *week.* If you get paid 1½ times your salary for all hours above your normal forty hours per week, how much money would you make for:
      1. ten hours overtime in one week?
      2. fifty hours of work in one week?
      3. one regular week and one forty-five-hour week?

   c.   If you have 10 percent of your salary deducted for Federal income tax, how much will be deducted? How much will be left?

d. If you have 5 percent of your salary deducted for Social Security (FICA) taxes, how much will be deducted?

e. If you have 3 percent of your salary deducted for State income tax, how much will be deducted?

f. If you have 2.65 percent of your salary deducted for the City wage tax, how much will be deducted?

g. After the Federal income tax, Social Security tax, State income tax, and City wage tax are deducted from your salary, how much will you have left?

h. If you were a policeman who started his shift at 8:00 a.m. and worked for 8 hours, at what time would you quit?

i. If you started work at 12:00 and worked 8 hours, with an additional ½ hour for lunch, at what time would you quit?

j. If after working for a month, you found that you had worked forty-two hours the first week, and fifty-six hours the second week, forty-eight hours the third week, and fifty-four hours the fourth week, what would be the average weekly hours you had worked that month?

k. What would be your salary for the month mentioned in problem J?

l. What would be your "take-home pay" (salary after deductions) for the month mentioned in problem J?

37. Get a newspaper and count the number of stories or articles in it. Then count only the ones which are related in some way to crime, criminals, police, prisons, laws, or law enforcement. What is this percentage? Measure and calculate the total space of the newspaper in square inches. Then measure the amount of space of the crime-related stories. What is this percentage? Do you think newspapers give crime stories:
    a. Too little coverage.
    b. Too much coverage.
    c. Just the right amount of coverage.
Write a paragraph explaining your answer.

38. Take a survey in your neighborhood. Find out how people feel about the police on the following continuum.

ALWAYS FAIR |—————————————————| NEVER FAIR
            1   2   3   4   5   6   7   8   9   10

Keep a record of the age of each person you interview and his or her answer. Compile the results. What is the average rating? Make a bar graph to display your findings. Where do you stand?

39. Do a survey of your classmates on the same issue as in

Activity 38. Use the same procedures. Compare the results. Share your findings with the class.

40. There are posters in the subway which say "Shoplifting Is a Crime." Do you agree or disagree with this? Find out exactly what happens if you are caught shoplifting. Do you have a criminal record after you are caught? How long do you have that record?

41. Some posters in the subway say "Shoplifters Take Everyone's Money." What does this mean? Do they take your money? Is there anything you can do about it?

(See following two pages.)

GRID FOR CRIME AND LAW ENFORCEMENT UNIT

UNIT OBJECTIVES	UNIT ACTIVITIES								41
	1	2	3	4	5	6	7		
1. To help students clarify their values with regard to:									
Policemen									
Reporting crimes									
Helping people in trouble									
Criminals/law breakers/ criminal suspects									
2. To help students improve their language arts skills in:									
Reading (vocabulary, figurative language)									
Writing									
Locating information									
3. To help students develop and understand the concepts of:									
Cause & effect									
Law enforcement									

4. To help students improve their computational skills in:									
Fractions									
Percentages									
Averages									
5. To encourage students to learn more about:									
The human body									
Hospital emergency care									
The Caribbean area									
Law enforcement									

Notes

1. Co-authored by Fred Harwood.

2. By concerns we mean the enduring kinds of concerns that are reflected in such questions as, "Who am I?" (concern for identity), "What is my relationship to others?" (concern for connectedness), and "How much influence and control do I have over my own life?" (concern for fate control). For more on this see Weinstein & Fantini, *Toward Humanistic Education*, Prague Press.

3. This step was suggested by Howard Kirschenbaum. It is adapted from a curriculum building process he has developed and has used in his own teaching.

4. Instructional Materials Center.

12. Adapting Curriculum to Serve Student Interests, Needs, Concerns, Goals, Values

NOTE: The following three strategies can be used by a teacher who is locked into a curriculum which must be covered. Their purpose is to help the teacher adapt and personalize the curriculum so that it relates to and, whenever possible, even serves student concerns, interests, goals, and values.

Every Lesson a Values Lesson

PURPOSE

There is no question that facts are important to education. Facts are the building blocks of our ideas about how and why things do what they do. But to teach only the facts is to miss the point of education. Unless a student learns how to *use* facts to build concepts, he becomes little more than an "educated fool" who can spout hundreds of facts which relate to nothing.

However, learning how to formulate concepts is not enough, either. Just- because a student can explain why a thing works the way it does does not mean he can translate it into practice, or even relate it to real situations around him. Unless the concepts he builds in his head are somehow related to his personal experience, his learning has probably not been internalized. And learning which is not internalized does not get translated into behavior. Education which does not eventually change the students' behavior is, to say the least, frivolous.

But changed behavior is still not enough. Another primary aim of the school should be to help each student define and become the kind of person he wants to be. That is to say, schools must help students examine how they intend to use the knowledge they have gained. Values, decision making, and moral development must be an integral part of the school curriculum.

The purpose of this strategy, then, is to help teachers turn every content lesson they teach into an opportunity for students to relate this content to themselves and their values.

PROCEDURE

Try adapting some of your own lessons into both academic and values lessons. First, look over the sample units provided on *pages 398-417*. Then, using the grid on *page 397*, do the following:

1. Select the subject matter topic, unit, problem, or theme you want to teach.

2. Start by writing in Column 1 the important facts you

want students to know or be aware of. Then translate the facts into questions or activities. *Fact* questions have right and wrong answers. Example: What powers does the Constitution give to each branch of government?

3. Move to *Concepts*, Column 2. Under this heading, list the important academic concepts that you want students to develop in the unit. Translate these into questions or activities. Concept questions do *not* have clear-cut, right-wrong answers. They require thinking which results in a reasonable explanation. Example: What are the differences and similarities between our system of separation of powers and England's parliamentary system?

4. Under the heading *Personal Experience*, develop a list of questions or activities which help the student relate the facts and concepts in columns one and two to his own *personal experience*. Example: The U.S. system of separation of powers provides for a system of checks and balances between the Legislative, Executive, and Judicial branches. Is there a system of checks and balances in your family? Who makes the rules? Who decides if they have been broken? Who decides the punishment? Who executes the punishment? Is there a "court of appeal"?

5. Finally, under the heading of *Personal Values*, develop a list of questions or activities which ask the student to make some evaluative statements, or to take a position on some values issues related to the subject matter of the unit. Example: Considering the facts which have come out of the Watergate affair, do you think the Executive branch of our government has become too powerful?

Why? If your answer is yes, what do you think should be done about it? Is there anything you can do?

In teaching the unit, we suggest that you generally start on a values inquiry level, since this tends to generate interest and involvement in the lesson very quickly. Then move to the concepts and facts levels. With practice, you will be able to change and mix levels at a moment's notice. Such lessons are likely to become the most exciting and involving you teach.

Just a word about selecting the unit of study. If you have a choice, we suggest you choose subject matter which lends itself to helping students relate to and internalize the content and which helps them develop value clarity.

Values Lesson Grid

ACADEMIC INQUIRY		PERSONAL VALUES INQUIRY	
FACTS	CONCEPTS	EXPERIENCE	VALUES

Adapted from a Unit on "The Progressive Era:

ACADEMIC INQUIRY	
FACTS	CONCEPTS
1. Can you name several traditions people lived by in the U.S. during the Progressive Era—1900-1917?	1. Choose one of these traditions and trace its roots. How did it get started in this country?
2. Who was Boss Tweed? Who was Plunkitt of Tammany Hall? Can you name several examples of government corruption during the Progressive Era?	2. Compare the kind of corruption in government during the Progressive Era with some current examples of corruption in government, e.g. Watergate, campaign dirty tricks, etc. How are they different? How does corruption get started?
3. What is a muckraker? Can you name several men who were considered muckrakers in the Progressive Era? What was the public's reaction to their muckraking? Name several reforms that resulted.	3. Compare the muckraking activities of the Progressive Era with the investigative reporting of today. How are they similar? How are they different? What do they accomplish? Are the reforms that are being considered as a result of the exposure of Watergate similar to the reforms which were instituted in the Progressive Era?

1900-1917" by Mitchell S. Itzko *(see bottom of page 401)*

PERSONAL VALUES INQUIRY	
EXPERIENCE	VALUES
1. Do you have any traditions that you live by? Does your family? How did they get started?	1. The following are a number of traditions which many men lived by in the Progressive Era. Do you think men should still live by them today? Which do you agree with? Which do you disagree with?
2. Do you know people who use their power and influence for their own personal gain without considering the welfare or interests of others? Have you ever acted this way? Have others treated you this way? What did you do about it?	2. Do you think corruption in our government can be eliminated? What safeguards do you think are needed? What can be done to prevent future Watergates? Can you do anything?
3. Have you ever written a letter to the editor (or to an organization, business, agency, or friend) expressing your outrage at something you thought was not right? What was the response? Do you think it did any good? Have you ever received such a letter?	3. A number of government officials, politicians, and critics have been critical of the press today for reporting "hearsay" without having the facts to back it up. Do you think newspaper reporters should be allowed to publish reports which start with a phrase like "According to reliable sources . . ."? Why or why not?

Adapted from a Unit on *Othello*

ACADEMIC INQUIRY	
FACTS	CONCEPTS
1. What is the structure of a Shakespearean tragedy?	1. In what ways are tragedies and comedies different? The same?
2. What was the plot of *Othello*?	2. What was the cause of Othello's poor self-concept?
3. Who were the major characters?	3. What were the motivations for Iago's hatred of Othello?
4. Give three well-known critical interpretations for Iago's behavior.	4. How do you explain Desdemona's behavior toward Othello's friend Cassio?

For further suggestions on how to develop and teach lessons on the facts, concepts, and values levels, we suggest you consult Harmin, Kirschenbaum, and Simon, *Clarifying Values Through Subject Matter.*

by Louise West   *(see page 402)*

PERSONAL VALUES INQUIRY	
EXPERIENCE	VALUES
1. What would you consider a tragedy in your life? What made it a tragedy?	1. Do you think that every person should experience tragedy? Some say it deepens our understanding of life. Do you agree?
2. Have you ever felt a strong dislike or hatred for another? What did you do about it?	2. How do you feel about interracial marriages? Would you marry someone from another race? Religion?
3. Have you ever been unfaithful to anyone?	3. How do you think you would react if your mate or best friend accused you unjustly of being unfaithful or disloyal?
4. Have you ever believed a story and later found it to be untrue? What did you do?	4. Do you think the telling of lies is ever justified?

SAMPLE UNITS DEVELOPED ON THE FACTS, CONCEPTS, EXPERIENCE, AND VALUES LEVELS

In a unit titled *The Progressive Era: 1900-1917*, Mitchell S. Itzko has students compare the Progressive Era with our own to illustrate such concepts as corruption, power, and reform. The content helps students develop their own value clarity on issues like social reform, abuse of power, corruption in government, and individual and civil rights.

The second example, *Othello*, developed by Louise West, is presented in the same format, using Shakespeare's drama to help students examine and explore their own experience and values on the subjects of prejudice, tragedy, faithfulness, and honesty.

The third example, by Jeanne B. Wright, employs a self-instructional format with various levels of questions mixed together on each task card. Titled *Japan: A Self-Directed Learning Experience*, the unit is an excellent example of the kind of personalized material that can be developed. We have included the task cards and activities for this unit.

From a Unit on Japan: A Self-Directed Learning Experience by Jeanne B. Wright

A Word About the Unit from Its Originator

This is a sample social studies unit on Japan designed for use as a self-directed learning experience. I have found it to be quite successful in my second grade class with eight capable and highly motivated children who agreed to work on the unit independently.

The following activities were printed on 4 x 6 cards and kept in a file box on the social studies table. The activity cards were arranged without a specific sequence. The children were permitted to select the activities that were of interest to them. Several of the activities were designed to involve the children in small groups.

Because no time limits were imposed, the children were allowed to establish their own pace. No minimum requirement on the number of cards to be completed was established, thus facilitating idiosyncratic learning. Each child kept a personal progress folder in which completed cards were stored.

Each child was encouraged to meet informally with me to discuss new learnings. Several of the eight children presented their learnings to other students in the class who were not involved in the self-directed unit. Thus, these children were used as resource persons by their classmates, who were involved in a more teacher-directed unit covering the same topic. While their classmates were involved with me, these eight children were free to use all of the resources and facilities available in the classroom.

Although I designed this self-directed unit for use with high achievers in second grade, it could easily be adapted for use in any elementary grade.

Resources Available in the Classroom:

FILMLOOPS: An Evening in a Japanese Family
             Harvest Festival in Japan
             Japan Gathers Food from the Sea
             A Japanese Family at Dinner
             Japanese Village School

FILMSTRIPS: Children of Many Lands—Japanese Children
             Children of Japan
             A Visit to Japan

SLIDES: Cherry Blossom Time in Japan

TEACHER-PREPARED PICTURE BOOKS WITH
SIMPLE NARRATION:

The Silkworm
A Visit to Japan
Growing Rice
The Flag of Japan
Japanese People at Home
Japanese Picture Words
Japanese Dishes

SCIENCE CHART: The Sun and the Earth

WALL MAPS: Japan
World

GLOBE

References Available to Children:

Text: Laidlaw Social Science Program, *Families and Social Needs* (1968).
Behn, H. *Cricket Songs: Japanese Haiku.*
Caldwell, J. *Let's Visit Japan.*
Coatsworth, E. *The Cat Who Went to Heaven.*
Godden, R. *Miss Happiness and Miss Flower.*
Issa. *Don't Tell the Scarecrow and Other Japanese Poems.*
Langer, P. *Japan: Yesterday and Today.*
Lewis, R. *In a Spring Garden.*
Lifton, B. *A Dog's Guide to Tokyo.*
Lifton, B. *The Cock and the Ghost Cat.*
Maisuzo, M. *A Pair of Red Clogs.*

Newman, R. *The Japanese: People of Three Treasures.*
Scholat, W. *Junichi, A Boy of Japan.*
Shirakiajawa, T. *Children of Japan.*
Visual Geography Series, *Japan in Pictures.*
Yashima, T. *Crow Boy.*

Geography

Japan has been called "a country of many islands." What is an island?   (F)[1]

Have you ever been on an island?   (E)

Do you think this is a good name for Japan? Why?   (C)

Locate Japan on the world map and on the globe.   (F)

Compare the size of Japan with other countries.   (C)

Color the Japanese islands on your map. Find the names of the four largest Japanese islands. Label them on your map.   (F)

What borders Japan?   (F)
     To the north _____
     To the south _____
     To the cast _____
     To the west _____

Do you know someone who has traveled to Japan?   (E) Talk to him or her about it and share what you learned with others.

Would you like to visit there someday?   (V)

What would you most like to see?   (V)

Read about the earthquakes and volcanoes in Japan in our picture book about Japan. *(F)* Do we have earthquakes and volcanoes in the United States? *(F)*

When it is daytime in Japan it is night in the United States. Why? *(C)* Talk with some of your friends. Find out by looking at the chart of the sun and the earth on the science table. What are the children in Japan doing now? *(C)* What would you like to be doing if you were in Japan now? *(V)*

There are many mountains in Japan. What is the tallest mountain in Japan called? *(F)* Draw a picture of this mountain. Is there always snow on top? *(F)* Have you ever been on a tall mountain? *(E)* Tell about it.

There is very little good farmland in Japan. Read the picture book of Japan and find out what is grown in Japan. *(F)*

Have you ever grown anything? *(E)*

If you could grow something, what would you like to grow? *(V)*

Industry

FISHING

View filmloop "Japan Gathers Food from the Sea." Why is fishing important in Japan? *(C)*

List the different fishing methods, or draw a picture showing them. *(F)*

How are the fish preserved for eating? *(F)*

Why were the fishing nets different colors?   (C)

What things does a fisherman need for his job?   (F)

Have you ever been fishing? What did you catch?   (E)

Would you want to be a fisherman?   (V)   What things would you like best about your job?   (V)

Draw a picture showing something you learned from the film. Write a sentence telling about it.   (C)

A special plant from the sea is used in many Japanese dishes, like sushi. What is this sea plant called?   (F)

Do you like to try new things to eat?   (V)

Would you like to try sushi?   (V)

Tell about a new food you once tried.   (E)

RICE

Rice is an important crop in Japan. The seeds are planted in seed beds. When they are tiny plants, they are planted in water-covered fields. These fields have a special name. They are called rice _____.   (F)

Look at the picture book of "Growing Rice." Read more about it in your social studies book. Look through the pictures of Japanese dishes. See how many look like they are made with rice.   (F)

Color the picture of the woman working in the rice field.   (E)

Draw a picture of your own.   (E)

Do you like rice?   (*V*)

Would you like to help your mother cook rice for dinner?   (*V & E*)

Tell her what you have learned about growing rice.   (*F*)

If you were planning meals for your family, how often would you have rice? Why?   (*V*)

SILK

Read about making silk in our picture book on the silkworm. Where does silk come from?   (*F*)

Look at and hold a silkworm's coccoon. How does it feel?   (*E*)

Shake it. What can you hear?   (*E*)

What do you think is inside?   (*C*)

Soak the coccoon in warm water for 10 minutes. Try to pull a single silk thread from the coccoon. With your scissors, cut open the coccoon. Examine the silkworm inside.   (*C & E*)

Silkworms eat all the time. What do they eat?   (*F*)

Would you like to raise silkworms? Why or why not?   (*V*)

Where is the silk cloth made?   (*F*)

Why do you think silk cloth is expensive to buy?   (*C*)

Color the picture of the silkworms eating.   (*E*)

The Flag

Look at the Japanese flag. Draw the Japanese flag.   (*E*)

Read the story of the flag of Japan. What does the red circle remind the people of?   (*F*)

The Cities

Japan has modern cities. The capital of Japan is the city of
_____ .   (*F*)

Look up Tokyo in the index in the book called *Let's Visit Japan*. Find out one fact about Tokyo that you could share with others.   (*F*)

In what kinds of houses do the people in the Japanese cities live?   (*F*)

How do they get to the store or to school?   (*F*)

List other kinds of transportation in Japan.   (*F*)

Would you want to live in a big city in Japan? Why?   (*V*)

What do you see in the pictures of the Japanese cities that we have in our cities too?   (*C*)

What can you see that is different?   (*C*)

View the filmstrip "Children of Japan" for more ideas.   (*C*)

What things in Japanese cities do you wish we had in our cities?   (*V*)

The Japanese Family

Japanese people live in families. What members of a family might live in a Japanese house?   (F)

What members of your family live with you?   (E)

Are there some relatives that do not live with you? List them.   (E)

How would you feel about having your grandparents live with you?   (V)

Most fathers in Japan go away from the house to work. Name some things Japanese fathers might do.   (F)

What does your father do?   (E)

Some Japanese mothers go away from the house to work, too. Name some things Japanese mothers who work away from the house might do.   (F)

Many Japanese mothers stay at home. What are some of their jobs?   (F)

What does your mother do?   (E)

BOYS: Would you like to do the same thing your father does?   (V)

GIRLS: Would you like to do the same thing your mother does?   (V)

View the film "Japanese Family at Dinner."

What did the father in the story bring to the children?   (F)

Does your father ever bring you a surprise present when he comes home from work?   (*E*)   What kind of surprise do you like best?   (*V*)

Why did the people in the film take off their shoes at the door?   (*C*)

What did the children do before dinner that you do too?   (*C*)

Does your father change into comfortable clothes when he comes home from work, like the father in the story did?   (*E*)

Does he read the newspaper after dinner?   (*E*)   What do you like to do after dinner?   (*V*)

How was the table at the Japanese family's house different from yours?   (*C*)

Draw a picture showing both types of tables.   (*C*)

What did they use instead of a fork when they were eating?   (*F*)

Try using chopsticks from the display table.   (*E*)

Do you think you could learn to eat using them?   (*E*) Which would you prefer to eat with, a fork or chopsticks? Why?   (*V*)

Help set up a corner of the room containing some of the things shown in the film.   (*E*)

Act out a part of the film with some of your friends.   (*E*)

Japanese Customs

View the filmstrip "Children of Many Lands: Japanese Children."

What do the children, Taro and Yukiko, do when they say hello and goodbye?   (F)

What do you do?   (E)

If Taro and Yukiko visited you, what would you ask them about Japan?   (E & V)

What would you tell them about life here in America?   (V & E)

Which of our customs are you most proud of?   (V)

Do you think Taro and Yukiko would make good playmates? Why?   (V)

What games do you both know how to play?   (C)

Look at the picture book about Japanese people at home. Where do they sleep?   (F)

Japanese Homes

Look at the floor plan of a Japanese house in your social studies book.

What room is also used as a bedroom?   (F)

Is this a good idea?   (V)

Do you have a room in your house that is used for sleeping only when a guest comes?   (E)

Does it look like the other bedrooms in your house?   *(E)*

Why are most Japanese houses smaller than yours?   *(C)*

Design a floor plan for a house in Japan.   *(C)*

Why do the Japanese houses have walls that can be slid open?   *(F)*

Is this a good idea?   *(V)*   Why?

View the filmloop "Evening at Home with a Japanese Family" for more information.

Every house in Japan has a special place of honor. This place is called _____.   *(F)*   Read about this place of honor in your social studies book.

Do you have a special place for guests at your house?   *(E)*   If you do, is it a comfortable chair, or a special seat at the head of the dinner table, or something else? Tell us about it.   *(E)*

Almost every house in Japan has a beautiful garden outside. Some have a little pond with a bridge to walk on.

Build or design a miniature Japanese garden.   *(C)*

Color the picture of the Japanese house and garden.   *(C)*

Tell your parents about our trip to the Japanese house in Fairmount Park.[2] Maybe they would like to visit it with you. You could show them around.   *(E)*

Pretend that you are a tour guide at the Fairmount Park Japanese house. What would you want to tell the people about and show them?   *(V)*

View the filmstrip "Japanese Children."

Flower arranging is a popular art in Japan. It has a special name. It is called _____ .   (F)

Look through the picture book of Japanese art.

Bring in a bowl and some real or artificial flowers. Put a soft piece of clay in the bowl to hold the stems. Try arranging the flowers into a centerpiece for our table.   (E)   Do you like flowers?   (V)   Which are your favorites?   (V)

Draw a picture of a Japanese-style flower arrangement. If someone has already made a centerpiece, maybe you could draw that.   (C)

View the filmloop "Harvest Festival in Japan." This tells about one of the Japanese festivals.

Tell us something that you learned from the film.   (F)

Draw a picture showing this festival.   (E)

What festivals do we have in the United States?   (F)

If you could plan a new festival for us to have, what would it be like?   (V)

Many cherry trees bloom in Japan in the spring. Read in your social studies book about the Cherry Blossom Festival.

What do the people do?   (F)

Draw or paint a picture of the cherry blossom tree.   (E)

Look at the box of slides showing the Cherry Blossom Festival in Japan.

Tissue paper blossoms can be cut and used to decorate our season tree. Ask Mrs. Wright to show you how to make them. (E)

There are special days in Japan for boys and girls. Read about them in your studies book.

Draw a picture of a fish kite. Color it with bright colors. (E)

The fish kite is shaped like a special type of fish. That fish is the _____. (E)

When is Boys Day celebrated? (F)   Is it fair not to have a Girls Day? Why? (V)

The Japanese people manufacture many things. Look at some of the things you have. Do any of them say "Made in Japan"? (E)   See how many different things you can find that were made in Japan. (E)

Japanese Schools

Children in Japan go to school, too. View the filmstrip "Schools in Japan."

How many days each week do the children in Japan go to school? (F)

What do the children wear to school? (F)

What subjects do you learn in school that Japanese children learn too? (C)

What do they learn that is different? (C)

Would you like to go to a Japanese school? Why?   (*V*)

View the filmloop "Japanese Village School" for more information.

What do Japanese children use instead of a pencil?   (*F*)

Would you like to be able to read and write in Japanese?   (*V*)

Look at the book of Japanese "picture characters."

Write a few words in Japanese and English.   (*E*)

This kind of writing has a special name. Read your social studies book to find out what it is. Japanese picture writing is called _____.   (*F*)

Japanese Dress

The people in Japan often dress as we do, but on special occasions they wear a beautiful silk _____.   (*F*)

Read about their special clothes in the book *Japan in Pictures*.

The wide sash and bow is called an _____.   (*F*)

Most of the people wear sandals called _____.   (*F*)

When the sandals have two blocks of wood on the bottom they are called _____.   (*F*)

Why do the Japanese sometimes need to wear the ones with the blocks of wood on the bottom?   (*C*)

Because the sandal strap goes between two of the toes, they

must wear a special sock that is like a mitten. These special socks are called _____.   (*F*)

Draw a Japanese woman dressed for a special occasion. Label the different parts of her outfit.   (*F*)

Do you ever dress for special occasions?   (*E*)   What kind of clothes do you like to wear best?   (*V*)

Would you like to dress in Japanese clothes?   (*V*)

Read the story, "A Pair of Red Clogs."

Religion in Japan

There is a famous statue in Japan of a religious leader. The statue is of _____.   (*F*)

The religion is Buddhism. The statue is so big that five children can sit on the thumb.

Read the book, *A Visit to Japan*. Find out more about this statue.

Write one thing that you learned from the book.   (*F*)

Color the picture of this famous statue.   (*C*)

What is something about America's religions you would like to tell a Japanese child?   (*V*)

Subject Matter Strategies

PURPOSE

Another method for integrating Values Clarification with subject matter is to use the valuing strategies. This helps students clarify their values and makes the subject matter come alive.

PROCEDURE

Step 1. Select the subject matter to be studied. We recommend that whenever possible, you select units, topics, and material which will help students to clarify their values. For example, a unit on ethnic differences in the United States is much more likely to help students clarify their values than a unit on the capitals and major cities of each state.

Step 2. Identify the values issues which grow out of the unit, topic, or material to be used. These may take the form of values dilemmas, various values articulated or implied by different characters, or values messages which the author of the material intends to deliver to the student, either overtly or covertly.

Step 3. Select a number of the Values Clarification strategies in *Values Clarification, Values and Teaching*, or this book which seem to lend themselves to the topic or materials selected. A variety of strategies should be selected so as to:

A. Help the student gain insight into:

1. What he values or prizes.

2. What he is willing to affirm.

3. Whether he makes his decisions and choices freely.

4. Whether he makes his choices from alternatives.

5. Whether he makes his choices after weighing the consequences.

6. Whether he acts upon his values.

7. Whether he acts upon his values in a consistent pattern.

B. Give the student an opportunity to:

1. Begin to articulate what he values and prizes.

2. Publicly affirm his values.

3. Choose and make his decisions of his own free will.

4. Choose from alternatives.

5. Choose after weighing the consequences of each alternative.

6. Act upon his values.

7. Act upon his values repeatedly and in a consistent pattern.

The following are two sample units which integrate values inquiry with academic inquiry. One is on a novel, *The Pearl*, by John Steinbeck; the other is on two chapters from a science text dealing with sound and communications.

A Unit on John Steinbeck's "The Pearl"
by Paul Solis-Cohen

I.   The General Aim of the Unit Is:

To provide for a study of *The Pearl*, viewing similarities and differences in the way we, the characters in the book, and the author, think, believe, and behave.
The Pearl, viewing similarities and differences in the way we, the characters in the book, and the author, think, believe, and behave.

II.   The Specific Aims of the Unit Are:

A.   To encourage examination of our lives and the lives of other people.

B.   To teach how the experiences of people affect who they are.

C.   To encourage clarification of our own values.

D.   To find out where knowledge deficits exist.

E.   To discover points of interest and degrees of experience.

III. Materials and Strategies Used:

    A.   *The Pearl* by John Steinbeck.

    B.   Values Clarification Strategies:[3]

        1.   Value Survey.

        2.   Forced Choice Ladder.

        3.   Values Voting.

        4.   Values Continuum.

        5.   Proud Whip.

        6.   "I Wonder . . . " Statements.

        7.   "I Urge . . . " Telegrams.

        8.   Alternative Action Search.

        9.   Consequences Search.

     10.   Kino's Values Grid.

     11.   Baker's Dozen.

IV. The Activities Are Designed to Teach the Following Skills:

    A.   Listening:

        1.   To themselves as they express ideas.

        2.   To the views of classmates in small groups.

        3.   To the views of classmates in the entire class setting.

    B.   Writing:

        1.   Paragraphs.

        2.   Book report or composition.

    C.   Reading:

        1. The novel itself.

        2. Critical reviews on the novel.

    D.   Speaking:

        1. In a small group.

        2. In the entire class setting.

V.   Follow-Up Activities

    A.   Composition or book report emphasizing personal values.

    B.   Choosing and reading another novel about the life and problems in a foreign culture.

Value Survey (an introduction to the novel)

Rank these values in the order of their importance to you: 1 is the most important, and 10 is least important. Discuss your rankings in groups of three.

    _____ An obedient spouse.

    _____Being close to members of your community.

    _____An exciting job.

    _____Giving whatever you can to your children.

    _____Killing to protect your property.

———————— A peaceful life.

———————— A rich life.

———————— A risky job.

———————— Killing to "save face" in your community.

———————— Marrying someone who can help you with your job.

Forced Choice Ladder (Chapters 1 & 2)

Place all of the characters you met in Chapter 1—Kino, Juana, Coyotito, Doctor, Doctor's Doorman, Juan Thomas, and The Four Beggars—on a ladder according to the strength of your feelings about them, either liking or disliking.

Compare and discuss your responses in groups of six.

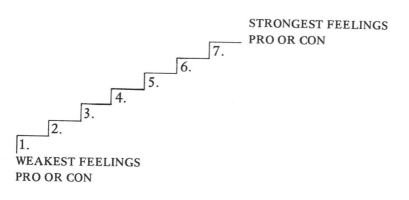

STRONGEST FEELINGS
PRO OR CON

7.

6.

5.

4.

3.

2.

1.

WEAKEST FEELINGS
PRO OR CON

Values Voting (Chapters 1, 2 & 3)

The teacher says to the class, "I will read you ten questions. If you strongly affirm, raise your arms and shake your hands in the air. If you mildly affirm, raise your arms and place your thumbs up. If you mildly disagree, thumbs down. If you strongly disagree, show an active thumbs down. If you want to pass, take no action at all."

The teacher then reads the following questions for voting:

1. Do you get up in the morning when the stars are still out?

2. Would you like to live on a beach?

3. Would you like to live in a brush house in a warm climate?

4. Do you find that facial expressions àre often more expressive than words?

5. Would you suck the poison from a scorpion bite on your child?

6. Would you suck the poison from a scorpion bite on a stranger?

7. If you were a doctor, would you turn down a patient who was "broke"?

8. Would you enjoy being a pearl fisherman?

9. Would you tell "the town" if you found something of tremendous wealth?

10. Do you believe that great wealth will "turn people's heads"?

Class discussion follows.

Values Continuum (Chapter 3)

Is the discovery of one's tremendous wealth a blessing, or does it mean one's sure destruction?

These two positions are at different ends of the lines below. Points are marked in between them. Circle the point that best represents where you stand on this issue. Then discuss your markings in groups of three. Discussion with the entire class will follow.

A LOT OF $ WILL PROTECT YOU FROM ILLNESS	├─┼─┼─┼─┼─┼─┼─┼─┤	A LOT OF $ WILL HASTEN YOUR DEATH

A LOT OF $ WILL KEEP YOU FROM BEING INSULTED	├─┼─┼─┼─┼─┼─┼─┼─┤	A LOT OF $ WILL CAUSE PEOPLE TO INSULT YOU ALL OF THE TIME

A LOT OF $ WILL CAUSE YOU TO BE ENERGETIC	├─┼─┼─┼─┼─┼─┼─┼─┤	A LOT OF $ WILL MAKE YOU LAZY

A LOT OF $ WILL INSURE THAT YOU WILL NEVER BE LONELY	├─┼─┼─┼─┼─┼─┼─┼─┤	A LOT OF $ WILL CAUSE YOU TO BE LONELY

"I Wonder . . . " Statements

You have read the first half of *The Pearl*. You have discovered much about the life of Kino: his town, his family, and his particular dilemmas. Here is a chance for you to raise questions about what has taken place so far.

Complete the following sentence stems:

I wonder if . . .

I wonder why . . .

I wonder whether . . .

I wonder about . . .

I wonder when . . .

Discuss in groups of six.

Proud Whip (Chapter 4)

Pretend you are Kino. What did you do in this chapter that you are proud of? You will be called on in order around the room. You may pass if you choose.

Sample statements made by students:

I was strong in my demands when selling the pearl.

I did not lose my temper when intimidated.

I did not accept a sum which I didn't believe to be fair.

I fought to protect my possessions.

"I Urge . . ." Telegrams (Chapter 5)

When you reach the end of Chapter 5, write a telegram to Kino, Juana, Juan Thomas, and the town council, beginning with these words "I urge you to . . . ." The message should consist of less than fifteen words. Share your "I Urge . . . " Telegram with the class.

Alternative Action Search (Chapters 5 & 6)

In Chapters 5 and 6, Kino is faced with a difficult decision: whether to stay or run away because he killed someone and lost his house. Write out briefly what you would do if you were in his situation.

Break up into groups of three or four to discuss your proposals. Try to decide on a solution that would be most desirable.

Consequences Search (Chapters 5 & 6)

Make a grid, and in the appropriate spaces place the three most feasible solutions to the problem faced by Kino at the end of Chapter 5—whether to run or stay. Use the alternatives you decided upon in the *Alternatives Action Search*. For each of the three alternatives, list as many consequences as you can think of.

Work in groups of three. Then discuss with another group.

Consequences Grid

ALTERNATIVE NO. 1	ALTERNATIVE NO. 2	ALTERNATIVE NO. 3

Kino's Values Grid (Entire novel)

Construct a values grid for Kino. List five to eight issues that he was faced with in the story and decide if these represented values for him. If they did, check the appropriate box on the right-hand side of the grid.

1. Was he proud of his position?

2. Did he publicly affirm his position?

3. Did he choose his position from alternatives?

4. Did he choose his position after considering the pros and cons and consequences?

5. Did he make his choice freely?

6. Did he act on or do anything about his apparent belief?

7. Did he act in a repetitive way, patterned and consistent?

ISSUE	1	2	3	4	5	6	7
1.							
2.							
3.							
4.							
5.							
6.							
7.							
8.							

Now use the same values issues that Kino confronted and do a values grid for yourself. Share in groups of three.

Baker's Dozen (Follow-up)

Kino, the other pearl fishermen, and their families lacked many of the conveniences that we use every day. Let's look at some of them.

Make a list of 13 things you yourself use around your house which are run by electricity. Then draw a line through the three things you could live without most easily. Circle the three which you find most precious, the ones you would least want to give up.

Volunteers will be asked to read their crossed-out and circled items to the class.

Incorporating Values Clarification Strategies into Two Sixth Grade Science Units by Warren M. Benedetto

TEXTBOOK: *Science for Today and Tomorrow*, Herman and Nina Schneider.

GRADE LEVEL: Six.

UNITS: Sounds and Communication.
Radio and Television.

MAJOR TOPICS: Telephone.
Public Address Systems.
Telegraph.

Phonograph Records.

Tape Recorders.

Radio.

Television.

STRATEGIES USED:[4]   Values Voting.

Rank Order.

Values Whips.

Public Interview.

Partner Risk or Sharing Trios.

Alternatives Search.

Three Characters.

Percentage Questions.

Unfinished Sentences.

Strongly Agree/Strongly Disagree.

Sensitivity Modules.

Are You Someone Who . . .?

Values Voting

Teacher reads the list below. Students raise their hands if they agree with the statement, put thumbs down if they disagree.

SAMPLE VOTING LISTS

How many of you:

- Prefer to be alone most of the time?

- Enjoy sharing what you know, think, and feel?

- Think that it is important to communicate with other people?

- Feel that the telephone is a good way to communicate?

- Like to listen to phonograph records?

- Have your own radio?

- Enjoy watching T.V.?

- Think that there are many different ways to communicate?

How many of you:

- Think that every family should have a telephone?

- Feel that a child of your age should have a private line?

- Think that it is OK to listen in on a phone call if there is a good reason?

- Feel that the use of the telephone should be limited to emergencies?

- Have ever received an obscene or threatening telephone call?

- Would prefer a small transistor radio to a table model?

- Enjoy listening to the radio?

- Turn up the volume when your favorite song is played on the radio?

- Watch T.V. more than two hours per day?

- Like T.V. commercials?

- Think that a child your age should have his own T.V. set in his bedroom?

- Like black/white T.V. programs better than color shows?

- Feel that every home should have a color T.V.?

- Enjoy listening to phonograph records?

- Think a record album is a good investment?

- Think a person's voice should be taped without his knowledge and consent?

Rank Order

Teacher reads three items. Students rank the items according to their own personal preference. Discussion can follow.

SAMPLE QUESTIONS

Which would you prefer?

- Making a long distance phone call to a famous person.

- Receiving a phone call from your best friend.

- Placing a phone call to a relative in the same town.

How late should a child your age be permitted to watch T.V. on a school night?

- 9:00 p.m.

- 10:00 p.m.

- Own choice.

What kind of T.V. programs do you like best?

- Westerns.

- Comedies.

- Cartoons.

How would you prefer to spend a rainy Saturday afternoon?

- Listening to the radio.

- Watching T.V.

- Listening to phonograph records.

What kind of music do you like most?

- Rock.

- Jazz.

- Soul.

Values Whips

Teacher asks a question and quickly whips around a

portion of the class. Students give their answers in a sentence or two. Students may pass.

SAMPLE QUESTIONS

What would you do if you caught your little brother/sister (big brother/sister, parents) listening in on an extension phone to a conversation with your best friend?

If you wanted to share a secret with someone, how would you communicate with the other person?

What would you do if you disliked the show on T.V., but were not permitted to change the channel?

What would you do if your favorite phonograph record was broken intentionally by your little brother/sister, (big brother/sister, parent, friend)?

What would you do if you received an obscene telephone call?

What would you do if you found some change in the coin box of a pay telephone?

How many telephones should a family have?

What are the advantages/disadvantages of having a telephone in your bedroom?

If your two favorite T.V. programs were on at the same time, how would you decide which one to watch?

What kind of music do you like best?

What would you do if you discovered that your best friend (stranger, parents, police) had tape recorded a private conversation without telling you?

Public Interview

Teacher chooses a student volunteer and interviews while rest of class listens. Student may pass on any question.

SAMPLE QUESTIONS

Should a child your age be limited to a specific number of telephone calls per evening? Explain.

How long should an "average" telephone call last?

What are your three favorite T.V. programs? Why do you like them?

How much time should a child your age spend watching T.V.? How much T.V. will you let your child watch?

What do you usually do when the news report comes on the radio?

Do you feel T.V. has helped or harmed our society? Explain.

Who is your favorite recording artist?

Do you think that you would like to be in a group that cuts records? What kind of group?

If you were permitted to arrange one evening of T.V. programs, which shows would you include?

Which T.V. program do you dislike most? Why?

Partner Risk

Teacher divides class into pairs or trios and gives a topic to be discussed.

SAMPLE TOPICS

Tell about a telephone conversation that you've had recently which made you very happy (sad, scared, upset, etc.).

Share your opinion about making annoyance telephone calls.

Describe how you think you would feel if you were "paged" on the school P.A. system and told to report to the principal's office immediately.

Describe how you would feel and what you would do if you discovered that your best friend had stolen your new transistor radio.

Tell how you would feel and how it would affect your life if your favorite recording artist died from a drug overdose.

Describe how your life might change if you did not have a T.V.

Share your opinion about showing "X" rated films on T.V. during "prime" time (any time).

Alternatives Search

Teacher gives class or small groups a "problem." Students see how many alternative solutions they can come up with.

SAMPLE TOPICS

How many ways can you think of to stop annoyance and/or obscene telephone calls to your house?

What can you do to prevent objectionable programs from being shown on T.V.?

If T.V. instructional programming were your goal, and your resources were unlimited, how would you set up educational programs for children your age?

If you had the opportunity, how would you change T.V. programs so they might be more appealing to children your age?

Three Characters

Students share and discuss their answers.

SAMPLE QUESTION

If you had the opportunity to be like a person on T.V., who would you most like to be? Least like to be? The person most like you?

Percentage Questions

Students share and discuss their answers.

SAMPLE QUESTIONS

What percentage of:

- Your allowance should be spent on phonograph records?

- Your free time do you spend watching T.V.?

- Your free time do you spend listening to phonograph records (radio)?

- Your free time do you spend talking on the telephone?

- Telephone calls received at your house are for you?

- T.V. programs watched at your home are ones you've selected?

Unfinished Sentences

Students finish the sentence stems and discuss.

SAMPLE SENTENCE STEMS

If I had my own telephone I would . . .

If the telephone company charged me 20¢ for a call I didn't make, I would . . .

When I hear my name on the school P.A. system, I . . .

The kind of music I like best is . . .

My favorite record is . . .

I usually listen to the radio . . .

I like/dislike small transistor radios because . . .

A T.V. program that I don't want to miss is . . .

If I could phone anyone in the world free of charge, I would call . . .

If I received an obscene phone call, I would . . .

If I knew that three of my friends were in the habit of making annoyance calls, I would . . .

If my best friend dared me to make a bomb-scare call to a

school (hospital, mental institution, factory, etc.), I would . . .

P.A. systems are necessary/unnecessary because . . .

The kind of music I dislike most is . . .

My least favorite record is . . .

The best night to watch T.V. is . . .

Strongly Agree/Strongly Disagree

Students indicate by coding whether they strongly agree (1), agree somewhat (2), disagree somewhat (3), or strongly disagree (4) with the statement. Discussion follows.

SAMPLE STATEMENTS

Most phone calls are too expensive.

Telephone poles and wires are aesthetically displeasing to me.

It is all right to make obscene telephone calls once in a while.

Every child my age should have a phonograph.

Most recording artists abuse drugs.

Male recording groups are better than female groups.

Cartoons are too childish for me to enjoy.

"X" rated programs should not be shown on T.V.

There are too many commercials on T.V.

T.V. newscasts are boring.

Sensitivity Modules

Students are to do a module and then discuss it in class.

SAMPLE EXPERIENCES

Don't use the telephone for three days.

Interview a person who did not have a telephone when he/she was your age.

Keep a record of the number of phone calls received and made in your home for one week. Include who they were from and who they were to.

Visit a telephone company and watch the operator at work. Would you like to have her job?

Watch a pole climber repair a telephone line. Talk to him about his job. Ask him to show you the different equipment used.

Ask the school secretary to show you how the P.A. system works.

Ask the principal for permission to use the school P.A. system to make an approved announcement.

Visit a record manufacturing company and observe how records are made. Talk to some of the employees to find out what they think of their job.

Take a trip to a recording studio. Try to talk to some of the recording artists to determine how difficult it is to "cut" a *hit* record.

Visit a store that sells records. Talk to the manager. How

does he select the records to purchase? What does he do with the records he can't sell?

Spend a few hours in a factory that manufactures phonographs (radios, tape recorders, televisions).

Visit a radio station. Strike up a conversation with the disc jockey, if possible. What does he like most (least) about his job?

Ask your parents to take you for a three-hour drive. Do not play the radio!

Don't watch T.V. for one weekend. How did you spend your time?

Are You Someone Who . . . ?

Students answer YES, NO or MAYBE, and then discuss.

SAMPLE QUESTIONS

Are you someone who . . .

- Likes music?

- Spends too much time watching T.V.?

- Seldom listens to the radio?

- Makes annoyance telephone calls?

- Is likely to spend most of your allowance for phonograph records?

- Turns off the T.V. when the newscast is being shown?

- Enjoys records only at peak volume?

- Insists on viewing T.V. programs you like regardless of how the rest of your family feels?

- Will probably cut a record someday?

- Enjoys watching educational programs on T.V.?

- Would make a long distance call on a friend's telephone without telling him/her?

Simulation

PURPOSE

Simulation is a technique for modeling and learning about some aspects of the real world. Because this learning is active rather than passive, it is likely to be internalized. This strategy is designed to teach a basic method for putting together simple simulations.

PROCEDURE

After selecting the unit of study, decide what you want to simulate. What are your goals and objectives? What do you want students to learn from the game? Since our focus here is on both values clarification and subject matter, your goals and objectives should include both.

Decide what is important to give reality to the situation

that is to be simulated? Give enough details about the situation so that students can identify with and relate to it. This might include descriptions of people, places, events, things, etc. Often these details are presented in written form, as a scenario.

Specify the action to be taken or the interaction that is needed in the simulation. What is to be done, by whom, when? What are the rules or guidelines which students are to follow during the simulation activity?

Then try out the simulation. Take careful notes of what happens. Evaluate the simulation in terms of your purposes, goals, and objectives. Redesign the simulation if needed.

The following is an example of a simple simulation designed by an economics teacher. *"Glub"—The Island Simulation,"* by Steve King, helps students become more clear about what values they prize, and how they choose and act upon these values.

"Glub"—The Island Simulation
by Stephen J. King

This unit is designed as a series of simulations set up to introduce the student to some fundamental concepts necessary to the study of economics.

I. *Objectives*—To help students:

    1. Gain a clearer understanding of fundamental economic concepts, e.g., scarcity, ownership, exchange.

2. Gain insight into their own values and the values of others which affect the making of economic decisions.

3. Learn to organize their thoughts, both in writing and orally, make logical decisions, and work more effectively in groups.

II. *Reason for Simulation Strategy*

1. To provide greater interest and motivation by setting up hypothetical situations which students can easily relate to.

2. To use as a springboard for further reading and discussion of economic issues.

III. *Procedures*

1. Divide class into groups of five or six.

2. Give out *Student Introduction Sheet.*

3. Give out *Activity I: The Suitcase Exercise.*

4. Give out *Activity II: Five People Exercise.*

5. Give out *Activity III: First Thing Exercise.*

6. Give out *Activity IV: Planning Stage Exercise.*

7. Give out *Activity V: Tree Exercise.*

8. Give out *Activity VI: The Two Hens Exercise.*

9. Give out *Activity VII: The Fish and Hens Exercise.*

Student Introduction Sheet

You are going to be presented with a series of hypothetical (make-believe) situations. You will be asked to place yourself in these situations as though they were actually happening now. The exercises will be done in groups, and you will be asked to make decisions both on your own and as a member of the group.

Activity I: The Suitcase Exercise

You are unhappy with life here in the United States. The noise, confusion, tension, and violence are getting you down. You have been discussing the possibility of finding a small island, far away from everything, where you can escape the problems here at home.

A friend of yours feels he has just the kind of place you are looking for and gathers together a group of people, including yourself, who will be interested in making the move. A decision is made to leave the United States and start a new life on this far-away island.

The island is named Glub, and a wealthy man has donated a boat in which to make the trip. About 50 families numbering about 125 people decide to make the trip to Glub. Since space on the ship is limited and adequate supplies of food must be brought for all, each person is allowed to bring only *one suitcase* carrying his belongings.

Instructions:

1. After you have read the above, I want each of you to make a list of what you would bring along in your one suitcase.

2. After you have made the list, discuss it with the rest of the people in your group.

3. Has the discussion made you want to change any of your original decisions?

4. Appoint one person from the group to give a summary of your decisions to the other groups.

5. In a whole-class discussion, determine what should be taken on the boat in addition to food and personal belongings.

Activity II: The Five People Exercise

Instructions:

You find out that there is room for five more people on the boat. However, eight more people have asked to come along. The following list is a brief description of the eight people who have asked to come:

- A 30-year-old white doctor.

- A 60-year-old black minister.

- A 28-year-old black policeman.

- A 35-year-old black female singer.

- A white college student.

- A 34-year-old black nurse.

- A 45-year-old white nun.

- A 20-year-old unemployed black Vietnam veteran.

1. Each of you are to pick *five* people from the eight listed whom you would want to come on the trip.

2. Next, discuss your selections with the rest of the group.

3. Your group then should come to some consensus agreement as to which five people should be picked.

4. Write an essay explaining the reasons for your own choices, and include any observations you may have as a result of what happened in your group.

Activity III: First Thing Exercise

Glub is located in the South Pacific Ocean about 10,000 miles from the United States. You arrive after a long journey and find that everything your friend said was true. Glub seems to be an island paradise. It looks to be only a few miles wide, and apparently contains no people or animals. There is an abundance of trees and vegetation on the island which bear fruit. The waters surrounding the island are filled with fish. The climate is tropical, requiring a minimum of clothing.

Instructions:

1. What would be the first thing you would do after you have arrived on the island and observed the above?

2. Do you feel that the first step to be taken should be your own decision or one made by the entire community?

3. What subsequent steps would you take? Should these steps be taken by you or together with the entire community?

Activity IV: Planning Stage Exercise

Instructions:

1. Having discussed some of the steps which might be taken, your group is now going to make a decision as to what *plans*, if any, you would set up in order to live on this island. The plans don't have to be detailed. If you decide that it is not necessary to set up any plan at all, you must give reasons for your decision.

2. Have one person in the group write up the decision of the group.

3. Each group will then present its plan, or reasons for not having one, to the entire class. In the exercises that follow, you will stick with the plan that your group has devised.

Activity V: The Tree Exercise

You have now been living on the island for several weeks and are fairly well settled. So far, everything has gone fine. One morning, your neighbor wakes up and decides to chop down several small fruit trees and brings them to his house. He continues to do this for the next couple of days. You are concerned and are wondering what to do about it.

Instructions:

Consider the following questions:

1. Would you discuss the matter with your neighbor?

2. Would you tell him to stop?

3. Would you discuss it with other people?

4. What if he decides to keep on cutting trees?

Come up with some decision and discuss it with your group to see if you come to a joint agreement as to how the problem should be handled.

NOTE: Consider the original plan your group set up. Is your decision consistent with this plan? Or do you think you have to revise it? If so, how?

Activity VI: The Two Hens Exercise

There are two hens and one rooster on Glub. One of your neighbors found them in the area where he built his house and he has kept them. He now has eggs as part of his diet and is beginning to raise some chickens. He has not shared these with anyone, and is intent on keeping the hens and rooster to himself. You asked him for some eggs but he refused.

Instructions:

1. What action should be taken in this case? If none at all, explain your reasons.

2. Consider the following questions:
   Does he have a right to these hens and rooster? Why?
   Does he have a monopoly? (Look up the word *monopoly* to answer the question.) Would you do the same thing if you were in his place?

Write your own answers to the above questions and then discuss them with your group. Reach a group decision as to how you would solve this problem.

Activity VII: Fish and Eggs Exercise

We will assume that the decision was made to let your neighbor keep the hens and rooster to himself. You are a good fisherman, which he is not, and have plenty of fish to eat. Still, you crave some eggs.

Instructions:

Can you think of any way other than stealing or force that you can use to get some eggs? Discuss your solution with the rest of the group.

In writing, give your answers to the following questions:

1.   What is barter? Would barter be a good system on Glub?

2.   Do you think there should be some system of exchanging goods on Glub?

3.   What system do you think would be best?

4.   Would money be needed on the island? Why or why not?

Notes

1. F = fact level question or activity.

    C = concept level question or activity.

    E = experience level question or activity.

    V = values level question or activity.
2. In reference to a field trip arranged by the teacher.
3. A detailed description of these strategies and how to use them may be found in *Values Clarification*.
4. A more detailed description of these strategies and how to apply them in the classroom may be found in *Values Clarification*.

PART IV

PERSONALIZING CLASSROOM ORGANIZATION AND MANAGEMENT

13. *Introduction to Part IV*

In the personalized classroom, the organization and management should facilitate learning and personal growth. The needs and goals of both the students and the teacher should dictate the organizational and management procedures—not the other way around. Thus, like the curriculum, classroom organization and management must be flexible and open to continual change. There must be many opportunities for students to begin to direct their own learning, to practice making choices from alternatives, to decide for themselves which ways they learn best.

The teacher must use a variety of organizational and management styles, for students have different skills and different levels of dependence. Chapter 14 sets forth five such styles, and details a number of the teaching skills and strategies, such as learning centers and activity cards, needed to implement each style.

Chapter 15 deals with goal sheets and learning contracts, two of the most useful tools for managing a choice-centered classroom where students pace themselves and select or design their own learning activities based on their own goals and needs. Examples of a variety of goal sheets and contracts are presented with a discussion of how to use them.

Chapter 16 presents a number of additional strategies which are invaluable aids for managing the choice-centered classroom. They deal with such matters as evaluation, student record keeping, the use of groups, peer teaching, student projects, etc.

Chapter 17 deals with one of the main questions teachers ask us about choice-centered classrooms: "How do I handle discipline problems?" Actually, many answers to this question can be found in earlier sections of this book. The strategies which help relate the curriculum to students' needs and concerns are perhaps the most effective way of dealing with "discipline" problems, simply because when students are enjoying learning and can see purpose and meaning in what they are learning, most discipline problems disappear. Some of the communication strategies, such as active listening and "I messages," and some decision-making strategies, such as conflict resolution, are extremely effective in handling the problems which do occasionally arise. Another effective way of dealing with discipline in the choice-centered classroom involves letting students experience the consequences of their actions, and therefore take more responsibility for their own behavior. This technique is explained more fully in Chapter 17.

In the last section of this part of the book, Chapter 18, we discuss several ways that Values Clarification can be used in the choice-centered classroom. These include integrating V.C. into the curriculum, setting aside time for doing V.C. with the whole class or in small groups, and creating a "do-it-yourself" values center.

RATIONALE FOR A CHOICE-CENTERED CLASSROOM

Many teachers who have become very turned on to humanistic teaching approaches like Values Clarification remain reluctant to open up and individualize their classrooms. We are often asked why we so strongly advocate the use of a choice-centered classroom, one where students are encouraged to pace, select, initiate, design, and evaluate their own learning. The following is a brief rationale which sets forth some of the reasons we give for our advocacy.

Giving students choice in terms of what they will learn and how they will learn it is a logical extension of the valuing process. For one thing, it encourages students to begin asking the question, "What is worth knowing?" This in itself is a values search.

Moreover, the choice-centered classroom helps students learn to select from alternatives and examine the consequences of their actions. For example, students who do not use and manage their time wisely in the choice-centered situation often find themselves failing to meet their commitments at the end of the week or marking period. Rather than admonish these students, the teacher in the choice-centered classroom tries to help them solve the problem of their unfulfilled contract by seeking out the causes; perhaps they were not interested in the topic selected; perhaps they had not learned to pace themselves in doing their work; perhaps the work was too difficult or too easy; perhaps personal problems interfered. Through discussion, the teacher tries to help the student identify the causes for his failures and plan ways of achieving success the next time around.

A third product of the choice-centered classroom is student self-confidence. If a student is to become less of a *pawn* and more of an *origin*—that is to say, learn to choose freely—he must develop a strong and healthy self-concept. Perhaps nothing builds self-concept like giving students choices, which in effect says, "I trust you, and think you capable of making decisions about your own learning." When we make the learning decisions *for* students we are in effect conveying the message, "I *do not* trust you nor think you capable." The first approach serves to build self-concept, the second tends to tear it down.

Fourth, the choice-centered classroom teaches students responsibility. Many teachers believe that students must be forced to develop responsibility. Children, they argue, are naturally irresponsible; only through external direction and close monitoring can they be taught responsibility. We disagree with this view. Rather, we believe students become fully responsible only when they experience and understand the natural and logical consequences of their own choices, upon themselves and upon others. In the choice-centered classroom, the teacher does not direct the student's every move. By allowing the student a choice in behavior, and by helping the student to understand the impact of his behavior on himself and others, the teacher fosters *responsible* behaviors and attitudes.[1]

Fifth, the choice-centered classroom avoids the covert coercion some students feel to enter into a values activity which they would really rather sit out. When the whole class is involved in a values activity, many students are reluctant to pass even though the teacher stresses that they may do so. Thus, they participate half-heartedly or, in some cases, actually interfere with those students who do want to participate. By providing options or choices of learning activities in the classroom, those students who want to participate in a teacher-directed values activity can do so, while other students work at something else.

Sixth, the choice-centered classroom provides the most suitable kind of environment for the search for values. It serves to increase student interaction, thus providing opportunities for students to become aware of and discuss each other's beliefs and values. The informality and relaxed climate also encourage students to share more of themselves, increasing the likelihood that meaningful values issues will be raised, discussed, and clarified. And the emphasis on doing, student involvement, and student decision making increases the likelihood that students will take action upon their values, in the classroom and outside.

Notes

1. For an excellent defense of this position, consult Rudolf Dreikurs, *Children the Challenge*, New York, Hawthorn, 1964, pp. 76-85.

14. A Continuum of Classroom Organization and Management Styles and Strategies

The ultimate goal of the teacher in a choice-centered classroom is to eventually put himself out of a job—that is to say, to take students who are toally or partially dependent upon him for the direction of their learning and help them become self-directed, autonomous learners. Said another way, the goal is to teach students to *learn how to learn*.

FROM NO CHOICE TO FREE CHOICE: ONE STEP AT A TIME

This goal is not easily accomplished. The student who is totally or partially dependent must progress in steps which are often very small and sometimes painfully slow. What we are asking the student to do in the choice-centered classroom is to learn how to make sound choices or decisions about his own learning, and to begin to assume the major responsibility for his learning. Since there are so many decisions to be made and so much responsibility is involved, the task can be overwhelming if dumped upon the student all at once.

Another factor is that different students will learn or accept increased decision making and responsibility at different rates. Unless you have organized your classroom and curriculum to accommodate these different rates, the process of helping students become better decision makers or choosers can be a frustrating one for both you and your students.

Using A Continuum of Classroom Organization and Management Styles

Classroom learning can be divided into three parts: *planning, execution,* and *evaluation.* Planning involves all of the decisions that must be made by the teacher and/or student before the learning activity is begun. Execution is the actual carrying out of the plan. Evaluation involves an assessment of both the product which resulted and the process that was used in the planning and execution.

To ask a student who has never made any decisions about the planning, execution, or evaluation of his own learning to begin to make all of these decisions at once is in most cases unwise. It is simply too much for the student to handle. A better plan is to encourage the student to start making some decisions for himself in only one of the areas, such as execution. For example, the student might be allowed or encouraged to choose where he wants to work on the activity in the classroom, if he wants to work on it alone or with someone, and the speed or pace at which he will proceed through the activity. After he has learned to handle these choices responsibly, he might then be encouraged to choose his own learning activities from a number of specified alternatives, self-correct his work when it is completed, and

A Continuum of Classroom

STYLE:	*Teacher Designed & Directed Learning*	*Student Self-Paced Learning*

TEACHER
MAKES ALL ├─────────────┼─────────────┤
DECISIONS

DESCRIPTION:	Teacher uses conventional organization, management, and teaching procedures: rows facing teacher, lecture and recitation, control techniques, etc. All students learn the same thing at the same time at the same speed.	Teacher gives separate assignments to individual or small groups of students, then acts as a resource to help students who need help. Students work at their own pace, and gradually take charge of their own movement, interaction, record keeping.

WHO MAKES
WHAT DE-
CISIONS:

Planning:	Teacher	Teacher
Execution:	Teacher	Shared
Evaluation:	Teacher	Shared/Student

Organization and Management Styles

Student Self-Selected Learning	Student Self-Designed & Initiated Learning	Student Free Choice Learning

STUDENT MAKES ALL DECISIONS

Teacher uses learning centers with self-instructional task cards. Students choose their own learning tasks and work at their own pace. Teacher acts as a resource to help students who need help.	Students identify and design own learning projects or programs. Teacher helps to plan the project or program and acts as a general resource when students need help.	The student is free to plan his own learning; the teacher serves as a resource when needed.

Teacher	Shared	Student
Student	Student	Student
Shared/Student	Shared/Student	Student

so on until he is finally making all of his own decisions about what and how he will learn.

One very useful way to conceptualize this process and prepare a plan for moving students from making no choices to making free choices in the classroom is to develop and learn to use a continuum of organization and management styles. Several efforts have been made in this direction. For example, Muska Mosston[1] has developed a continuum of seven teaching styles which range from the teacher-centered *command* style to the *student-designed individual program* style. Silberman, Allender, and Yanoff[2] have developed three different teaching-learning styles—individual, small group, and whole group.

We have developed a continuum of five classroom organization and management styles *(see pages 462-463)*.

THE TEACHER DESIGNED AND DIRECTED STYLE

This style is in general use throughout most schools today. It depends on lecture and recitation as the primary instructional method, and reward and punishment as the primary motivational strategy. The classroom organization is usually that of straight rows lined up facing the teacher or chalkboard. Students are expected to remain in their seats for most of the period or day. Movement is limited and controlled by teacher permission. Generally, all of the students are expected to learn the same things, at the same time, in the same order, and at the same speed.

The teacher-directed style is the one many students and parents accept as the only legitimate classroom learning style.

For this reason, we recommend that you start the year or semester in the conventional "from the front" style. After a few weeks, when students have gotten acquainted with you and your expectations, start moving those who are ready into a new style of instruction.

By starting with complete control, you will be more likely to avoid the misconception (and problems which arise from it) that the choice-centered or "open" classroom is goof-off time, and a sign of the teacher's inability to enforce discipline. We have watched far too many teachers, after hearing about open classrooms, "open up" their classroom on an "anything goes" basis the first day of school, and spend the rest of the year trying to get control of the chaos which erupted.

STUDENT SELF-PACED STYLE

This next style on the continuum turns over many of the execution decisions to the student. This can be done gradually by giving more and more responsibility as the student is ready to handle it. The following is a list of execution and evaluation decisions that should eventually be shared with the student in this style.

1. *Pace:*   the rate of speed the student will progress through the activity or material.

2. *Location:*   where in the classroom the student will work on the activity or material.

3. *Movement:*   when and where the student will move around the classroom.

4. *Interaction:*   who the student will work with, talk with, seek help from.

5. *Correction:*   the student corrects his own completed work.

6. *Record Keeping:*   the student keeps a record of his own progress.

PROCEDURES FOR IMPLEMENTING
THE STUDENT SELF-PACED STYLE[3]

Step 1. Make a list of all the published, mimeographed/dittoed, and teacher-made materials available for use with your students. This might include textbooks, workbooks, individualized reading kits, paperback books, learning packets, activity cards, instructional games, film strips, audio tapes, etc. (Include textbooks or workbooks even if only one copy is available; in a self-paced classroom, not every student needs to work on the same material at the same time.)

Step 2. Categorize the above list by skill area or subject matter content. For example, a teacher might categorize his reading materials under vocabulary skills, comprehension skills, and work-study skills.

Step 3. Design an assignment sheet that blocks out a set or sequence of assignments for the student to follow independently at his own pace (or cooperatively with several classmates who are also at the same level). The following form may by used.

Student Self-Paced Assignment Sheet

NAME: _____ DATE: _____

TEACHER: _____ SUBJECT OR SKILL AREA: _____

Do assignment in:	Pages:	Do Activities #:	Answer Questions #:	Additional Directions:

Step 4. (Optional) Design a *Contingency Contract* for use with the assignment sheet. Procedures are outlined on *pages 491-496.*

Step 5. Allow students who can handle the responsibility to begin working independently or in small groups at their own pace. After diagnosing the student's needs and interests, fill out an assignment sheet, give him detailed instructions as to what you expect, e.g., whether he has choice of movement, interaction, etc.

(you may wish to control this at first). Then allow him to begin.

One simple way to begin the transition is to allow students who complete their "seat work" early to go to the back of the room and work on individual self-paced assignments. Then, gradually decrease the amount of seat work given and increase the self-paced assignments until your curriculum is individualized to the extent you think is best for your students. Self-paced instruction need not mean that small group or whole-class activities cease. There is a place and important purpose for these types of activities in the choice-centered classroom.

Step 6. When students can handle the responsibility, encourage them to begin correcting their own work and keeping a record of their own progress. One simple way to have students self-correct is to place the teacher's edition of texts and workbooks in the front of the room or cut them up and post the relevant portions. When students complete an assignment in the student edition, they can check their answers against the correct answers in the teacher's edition. A simple record form can also be developed for students to use to keep track of their own work *(see page 500).* The *Skills Grid, page 510,* is also a useful tool for helping students keep track of their own progress.

STUDENT SELF-SELECTED LEARNING STYLE

This style, in the center of the continuum, encourages the student to begin making choices about what he wants to learn. The choices are to be made within the specified limits set by the teacher or agreed upon by the student; but within these constraints, the student is free to select or reject any of the alternative activities and materials available. Thus the student is allowed to make the following decisions:

1. ACTIVITIES: which activities the student will select and complete (within the limits set).

2. PACE: the rate at which the student will progress through the activity or material.

3. LOCATION: where the student will work on the activity.

4. MOVEMENT: when and where the student will move around the classroom.

5. INTERACTION: whom the student will talk or work with.

6. CORRECTION: the student corrects his own work.

7. RECORD KEEPING: the student keeps a record of his own progress.

PROCEDURES FOR IMPLEMENTING
THE STUDENT SELF-SELECTED LEARNING STYLE

For the teacher, it is only a small step (at least from an operational standpoint) from the *Student Self-Paced Style* to the *Student Self-Selected Style*. (Psychologically it may be a large and difficult step for both the teacher and student, since it means the teacher gives up much control.) Rather than prescribing activities for each student, you simply design a means for informing students of what the options or alternatives are, and then let them choose their own activities.

The primary means we have used to implement this style in the classroom is the use of learning centers (or stations) containing self-instructional activity cards and packets (also known as task, problem, assignment, learning, or job cards and packets).

The simplest way to begin, perhaps, is to take a corner of the room or a bulletin board and turn it into a learning center by doing the following:

1. Place on 3 x 5 or 4 x 6 cards a number of self-instructional activities. Each activity should be placed on a separate card and posted. (Some teachers prefer to use dittoed activity sheets placed in a folder taped to the wall; this way, students may pull the sheet from the folder, still leaving numerous copies of the same activity for other students to pull. It avoids the loss of activities, for when a 3 x 5 card is destroyed or misplaced, the activity is no longer available.) Some centers contain as few as five activity cards; others may have fifty. We suggest starting with only a few at first so as not to overwhelm students with choice. Gradually increase the number as students' interests and needs dictate.

2. Provide space near the learning center for the books, materials, manipulative objects, plants, animals, etc. that will be used. These can be placed upon a table pushed against the wall or put on shelving constructed by students.

3. Make the center attractive. Near the cards, post pictures cut from magazines or posters which relate to the activities; or, attach the cards to the pictures—these can be laminated and used year after year. Post examples of students' work which grew directly out of the cards; this often interests students to try the activity. Students love to decorate these centers. In fact, once they get the hang of it, they can often write some excellent activity cards, and in some cases, even develop the entire learning center.

Writing Activity Cards

The success of the learning center is often dependent upon the quality of the activity cards. First, they must be clear and detailed enough so that the student can read them and know exactly where to find the materials, what to do, and how to do it. Second, the activities must be interesting and challenging enough so that the student will select them. (This does not have to be the case when using a "point contract" in conjunction with the learning center, since the points—not necessarily the activity itself—are the motivating factor which keeps the student at the task. If activity cards are to stand on their own, they must relate directly to the students' own interests, needs, and concerns; if students don't get very involved in the learning center, it is probably a sign of poor cards. Another possibility is that the center is of interest or concern to the teacher but not to his students.)

A variety of formats may be used; perhaps every teacher should find his own style of writing activity cards. We will outline the procedures for two types of formats, the simple and the detailed.

Simple Activity Cards. Simple activity cards are nothing more than a brief set of instructions telling the student what he is to do to accomplish the task or project. If materials are to be used, specify them. Label or number the cards so they may be easily identified or referred to. The following is an example of a simple activity card.

The Food We Eat[4]

QUESTION: What do you eat every day?

MATERIALS: Labels from food cans or boxes, a science book, and a good memory.

1. What did you eat yesterday? Try and remember everything you ate and write it down in your notebook.

2. Now, make four columns in your notebook and label them: (1) Carbohydrates, (2) Fats, (3) Proteins, and (4) Vitamins and Minerals. Try and place the food that you ate in one of the four columns. If you are not sure of where a certain food would go, look up the definitions of these types of foods; then try and decide.

3. Look at the labels from cans and boxes which once contained food. Find the ingredients on these labels, and, from this, place the foods in the proper columns.

4. As you know, you should try and eat some of each of these kinds of foods every day. What have you eaten so far

today? What will you have to eat to have a food from every category on your list (and in your stomach!)?

5. Look up scurvy and beriberi in your science book. These diseases are caused by not eating all of the foods that one should. Write a short description of each disease and its cause in your notebook.

Detailed Activity Cards. To construct a more detailed activity card, do the following:

A. Place the name of the activity at the top of the card.

B. Write a statement of the purpose of the activity; i.e., what the student can expect to learn from the activity.

C. List the materials needed to complete the activity.

D. Specify the steps or sub-tasks the student must follow to complete the activity.

E. Specify the evaluation criteria or procedure to be used.

F. Include some follow-up activities or questions which will help the student explore the topic or area further.

An example of a detailed activity card follows:

A. NAME: *Building a Piece of the World*[5]

B. PURPOSE: To develop an awareness of the land area and physical features of different countries (Earth Science).

C. MATERIALS: Large pinboard or thick piece of cardboard, 2' x 3'; molding clay; artificial plants, sticks, etc.; source book, e.g., geography text.

D. STEPS:

1. Get a source book with a relief map of the section of the world you want to make. Use a pencil to sketch the map on cardboard.

2. Use clay to build a model on the map you sketched.

3. Use colored clay to put in relief features such as mountains, rivers, lakes, and forests.

4. Use sticks, artificial plants, etc., to put in crops and other things you want to show.

5. Make a key or legend to indicate the different sorts of things on your map.

6. Name all the places or features you can.

E. EVALUATION: There will be a teacher-student evaluation as your work progresses.

F. FOLLOW-UP: Representations of products, rainfall, and other aspects of the country can be made.

CONCEPT QUESTIONS

1. What is topography? How does it determine the life styles of people living in the region?

2. What is weather?

3. What is climate? How does it differ from weather?

VALUES QUESTIONS

1. If you were to take a vacation to the country you drew, where in it would you want to visit? Why?

2. If you could change just one thing in the country you are now living in, what would it be? Why?

Developing a Learning Center

The same process that is used to develop a conventional unit can be used to develop a learning center, except that the activities are written in a self-instructional format. One of the most effective set of procedures for developing a unit that we have seen involves a ten-step process which can be used with students to jointly plan and develop the curriculum activities. For a description of these procedures, *see page 364.*

The physical location and appearance of the center will depend upon content and materials. Some centers can be posted on bulletin boards or room dividers, or walls, or be propped up on tables. Other centers will require the use of tables or shelves on which to place materials and apparatus. Whatever the location and appearance of your center, we suggest that you generally follow the guidelines below.

1. Make the center attractive. Pictures, color, and interesting shapes, designs, and physical objects help.

2. Title the center so that it can be easily identified and located. Use interesting, unusual, or provocative titles.

3. (*Optional*) Provide a statement of the purpose or objectives of the center.

4. (*Optional*) Provide suggestions for using the center, i.e., which activities are to be done first, which activities are required, if any, and so on.

The following is an example of a social studies learning center titled, *All About Me.*[6]

All About Me

Purpose: Upon completion of this center, the student will be aware of some of the things he or she values.

Do Your Clothes Speak?

INSTRUCTIONS

What we wear often tells something about ourselves; our clothes can talk in their own way. What do your clothes say about you? Do they say you are quiet or loud—sloppy or neat? Make a list of what you are wearing today. Next to each piece of clothing, write what you want it to say about you.

Show your list to a friend; see what he thinks your clothes say about you!

Friends

INSTRUCTIONS

Write something about each of the *best* friends you've had.

Why do think you became best friends?

What did you like about him or her?

What do you think he or she liked about you?

What do you think it is that makes two people best friends?

Three People

INSTRUCTIONS

If you could be someone else, what is the name of the person you would most like to be? Why?

What is the name of the person you would least like to be?

Who is the person who is most like you?

Why did you choose the people you did?

What Are You Proud Of?

INSTRUCTIONS

We all have something to be proud of. What is something you are proud of about:

    a. Your family.

    b. What you've done in school.

    c. A skill or hobby.

    d. Something you did that took courage.

    e. Something you made yourself.

    f. How you've changed to improve yourself.

    g. What you've done for someone else.

    h. What you gave to someone else.

    i. What is something else you are proud of?

Pie of Life

INSTRUCTIONS

Draw a circle like the one on *479*. This circle or pie represents how you spend your day. Each quarter of the pie stands for six hours of the day. Now, make slices in the pie; make the size of each slice stand for how much of your day you spend on or with:

    a. Sleep.

    b. School.

c. Friends.

d. Homework.

e. Playing or relaxing, alone.

f. Family.

g. Chores or jobs.

h. Other things.

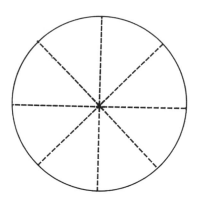

Do you like the way you spend your time? Would you like to change something? Make a new pie to show how you would like to spend your time if you could. Can you do anything about it? What?

The Magic Box

INSTRUCTIONS

Today you found a magic box. It can have anything in it you want, no matter how big or small.

What would you want in the magic box?

a. For yourself.

b. For your family.

c. For your best friend.

d. For your house.

e. For your neighborhood.

f. For your teacher.

g. For your school.

h. For your city.

i. For your country.

j. For poor people.

Life Line

INSTRUCTIONS

Draw a line across your paper. On the left side, put a dot and write your date of birth. On the right side, put another dot. This stands for when you will die. When do you think that will be? Now, put a dot on your life line for where you are right now.

Put an X on your life line for:

a. When you started school.

b. When you were very sick.

c. The saddest time in your life.

d. The happiest time in your life.

e. When you'll finish school.

f. When you'll get married (if you do).

g. When you'll start work.

h. When you'll have children; grandchildren.

Write a story telling about these times.

One Year Left

INSTRUCTIONS

You have just been to the doctor, and he told you that you have a rare disease. You only have one year left to live.

Write a story about how you would spend your last year.

    a. Where would you go?

    b. Who would you want to be with?

    c. Would you want to be alone?

    d. What would you want to finish before you die?

    e. What three special things would you want to do?

Life Inventory

INSTRUCTIONS

Answer these questions about yourself:

    a. When was the happiest time of your life?

    b. When was the saddest time of your life?

    c. What things do you do best?

    d. What things do you do poorest?

    e. What would you change about yourself, if you could?

f.   Whom do you trust with your secrets?

g.   When did you need to have courage?

h.   What makes you frightened?

i.   What is the greatest gift you could give someone?

j.   Who are you afraid of?

k.   Who would you like to grow up to be like?

l.   What is your biggest dream for the future?

m.   What do you know about yourself now?

STUDENT SELF-DESIGNED AND INITIALED LEARNING STYLE

In this fourth style, the planning decisions and methods of instruction are shared or turned over to the student. Rather than you initiating and planning the learning activities, the student is encouraged to plan his own program of study. The student comes to you with an interest area, topic, problem, or question he would like to explore; together, you and he formulate a program of study which is specific, meaningful, and within his capacity to accomplish. The following is a form which you may find useful to facilitate the process.

Student-Designed Learning Program Form[7]

NAME:_____ DATE:_____

TEACHER:_____ SUBJECT:_____

Instructions:

1. Select a problem concern, dilemma, question, or project and determine what you want to accomplish.

2. Ask questions that explore the possible things to learn about the problem, question, or topic.

3. Focus on specific questions to study about the problem or topic.

4. Make an overview of the possible resources—including reading, interviewing, use of mass media, and other activities—that can provide you with information about the topic.

5. Choose those readings, interviews, and other activities related to the specific questions you intend to address yourself to. Limit yourself to things that will help you accomplish your objectives.

6. Organize your reading, research, and activities.

7. Schedule time for study, research, and writing, and discipline yourself to this schedule. Change it only for good reasons.

8. Periodically, evaluate your work by comparing your real progress against your planned progress.

9. Determine how your completed project leads to further studies and further questions. A good project will often raise more questions in your mind.

10. Use the following form to prepare your plan of study.

   A.   *Name of the topic, project:*

   B.   *Questions I would like to answer from this project:*

   C.   *Materials I will use:*

   D.   *To demonstrate my learning, at the end of the project I will have completed:*

   E.   *I will complete the project by:* (date)

   F.   *Self-evaluation of how well I accomplished steps 2 through 5:*

   G.   *Teacher reaction:*

STUDENT FREE CHOICE STYLE

In this style, the primary goal of the choice-centered classroom—to turn the decision making over to the student—is achieved. Having *learned how to learn*, the student is free to plan, execute, and evaluate his own learning independent of your direction or guidance. Your job becomes that of act.ng as a resource and critic when and if the student needs your help. This does not mean, however, that you completely give up your check on the student. He should understand, before being given free choice, that if he is not doing well, you may think it appropriate to discuss the learning program with him.

Letting Students Choose Their Learning Style

One teacher we know[8] operates five mini-classrooms within his classroom simultaneously. In each of the mini-classrooms, a different teaching-learning style is in operation. Students are allowed to choose which learning style they prefer. In actuality, many students move back and forth between styles, depending upon their feelings of adequacy and upon the subject matter they are studying. Although this teacher is always encouraging students to move toward increased choice and decision making, none of the styles is valued above the others. Thus, students move freely from one style to another without feeling stigmatized. In fact, the teacher-control portion of the classroom (named the penalty box because of the students' interest in hockey) is a favorite place to "really accomplish something" for some students in the classroom. Here, they are given seat work which must be completed before they can talk to other students or move around the classroom.

The following series of room-arrangement diagrams shows the gradual move during the year from a teacher-centered classroom to a classroom in which there are a diversity of

Diagram 1

TEACHER DIRECTED LEARNING

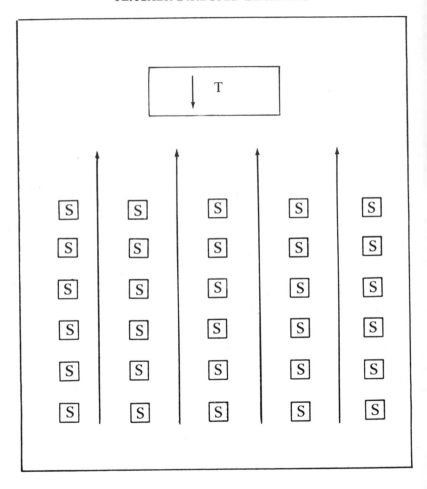

Diagram 2

TEACHER DIRECTED
LEARNING AREA

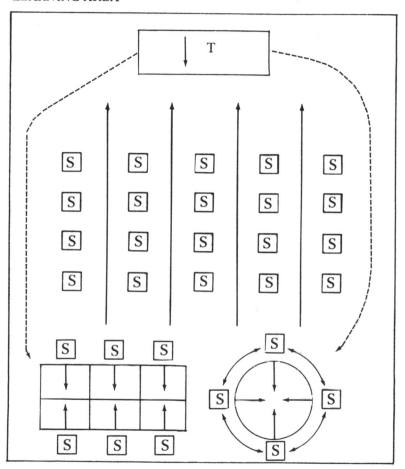

STUDENT SELF- PACED
LEARNING INDIVIDUAL
PRESCRIPTION AREA

STUDENT SELF- PACED
LEARNING GROUP
WORK AREA

Diagram 3

TEACHER DIRECTED
LEARNING AREA

STUDENT SELF-PACED LEARNING
INDIVIDUAL PRESCRIPTION AREA

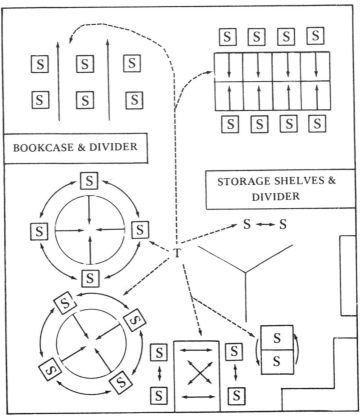

STUDENT SELF-
PACED LEARNING
GROUP WORK AREA

STUDENT SELF-SELECTED
LEARNING TASK &
ACTIVITY CENTER AREA

Diagram 4

TEACHER DIRECTED
LEARNING AREA

STUDENT SELF-PACED LEARNING
INDIVIDUAL PRESCRIPTION AREA

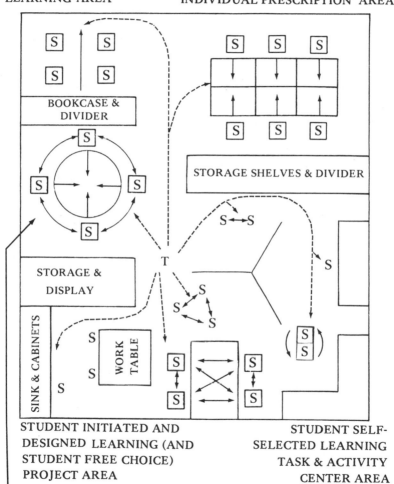

STUDENT INITIATED AND
DESIGNED LEARNING (AND
STUDENT FREE CHOICE)
PROJECT AREA

STUDENT SELF-
SELECTED LEARNING
TASK & ACTIVITY
CENTER AREA

STUDENT SELF-PACED LEARNING GROUP WORK AREA

teaching styles, each designed to give the student a different amount of freedom, responsibility, and decision making power.

Notes

1. *Teaching: From Command to Discovery*, Belmont, California, Wadsworth, 1972.
2. *The Psychology of Open Teaching and Learning: An Inquiry Approach*, Boston, Little-Brown, 1972.
3. We wish to thank Fred Harwood for teaching us this step-by-step process.
4. Developed by Sue Heineman and Fern Burch.
5. Developed by B. Hines.
6. Developed by Tina Haskins and Beverlee Hurwitz.
7. From materials developed by Frederic Harwood and Brenda McRae in an unpublished paper titled, "Planning Independent Study for Students in the Open Classroom."
8. Robert Muschlitz, Solanco High School, Quarryville, Pa.

15. Goal Sheets and Learning Contracts: Facilitating Student Self-Directed Learning

GOAL SHEETS[1]

One of the most effective techniques we have discovered for helping students learn to accept—and take—more responsibility for their own learning is a simple device called a goal sheet *(page 493)*. To use the goal sheet, the teacher simply asks each student to list his goals for the week (day, hour) and how he plans to achieve them. The goal sheets are then handed in to the teacher for review. The teacher can write notes to the student suggesting modification of the goals, resources to be explored, or any other pertinent information; or the teacher can arrange a conference with the student to discuss his goal sheet. Some teachers prefer to use a long-range goal sheet *(page 492)* to help students set their overall goals and a short-term goal sheet *(page 493, bottom)* to help students specify and plan more manageable weekly or daily goals.

Goal sheets can even be used with very young children. For example, a kindergarten teacher[2] we know sets up an individual goal conference each week for each child. Since her children cannot write, she enters the goals upon the goal sheets for them. *See page 493-4* for an example of one child's goals. In addition, she has each child evaluate his or her own progress with the form provided on *page 494.*

The great thing about goal sheets is that they truly help students realize that they can direct their own learning. In addition, goal sheets are very consistent with the valuing process upon which this book is based. Goal sheets help students learn to *choose*, since they must ask the most difficult question in education, "What is worth learning?" And goal sheets help students to *act upon their choices* by setting and achieving their own learning goals.

Form 1

Long Range Goals and Planning Form

NAME _____ COURSE _____

1. My long range goals and objectives for the course are to:

2. My specific plan of action for achieving these goals and objectives (please provide as much detail as possible).

Form 2

Weekly Goals Sheet

NAME_____ COURSE_____

Goal(s) for week of_____:
Specific steps I plan to take to achieve the goal(s):

Goal(s) for week of_____:
Specific steps I plan to take to achieve the goal(s):

Goal(s) for week of_____:
Specific steps I plan to take to achieve the goal(s):

Form 3

Goals for the Time Period_____ to _____

NAME Terri W.

Goal: Make things with play dough
Make ABC's with play dough

Goal: Learn to do hard math

Like $+\frac{2}{3}$ $+\frac{4}{4}$

Make work sheets for concepts

Goal: Learn lower case ABC

Form 4

Goals Evaluation

NAME _____

1. How are you doing on your goals?

2. Do you feel you could do better?

3. How do you feel you are doing in school?

1	2	3	4	5

MY BEST   MY WORST

4. How do you feel about school?

1	2	3	4	5

LOVE   HATE
SCHOOL   SCHOOL
LAURA   HARRY

THE LEARNING CONTRACT

The learning contract is another useful tool for managing the choice-centered classroom, and for teaching students to live with the logical consequences of their choices. The contract allows both the teacher and the student to specify in advance their expectations concerning the quality and quantity of work to be completed, the date of completion, and the payoff. When the parties come to an agreement about the terms of the contract, each affixes his signature to indicate commitment. If the student fails to meet the terms of the contract, he must live with the logical consequences—no payoff. Thus, the teacher can be more objectively involved in the relationship than he could if he had ordained the work to be done and then meted out the punishment (in the form of a low grade) when the student failed to perform.

With the contract, the student is likely to see and accept the fact that he, not the teacher, is responsible for his success or failure. If the student does fail, the contract allows the teacher to continue to express his faith in the student's ability to succeed, and to give the student encouragement for the next contract.

The learning contract is also an effective tool for helping students learn to set and achieve their own learning goals. For a sample contract, see below.

Sample Contract

I,_____ do agree to earn the letter grade ____ during this contract period ending_____(month) in the year_____. I further agree to present to the teacher all of my work in acceptable form on or before the due date. The following is a brief description of the work or project I am undertaking:_____

_____

_____

Signed on this____day of_____in the year_____.

_____   _____
SIGNATURE OF TEACHER   **SIGNATURE OF STUDENT**

Notes

1. Our thanks to Elliott Seif for introducing us to goal sheets.
2. Elaine Scott, Crescent Lake Elementary School, Waterford, Michigan.

16. Developing and Managing a Choice-Centered Classroom

Student Progress Folders and Charts

PURPOSE

Keeping track of student progress can be a major stumbling block in the choice-centered or individualized classroom. The teacher must develop a systematic but relatively simple way of getting a good picture of a student's development at a moment's notice. We have encountered no better system than student folders and charts.

PROCEDURE

Provide each student with a manila folder or large brown envelope with his or her name on it. In this folder, each student is to keep all of the written work he or she completes.

Develop a filing system. Some teachers and students like to turn one drawer of a filing cabinet or a cardboard box into a public file where both the teacher and students have access to the file at any time. Other teachers, for various reasons, prefer a more private system. In this case, an In/Out basket can be used by having students place their completed work or folders in the In basket. After you look over an individual's work, place the completed work in the student's folder or return the folder to the student via the Out basket.

In addition to written classwork, five other items should be kept in the folder:

1. All completed copies of the progress forms *(see pages 505-509)*.

2. A copy of the skills grid *(see page 510)*.

3. Diagnostic worksheets and results.

4. Copies of all goal sheets or negotiated learning contracts *(see pages 491-496)*.

5. Anecdotal notes and records.

An optional procedure is to set up a class progress chart. The activity chart lists all of the activities, projects, assignments, games, etc. in the classroom; you indicate each student's completion of the activities by noting the date of completion in the space provided. *(See Figure 1 on page 499.)* The daily chart can be used when there are too many activities in the classroom to list them all. Instead, have each student note in his or her folder the activity completed each day or period by making notations in the space provided. *(See Figure 2 on page 500.)* This can then be kept in the student's progress folder.

Figure 1: Activities Chart

NAME OR NO. OF ACTIVITY

Student's name	1	2	3	4	5	6	7	8	9
1.									
2.									
3.									
4.									
5.									
6.									
7.									
8.									
9.									
etc.									

(enter date or check mark
when completed)

VARIATION[1]

Reproduce Figure 3 *(page 501)* with the names of your students, one per box. Leave enough space to jot a few words, or a sentence or two. Each day, try to make some notes to yourself about how and what each child is doing.

Then, at the end of the week, review your chart and note any patterns, particular difficulties, etc., and make a plan for dealing with them. This variation is also a good way to check yourself to see if you are spending too much time with some students while neglecting others.

Figure 2: Daily Chart

Name:_____

Teacher:_____

Subject:_____

Instructions: Please keep a record of your completed activities and projects on the form below. Write the name of the project, task card number, book and page numbers, etc. in the box of the day you completed the activity.

MON	TUE	WED	THU	FRI

Figure 3

CHILDREN'S NAMES	MON.	TUES.	WED.	THURS.	FRI.
Judy					
Bob					
Margaret					
Jeff					

Monday

JUDY	Having difficulty with compound words; still very fearful of making mistakes.

Student Planning, Evaluation, and Advisory Committees

PURPOSE

One key to operating a successful choice-centered classroom is to delegate responsibility. Our experience is that students, even very young ones, can be given a great deal of responsibility in the classroom. Not only does the practice remove what would be an overwhelming load from the teacher's shoulders, it is also educationally sound: increased student responsibility tends to increase student involvement and self-confidence. One way to begin delegating responsibility is to set up student committees and assign them various classroom functions.

PROCEDURE

Make some decisions about what you think your students are capable of handling in terms of classroom organization, management, and development. You may wish to consider the following areas:

1. Record keeping.

2. Correcting student papers.

3. Planning various classroom activities, games, parties, etc.

4. Writing task cards.

5. Arranging and decorating the classroom.

6. Planning field trips, camping trips, etc.

7. Advising on student disciplinary action and situations.

8. Student government in the classroom, town meetings, etc.

9. Ombudsman committee.

10. Negotiating learning contracts.

11. Hearing and evaluating student reports.

12. Planning academic projects, thematic units, etc.

13. Classroom maintenance.

14. Operating and caring for equipment.

15. Setting up and running a classroom library.

16. Care and feeding of plants and animals.

17. Building storage shelves, study carrels, class-room dividers, etc.

18. Establishing and maintaining a storage system for materials, games, & equipment, etc.

19. Others you can add:

Form committees around the areas you think might be feasible. Start gradually, with one or two committees. Let students volunteer, or appoint a chairman and let him pick his own committee. Committees of two to five members work best, unless there is a major amount of work to do.

Spend some time helping the committees get organized. Make sure the members know their responsibilities and limits, and what you expect of them in the way of performance. With students who have not been given much responsibility in the past, do not be disappointed if they muff it the first time. Sit down with them and discuss the problems they encountered, and what could be done to remedy the situation. Then give them another chance. Be sure to make your expectations and your limits explicit. You'll help to avoid disappointment, hurt feelings, and guilt for all parties concerned.

Student Progress and Evaluation Conferences and Forms

PURPOSE

A primary goal of the choice-centered classroom is to make real and significant contact with each student. To that end, this is a useful strategy.

PROCEDURE

Find time for a conference. This is not an easy task: individual conferences take time, and time is what the teacher has least to spare. Some teachers, however, feel so strongly about individual conferences that they feel at least one ten-minute conference per student per week is a necessity. We feel individual conferences are important, but only as needed. We recommend that the teacher plan at least two formal, individual, ten-minute conferences per six-week period per student: one to be scheduled the first week of the period to get the student started, and the other at about the fourth week to discuss the student's progress. Informal conferences then can be held more frequently as individual students need them. We find some students need daily individual conferences while others rarely need to see the teacher.

Develop a progress-and-evaluation form which students complete before or during the individual conference. We recommend using something like the forms on *pages 505-509* which can be dittoed and kept in students' individual folders.

When you schedule the individual conferences, let students know their times well in advance so that they can prepare for them. The conference is then used to discuss any of the following:

A. Student's in-progress or completed work.

B. Comments made on the progress-and-evaluation form *(see pages 505-509 for models)*.

C. Problems the student is encountering with his academic work.

D. Personal problems the student may be encountering in the classroom or outside.

Progress and Evaluation Form No. 1

NAME:_____   DATE: _____

TEACHER:_____   SUBJECT:_____

1. I am:

          _____

      1   2   3   4   5

      VERY PLEASED   VERY DISPLEASED
      WITH MY WORK   WITH MY WORK

2. I feel that:

    ____I was not able to devote the time to the work that I wanted to or that was needed.

___ I was not very interested in the work.

___ The work was too difficult for me at this time.

___ The work was too easy and did not challenge me.

___ Other:

3. I would like to:

___ Go on to something new or different.

___ Re-do the work.

___ Do more of the same kind of work.

___ Other:

4. The thing that was the hardest for me to do was

_____

5. One thing I learned was _____

6. One thing I really enjoyed was _____

7. I hope that_____

Progress and Evaluation Form No. 2[2]

NAME OF STUDENT_____ SUBJECT_____

INSTRUCTOR _____

*Goals set by student and teacher:*_____ *Date*_____

_____

_____

Student Self-Evaluation (1 = absolute yes; 8 = absolute no):

	STUDENT'S OPINION	TEACHER'S OPINION
I give my best effort to the work I have chosen for this course.	1 2 3 4 5 6 7 8	1 2 3 4 5 6 7 8
I spend my unscheduled time wisely and efficiently for the work I have chosen for this course.	1 2 3 4 5 6 7 8	1 2 3 4 5 6 7 8
I use my scheduled time for this course to take advantage of the teacher's help.	1 2 3 4 5 6 7 8	1 2 3 4 5 6 7 8
I have made an effort to arrive at goals that are important to me.	1 2 3 4 5 6 7 8	1 2 3 4 5 6 7 8
I am satisfied with my progress toward the goals I have set for myself.	1 2 3 4 5 6 7 8	1 2 3 4 5 6 7 8
I rate the depth and extent of my independent work.	1 2 3 4 5 6 7 8	1 2 3 4 5 6 7 8

In relation to the goals I have set for myself, I believe that I have achieved the following level (check):

I know the important facts involved.   _____   _____

I am able to understand the meaning of facts by relating them to each other.   _____   _____

I am able to analyze my understandings in order to apply them to problems in this area.   _____   _____

Comments by the teacher:

Disposition of student effort:
__ Discontinued   __Continuing   __Completed   __ Hours Credit

Progress and Evaluation

NAME:_____COURSE/SESSION:_____

DATE:_____ INSTRUCTOR:_____

Statement

1. I want to assume the responsibility for my own learning.

2. I have assumed the major responsibility for my own learning.

3. I have set definite and concrete goals for myself.

4. My goals are clear and realistic in that I have a good chance of/ I am achieving them, given such constraints as time, resources, etc.

5. I am pleased with the goals I have set for myself.

6. The goals I have set for myself are challenging and will make/are making a significant difference in my behavior.

7. I am pleased with my present progress in achieving my goals.

8. I am being blocked in my progress toward achieving my goals.

9. This blockage is currently beyond my ability to remove.

Form No. 3

Strongly Agree

Strongly Disagree

1	2	3	4	5

1	2	3	4	5

1	2	3	4	5

1	2	3	4	5

1	2	3	4	5

1	2	3	4	5

1	2	3	4	5

1	2	3	4	5

1	2	3	4	5

Skills Grid

PURPOSE

The skills grid has multiple uses. It can be employed for evaluation and record keeping, as an index of available materials and resources, and as a self-instructional device. It also serves as a useful cognitive map of basic skills in the choice-centered classroom.

PROCEDURE

Make a grid like the one on *512-515*. On the left of the grid, list the important skills you think should be taught in your classroom. Across the top of the grid, list the major resources you have available which deal with these skills. If you have only one or two texts and workbooks, your next step is to locate more sources. If you are working in an individualized or choice-centered classroom, you can use broken sets of texts and workbooks since not all thirty students need the same book at the same time. In fact, the best source is a teacher's edition since it can be used by students to self-correct their work.

Then, index each of the skills listed on the left of the grid by locating the pages in the texts and workbooks which deal with that particular skill. This can be a time-consuming job if done all at once. For this reason, you may be reluctant to undertake the task until you know you have the time to do it. This could mean that it will never get done. Rather than put it off, we suggest that you set up the grid and do a little of it at a time. An easy way to accomplish the task might be to start by selecting (1) those few skills which you consider most important and (2) the texts and workbooks with which you are most familiar.

Using the Skills Grid for Individual Prescription

Once you have diagnosed a student's skill needs, the next step is to turn to the skills grid and assess which texts, workbooks, packets, etc. listed on the grid will be most helpful. If one set of materials fails to secure the results, another set of resources may be tried. The skills grid is a handy reference since you know exactly what available tools you have.

Using the Skills Grid as a Self-Instructional Tool

The skills grid can be posted or dittoed for students to use as a ready reference. Thus, a student who becomes aware of or feels the need to develop his skills in a certain area can turn to the skills grid to locate materials which can be used for self-instruction.

Using the Skills Grid for Evaluation and Record Keeping

An additional two columns can be added, one on each side of the skills grid. Then reproduce the skills grid and keep a copy in each student's progress and evaluation folder.

The left-hand column is used to indicate when the student mastered the particular skill on the grid. The right-hand column is used for notes concerning the problems encountered, degree of proficiency, etc.

A Skills Grid of Calculations for

SPECIFIC SKILLS	RESOURCES Related Math. for Carpenters— American Technical Society	Practical Math.— American Technical Society	Practical Problems in Math. for Carpentry—Delmar
1. Measuring Squares	69-70	443	60-63
2. Working Square Roots	53-54	289	80
3. Measuring Rectangles	71-72	443 458-459	84-85
4. Measuring Triangles	73-75	444-446 452-458	86-88
5. Measuring Parallelograms	77-78	443 458-459	89-91

Material Estimation Used in Carpentry[3]

Basic Math. Simplified— Delmar	Individualizing Math.— Addison-Wesley	General Math. Ability— Cowles	Fundamental Math.— Holt, Rinehart, & Winston	Introduction to Math.— Encyclopaedia Britannica	Math. for Tech. & Voc. Schools— John Wiley & Sons	Introduction to Industrial Math.— Scott Foresman	Spectrum Math. Series— Laidlaw Bros.
116-128	M. Geom 15-20 29-32	85	161-164	Ch. 23 670-702		140-141	133-138
305-308	square 20-32	86	222		78-83	122-125	
116-121	M. Geom 21-24 29-32	152	158-160	Ch. 23 670-703	70-78	220	143-144
123-124	angles 13-18	167	164-167	Ch. 23 670-703	91-103	212 223-228	127-131 145
121-123		151-156		Ch. 23 670-703		220	149-151

A Skills Grid of Calculations for

RESOURCES	Related Math. for Carpenters—American Technical Society	Practical Math.—American Technical Society	Practical Problems in Math. for Carpentry—Delmar
6. Measuring Board Feet	135-140		64-69
7. Measuring Bridging	151-154		
8. Measuring Roof Pitches	175-176		
9. Measuring Rafters	177-180		116-121
10. Estimating Number of Roof Rafters	181-184		
11. Estimating Flooring Area	191-192		107-109
12. Measuring Height & Width of Stairs	193-194		148-150

Material Estimation Used in Carpentry

Basic Math. Simplified— Delmar	Individualizing Math.— Addison-Wesley	General Math. Ability— Cowles	Fundamental Math.— Holt, Rinehart, & Winston	Introduction to Math.— Encyclopaedia Britannica	Math. for Tech. & Voc. Schools— John Wiley & Sons	Introduction to Industrial Math.— Scott Foresman	Spectrum Math. Series— Laidlaw Bros.
116-128					181		
		168	224-227		85-90	213	
	angles 17-19	169	224-227		85-90	213	
	angles 17-19						
					183		
						214	

Peer Teaching Through Mini-Workshops[4]

PURPOSE

One of the major advantages of a choice-centered classroom is that students learn from each other. The freedom of movement and interaction allows students to work on projects together and give each other help and feedback. This strategy facilitates the process of peer teaching.

PROCEDURE

Have each student make two lists, one of the things he would like to learn and the other of things he would like to teach someone. (Or, do the same thing with a large group, using sheets of newsprint.) Combine the individual lists onto a piece of newsprint and post. Explain to the class that certain times of the day or week will be set aside for mini-workshops in which students may learn or teach about any topic that appears on the list. (Additional topics may be listed at any time.) Stress that students will have the major responsibility for staffing and teaching the mini-workshops. Then, you may either (1) select a student committee and give them the responsibility for setting up and managing the mini-workshop operation, or (2) complete the following steps:

Step 1: *Developing a schedule.* We suggest using a schedule like the one on *522.* It provides a great deal of flexibility and allows several workshops to be offered simultaneously. The student(s) or teacher wishing to offer a workshop simply blocks in the amount of time he or she needs, lists a title and description of the workshop, its location, and who will be teaching the session.

Step 2:   *Setting up the schedule and enrolling students in the mini-workshops.*   On a large piece of oaktag, glue or staple numerous pockets in which 3 x 5 cards can be placed (small manila envelopes can serve as pockets). Also, attach a copy of the schedule and post the whole thing, which should look like the figure on *page 520.* Place a stack of 3 x 5 cards nearby, and post the following instructions for those students who want to offer a mini-workshop.

Instructions for Offering a Mini-Workshop

A. On the mini-workshop schedule, block in the time needed for offering the workshop. Include a title and a brief description of the workshop, its location, and who will be teaching it.

B. Decide what is the maximum number of people who can enroll in the workshop. Then, take the same number of 3 x 5 cards and list the title of the workshop on each one. Write the title at the very top of the 3 x 5 cards, turned lengthwise (so that the title shows when the cards arc in onc of thc pockcts). Placc thc cards in a pockct on the oaktag; they will serve as admission cards to the workshop.

C. Any time prior to the workshop, you can check to see how many students have enrolled simply by counting the number of cards that remain in the pocket and subtracting this number from the number of cards that was originally placed there. If no cards remain, the workshop is full. If no one, or too few students, enroll, simply cancel the workshop by notifying those students who have enrolled.

Instructions for Enrolling in a Mini-Workshop

A.   Look over the mini-workshop schedule and identify the mini-workshop(s) you wish to attend.

B.   Then, look in the pockets on the oaktag to see if there are any 3 x 5 cards with the title(s) of the workshop(s) you wish to attend. If cards are left, pull one for each of the workshops you wish to attend. The card(s) will serve as your admission card(s).

C.   If there are no cards left, this means that the workshop is full. If you still wish to take the workshop, put your name and the name of the workshop you want to attend on a 3 x 5 card and place in the pocket marked *Requests for a Repeat Performance.*

ADDITIONAL SUGGESTIONS

We suggest that the first few times, only one column appear on the scheduling form. As students become familiar with the process, add a second column. Then, add a third or fourth if needed. Too much choice in the beginning can create difficulties for students who don't know how to make choices.

Ongoing workshops can be automatically blocked into the schedule by X-ing out the time needed in one of the columns prior to putting the schedule up.

Leader Feedback Form

LEADER'S NAME(S):_____ SESSION:_____DATE:_____

The leader(s) was/were:	I AGREE STRONGLY	I AGREE SOMEWHAT	I'M NEUTRAL OR UNSURE	I DISAGREE SOMEWHAT	I DISAGREE STRONGLY
Prepared	1	2	3	4	5
Helpful	1	2	3	4	5
Expert in knowledge	1	2	3	4	5
Enthusiastic	1	2	3	4	5
Sensitive to my needs	1	2	3	4	5
Prepared to suggest follow-up activities	1	2	3	4	5
Interesting	1	2	3	4	5

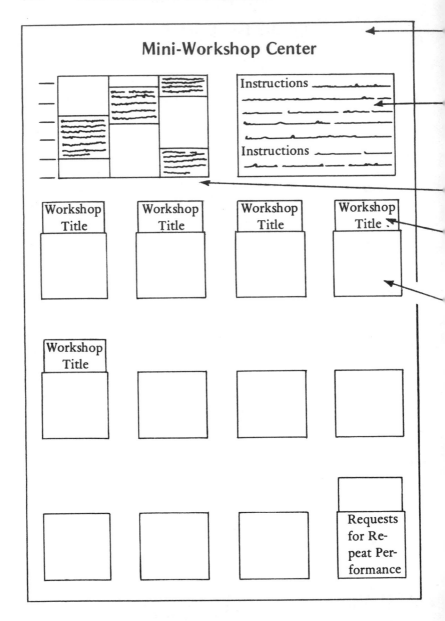

———— LARGE SHEET
OF OAKTAG

INSTRUCTIONS
———— FOR OFFERING &
ENROLLING IN
A MINI-WORK-
SHOP

———— MINI-WORKSHOP
SCHEDULE

———— 3 x 5 CARDS WITH
TITLE OF WORK-
SHOP

———— POCKETS FOR
3 x 5 CARDS

Advanced workshops can be offered by listing the prerequisites. We suggest these be kept to a minimum, however. Too many prerequisites can lead us back into the very thing we are trying to get away from, "closed education."

Use the mini-workshops as a way of scheduling guest speakers into the classroom. Parents, other teachers, ministers, community workers, businessmen, tradesmen, etc., love to come into the classroom and speak or demonstrate their hobbies and areas of special interest.

On *page 519* is an evaluation form which can be used by mini-workshop participants to give feedback to the leader(s).

Mini-Workshop Scheduling Form

Instructions: Schedule a workshop by blocking out the time needed in one of the columns below.[5] (If space is not available, you will have to wait until a new schedule appears.) Then, list the title of the workshop, a brief description, its location, and who will be teaching it.

DATE: _____

9:00 —			
9:15 —			
9:30 —			
9:45 —			
10:00 —			
10:15 —			
10:30 —			
10:45 —			
11:00 —			
11:15 —			

Using Groups in the Choice-Centered Classroom

PURPOSE

Many teachers have tried group work in their classrooms and have given it up because "it just doesn't work." In one sense, these teachers were right. Throwing a group of children or adolescents together and expecting them to function without conflict and friction is very unrealistic, especially if they are low-achieving or non-achieving students. In the first place, some students do not function well in groups even with adult leadership: they simply do not have the necessary social skills to allow them to relate. A second reason groups often do not work is that the teacher does not understand what is needed to make a group function effectively. This strategy is designed to help the teacher use groups more effectively.

PROCEDURE

The first thing to do is to realize that many things must happen for a group to function effectively. For example:

1. Group members must trust and respect one another.

2. They must share some common goals and concerns.

3. They must be willing to see each other's points of view and give ground or compromise when it is appropriate to do so.

4. The task they are undertaking must be clear and accomplishable.

5. Leadership functions such as keeping the group on the task, watching the time, etc., must be performed either on a shared, rotating, or fixed basis.

If any of the above principles is violated, the group is likely to face difficulty.

The first procedural step in using groups is to form the groups. Because students who choose to work with each other are much more likely to trust and respect each other than groups which the teacher forms, we recommend that groups be formed by the students themselves. Size is a somewhat important element. If the task to be performed or the project to be developed is a simple one, three to five students make a nice-sized work group. If it is a problem-solving situation which requires considerable group input and participant contribution, five to nine students are perhaps ideal.

Next, help the group get clear about its purpose. Unless the members of the group understand, agree upon, and are committed to the same goals and objectives, little headway will be made on the task or problem. Time spent helping the groups get straight about their purpose will be time well spent.

The final step is trouble shooting. Understand that when people work together in groups, problems will inevitably arise. Expect them, and be ready to help the group work through the difficulties they face. Try to get to the root causes of the conflict rather than deal with the surface causes which are only the symptoms of deeper group problems. Some knowledge, and if possible, some training in group processes is very helpful here.[6] If you have neither, we recommend reading *Group Development*, published by The National Training Laboratories as a primer in group dynamics. *Learning Discussion Skills Through Games* (Stanford) is also helpful in teaching students to work more effectively in groups.

The following is a useful diagnostic tool for helping groups become aware of and deal with the problems they face.

A Checklist of Group Difficulties[7]

Part I: Assessing the Symptoms

Instructions: First, spend some time observing the group at work. Note the difficulties the group faces and, on the sheet below, the symptoms which you observe. Then, go to parts II & III for a suggestion of possible diagnoses and courses of action.

_____ 1.   Ideas are rejected because they seem impractical or unworkable; students complain that the group is too small to get the job done; students complain that there is not enough time to do the job; confusion exists as to what is the group's task.

_____ 2.   Students rush to attack each other's ideas and suggestions; students refuse to listen to each others' ideas and suggestions; students make little or no attempt to get on with the task at hand; there is a great deal of side taking and clique formation.

_____ 3.   Each student has his or her own idea as to what is best; students talk "past" each other, with no one really listening; students seem interested only in making their own points.

_____ 4.   Students seem to care very little about what is going on in the group; no one is willing to do the work that needs to be done; ideas and suggestions seem to fall on deaf ears; students seem more interested in talking about other things than the issues at hand.

_____ 5.   Students "tip-toe" around the task; students are overly friendly and polite; agreement is easily reached with very little probing into the issues involved.

_____ 6.   The group discussion is controlled and dominated by a few students who seem to be in disagreement no matter what issues arise; except for a few vocal students, most of the group members have lost interest in the discussion/task.

Part II: Making A Diagnosis

If you checked item:

1   the group may feel that its task is too difficult, unclear or upsetting. *(Diagnosis A)*

2   students may be using the task to gain status in the group. *(Diagnosis B)*

3   students may be operating from different frames of reference. *(Diagnosis C)*

4   students may feel the group task is of little or no interest or concern. *(Diagnosis D)*

5   students may be more concerned about maintaining friendly relations in the group than working on the task. *(Diagnosis E)*

6   a win/lose attitude on the part of a few students may be producing apathy in the rest of the group. *(Diagnosis F)*

Part III: Doing Something About the Problem

If your diagnosis is:

(A)   report your findings to the group and check out their perceptions. If the task or problem is unclear, help them nail it down. If they feel the task or problem is impossible, help them identify the resources needed to solve it, *or* to redefine the task or problem. If the task or problem is disturbing, help them discuss and then finally resolve the part that is disturbing.

(B)   help members find ways to gain status in the group which are constructive rather than destructive. Perhaps roles can be suggested (with the appropriate titles for the age levels of the group members), e.g., Time Keeper, Sergeant at Arms, Fact Finder, Recorder, Process Observer, Message Runner, and so on.

(C)   help members learn to use *Active Listening* and *The Positive Focus Game. (See pages 70 and 56, respectively.)* Perhaps have another group observe, using the *In/Out Group* strategy *(see page 54)* and give feedback.

(D)   check out your perceptions with the group. If your diagnosis is accurate, help them find a more meaningful goal.

(E)   use *Active Listening (page 70)* to help the group work through and resolve its fears.

(F)   help the dominant members see what they are doing to the group and/or use *The Conflict Resolving Game (page 75)* to help work out the difficulty.

ADDITIONAL SUGGESTIONS

Feelings of identification and belongingness can be strengthened by encouraging the groups to create names, symbols, badges, patches, etc., which identify them and their membership. This can lead to problems of clique formation, but we feel that sometimes the benefits to be derived in terms of increased satisfaction of needs are worth the risks.[8]

The following are two quick and simple feedback forms which can be used to help you and the group gather data for reviewing the group's progress.

Feedback Form No. 1

1. Given your learning goals, how satisfied were you with your group during this session?

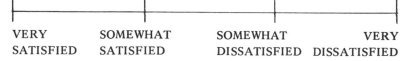

VERY   SOMEWHAT   SOMEWHAT   VERY
SATISFIED   SATISFIED   DISSATISFIED   DISSATISFIED

Why did you answer as you did?

How could your group function better to achieve its purposes?

2. Taking the role of an outside observer for a moment, how would you evaluate the progress of your group on its task?

GOOD PROGRESS   POOR PROGRESS

If, as such an observer, you were asked to make some helpful comments, what suggestions would you make to the group?

3. The most important learning for me this session was:

4. Other comments:

Feedback Form No. 2[9]

How do you feel?

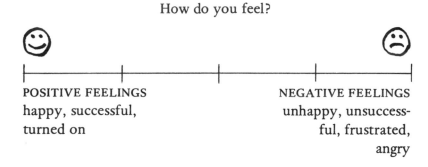

POSITIVE FEELINGS
happy, successful,
turned on

NEGATIVE FEELINGS
unhappy, unsuccess-
ful, frustrated,
angry

How involved are you?

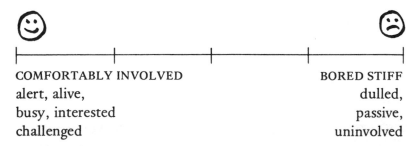

COMFORTABLY INVOLVED
alert, alive,
busy, interested
challenged

BORED STIFF
dulled,
passive,
uninvolved

Community Meeting[10]

PURPOSE

Nothing clears the air like a regular community meeting (or classroom meeting[11]) in which all can speak their mind freely without fear of ridicule or retaliation. Many classroom problems can be worked out in such an arena. As well, the teacher can receive valuable feedback upon which to base future planning or modify his behavior. The community meeting also builds a strong feeling of community in the classroom.

PROCEDURE

Introduce the concept of a community or town meeting. One way to do this, especially in a social-studies classroom, is to do a unit on the use of town meetings as a method of self-government; study the small New England villages and communities where the concept of the town or community meeting was—and in some areas still is—practiced extensively.

Set aside a period of time each week for the community meeting. Friday is a good day, since the week's activities can be reviewed and discussed. The community meeting is implemented in the following way:

1. An open agenda is established by using a chalkboard. To place an item on the agenda, a group member simply writes his topic on the chalkboard and the amount of time he thinks will be needed to discuss the item. If no agenda items appear on the chalkboard, the meeting is not held.

2. After all agenda items have been established, the group decides upon the amount of time needed for conducting the meeting. The meeting is adjourned at the end of the time specified, after which evaluation takes place.

3. While an item is on the floor, the group member who placed that item on the agenda is chairman. The agenda is worked through in a sequential fashion.

4. Upon the close of the agenda part of the meeting, or at the close of each item on the agenda, the process is evaluated: members identify what and who was helpful or not helpful.

The following rules are to be posted and followed during the meeting.

1. *Membership:* Each individual, no matter what his status in the organization, has equal influence in making decisions. No one member is permanent leader or chairman. Any individual may speak on the agenda item at any time.

2. *Keeping an open agenda:* An open agenda means any individual has a right to put up an item on the agenda, as long as the item concerns most members of the group. This rule prevents a few persons from dominating the group interaction and stifling the full

expression of feelings. The person raising the agenda item is to state his issue, problem, or concern and his expectation concisely. The group is then to ask him questions and attempt to help him clarify his thinking and feelings before stating their own feelings or solutions.

3. *Decision making:*   The community meeting is not a place for technical decisions or for friendly chats. It is a place for decisions by consensus concerning vital issues or problems facing the community. The community should delegate technical implementation of policy decisions to individuals or committees.

4. *Sharing feelings:*   Perhaps the key element is the expression of feelings on each agenda item. Each person speaking must state his own feelings directly and clearly. The group member who raised the agenda item is responsible for assessing feelings.

5. *Use of consensus:*   Only issues which affect the class organization, the group, or individual group members are appropriate agenda items. Therefore, if the decisions are to be carried out, it is important that most or all members are willing to support them. This may mean compromise and/or some delay in implementing decisions, since consensus is difficult to reach; however, the additional time spent gathering support by use of consensus will, in

the long run, pay off. Majority vote is therefore to be avoided, unless as a last resort for pressing decisions.

Student Projects

PURPOSE

Students' self-esteem is often dependent upon their feelings of achievement and success. The need for achievement, however, cannot be satisfied by simply multiplying successes. This may build the self-concept of failing students, but it is hardly appropriate for highly successful advanced students. These students seek the challenge of difficult problems and projects in which the risks of failure are moderate to moderately high. The projects which follow provide this type of challenge. In addition, they provide students with many opportunities to explore, clarify, and act upon their values.

PROCEDURE

You can help to encourage the development of students' self-esteem by turning students on to challenging and moderately difficult projects or problems. These might take the form of independent study or group projects. There is no easy rule for determining what will be a moderately challenging problem or project. This will depend upon the skill development, feelings of self-adequacy, and interests of individual students. The following are some examples of projects and problems which may be used successfully.

STUDENT PROJECTS

1. Set up and manage a class radio station.

2. Organize and edit a class newspaper.

3. Organize and direct a class play to which the public is invited.

4. Make an 8mm film (for example, a ten-minute history of the U.S., or "The Story of Our Town").

5. Plan and organize a class money-making project.

6. Plan and organize a class trip; make the reservations, arrange transportation, tours, etc.

7. Organize and run a one-day workshop on some topic (for example: black history, environment, economics) for which community experts are invited to talk to the class.

8. Design and build a learning center for the classroom.

9. Build a piece of equipment or furniture for the classroom.

10. Organize and set up a class paperback book library.

11. Set up a youth employment or tutoring service.

12. Plan a parent resource program; find out things parents are skilled or experienced in and invite them to share these with the class or school on a regular basis.

13. Survey the community on an important issue; have the results published in the local newspaper.

14. Start a drive or movement to solve a community

problem (for example: getting a new traffic light installed, improving a park).

15. Plan and organize a science fair, or art/hobby exhibition.

16. Write a one-act play and direct it.

17. Write a short story or poem and try to get it published.

18. Set up and run a Values Clarification workshop for students and their parents.

19. Organize a camping trip for the class.

20. Organize and take part in a TV show to be broadcast weekly or daily on the school closed-circuit system during homeroom period.

21. Do a photo study or essay on the school, the community, or a topic of your choice.

22. Edit a class literary magazine to include class members' compositions, short stories, poems, etc.

23. Start a class or school store; keep the inventory, etc.

24. Start a class or school business; use student labor.

25. Grow a garden on an unused plot of land in the community.

26. Build a neighborhood playground from scrap material or start a recycling center.

27. Start a rap room or peer counseling program.

28. Organize an after-school recreation program for younger students.

29. Plan an exchange program with another school.

30. Investigate and try to solve an ecological problem in your community, e.g., soil erosion, polluted stream, etc.

31. Write or tape a history of your community by interviewing the older people in the community.

32. Do a "Ralph Nader" study on some consumer issue in your community (Do stores raise prices on the days welfare checks are distributed? Are newspaper advertisements "come-ons"?).

33. Get together with several students and invest in the stock market; or use play money and keep records yourself.

34. Plan a heritage pot luck dinner in which each student brings a dish which represents his ethnic or cultural background.

35. Plan and carry out an overnight canoe trip for a small group of students with an experienced leader.

Many of the challenges, however, will be of a personal nature rather than academic. Students may want to achieve goals in swimming, chess, or football, or overcome personal problems like losing weight, or travel cross-country by bike, or race sailboats, or mountain climb, or hundreds of other things. Thus, helping students learn how to set and achieve personal goals also serves to meet their achievement needs. The goal-setting strategies in Chapter 9 are useful in this respect, as is a book entitled *Teaching Achievement Motivation* (Alschuler, et. al.).

Notes

1. We learned this variation from Elliott Seif.
2. This form is in use at the Archbishop Rummel High School, Omaha, Nebraska.
3. Developed in an Adult Basic Education Workshop, Temple University.
4. The idea for this strategy comes from Val Mulgrew, Director of the Mini-School, Washington Township High School, Sewell, N.J.
5. Additional (or fewer) columns may be added to the schedule, depending on the number of students in the class or group.
6. For further information write the Department of Psycho-Educational Processes, or the PEP Center, Larry Krafft, Director, Temple University, Philadelphia, Pa.
7. This checklist is a synthesis of ideas presented in "How To Diagnose Group Difficulties," by Bradford, *et. al.* in *Group Development,* National Training Labs, Washington, D.C., 1961, and Blake and Mouton, *The Managerial Grid,* Gulf, Houston, Texas, 1964.
8. This conclusion is limited to schools where gang violence is not a problem.
9. Merrill Harmin's 2D Rating Scale.
10. Developed by Leland Howe and Saville Sax, NEXTEP Fellowship Program, Southern Illinois University, Edwardsville, Ill.
11. For a detailed discussion of how to use classroom meetings, see Glasser's *Schools Without Failure.*

17. Discipline in the Choice-Centered Classroom

Perhaps the greatest single difficulty teachers face in setting up a choice-centered classroom is that often many students resist—and/or do not know how to handle—the freedom and responsibility they are given. This is understandable, since in many of the homes and classrooms in this country, children are given only a very small range of things about which they can make their own decisions. When confronted with a situation in which they must begin to make many more choices than they are used to, some simply cannot handle it. They may withdraw; they may become overly aggressive or hostile; they may become anxious and frustrated; or they may simply make unwise choices.

The teacher who understands this problem does not rush into the choice-centered classroom. Rather, he or she prepares students by discussing why and what he or she intends to do long before actually doing it. Then, choices are provided gradually, and only to students who seem ready to handle them. At first, the student is offered a choice of only two alternatives in a specific area. If the student handles them, the alternatives become three, four, five and so on.

When a student has difficulty, the teacher lets him drop back, and when he appears to be ready to advance, once again encourages him.

Of course, even when a teacher follows this plan carefully, there will be times when some students are disruptive of the efforts of others in the class. In a choice-centered classroom, where we encourage students to take responsibility for their own behavior and to make decisions on their own, many of the traditional ways of dealing with these "discipline problems" seem inappropriate. Therefore, we have turned to the work of Rudolf Dreikurs[1] for two alternative ways of handling classroom problems. (These are in addition to "I messages," active listening, and no-lose conflict resolution, which we discussed on *pages 65-79.*)

DELIMITING OR SPECIFYING THE CHOICES

One of the simpler techniques in moving students toward more choice is the technique of delimiting the choices in any given situation. Rather than directing or ordering the students' behavior, the teacher gives the student a specified number of choices in a given situation and lets the student choose which one he wants to take. The choices may only be two, or three, or whatever is appropriate to the situation. For example:

A small group of students working together on a project is disturbing others in the class. The

teacher turns to them and gives them a choice—
"We must have it quiet in here so others can work:
you can talk quietly or work separately"—instead
of giving them an order like, "Be quiet!" or,
"Let's break it up and work separately!"

The technique serves two purposes. One, it lets a student
be "his own man." By giving students a choice—even when
the choices are limited and not the ones the students might
prefer—the teacher recognizes the student as a person who
can make decisions and direct his own life. It serves to
convey a message of trust and helps to meet the students'
need for control of their own fates. Second, the fact that the
students have a say in the matter usually helps the teacher
avoid the power struggle which is so pervasive in American
classrooms.

The following are examples of situations in which the
teacher gives the students a set of limited choices rather than
ordering or directing their behavior.

> To a student who is throwing blocks: Instead of
> saying "Stop throwing those blocks!" say "Dennis, blocks are not for throwing. You can choose—
> you may build with them or you may put them
> away."

> To a student who has thrown paper on the floor in
> defiance of the teacher: Instead of saying, "Pick
> up that paper!" say "You may pick up the paper
> now or stay and pick it up after class."[2]

Letting Students Experience the Natural or Logical Consequences of Their Choices

In many homes and schools, punishment is the primary means of controlling children's behavior (or, as some would put it, teaching students responsibility). Many of the humanistic psychologists (Rogers, Maslow, Dreikurs) feel that this effort is misguided and misdirected. Instead, they suggest the use of more humanistic methods. One of the most useful of these is to let children experience the natural or logical consequences of their own actions. *See pages 543-544* for examples.

Once the teacher learns to let students experience the natural or logical consequences of their choices, the problem of classroom discipline practically disappears. The technique is also a primary means of helping students learn to make free and wise choices in the choice-centered classroom. A student who is allowed to experience the consequences of a poor choice will undoubtedly learn more about choosing than one who is constantly "programmed" by the teacher and prevented from making any poor choices.

Weighing the consequences of one's choices is an important step in decision making and in the valuing process, yet we find it is one of the most difficult for young people to understand. Perhaps this is because, from a very early age, many children in our society are shielded from the consequences of their decisions and actions by what adults call "discipline." For example, a toddler approaching a hot radiator is told to stay away and then spanked if he doesn't, because "after all, we have to protect him." If, instead, he was told that the radiator was hot and that it would hurt if he touched it, and then was allowed to touch it and experience the consequences—getting burned—he wouldn't have to be told again why he shouldn't touch hot things! (Of course, we are not talking about allowing real physical harm to the child. If a child persists in running into the street when allowed to play outside, then "logical" consequences would have to replace "natural" consequences, i.e., the child is told that if he does it again, he will not be allowed to play outside for the rest of the day. The child would thus suffer the "logical" consequences of his behavior.)

Using Natural or Logical Consequences in the Classroom[3]

To understand how natural or logical consequences are used in the classroom, let's examine the following situations.

SITUATION NO. 1

The teacher has given the students ten minutes to put away their art projects and clean up the room before going to gym. Several students are still goofing around at the end of the ten minutes. Instead of reminding them or reprimanding them, the teacher uses logical consequences. Those who have put their projects away and cleaned up are allowed to go to gym. Those who have not must remain behind and miss gym. The problem does not happen again.

SITUATION NO. 2

Students have not been taking very good care of the classroom. Equipment is not put away, materials are left strewn on the tables, paint cans are left uncovered, etc. The teacher has been wearing herself out cleaning up after them. Finally, she decides they must live with the consequences of their actions. She leaves the room just the way they left it. The next morning, children complain because they can't find the materials they need, the paint is all dried out and so forth. Later in the day, she holds a class meeting at the students' request. The problem is discussed and students decide to take more responsibility for keeping the classroom organized.

SITUATION NO. 3

Several students are in the habit of coming in late after recess. They are told that it is not fair to the other children for the teacher to take time away from the class to go over the work again just because these students wanted a little extra time to play. The next day, the same students come in late again. The teacher refuses to explain the assignment, instead telling them they will be given the assignment as soon as the class is dismissed, and that they will be expected to finish the work before they leave. So ends the problem.

In each of the above situations, the teacher lets students live with the natural or logical consequences of their behavior or the situation. When the students "goofed off" (Situation No. 1), logically they were not ready to go to gym class. Had the teacher retreated or given them punishment, the problem would undoubtedly have continued and become a power struggle. The same is true of Situation No. 2. The consequences of not putting things away is that one must live in a messy room where things are hard to find. The students learned the lesson without the teacher having to moralize or punish them. In Situation No. 3, the teacher refused to give the late students extra attention; thus they had to adjust themselves to the class schedule or stay after school. This was not a punishment, but simply the results of the situation; any power struggle that might have developed if the teacher had tried to force the issue was avoided.

Notes

1. *Psychology in the Classroom*, Rudolf Dreikurs, New York, Harper & Row, 1957.

2. For a more detailed discussion of this technique and additional examples of how to use it, see Rudolf Dreikurs, *Children the Challenge*.

3. For a detailed discussion of this topic and many more examples of how to use it in the classroom, see Rudolf Dreikurs, *Psychology in the Classroom*.

18. Using Values Clarification in the Choice-Centered Classroom

In our minds, there are at least four ways the teacher can go about building the valuing process of *choosing, prizing,* and *acting* into the choice-centered classroom. Though it is the ultimate aim, the most difficult way to do this is to make Values Clarification an essential part of every activity, every learning center, every task card, and every project—that is to say, Values Clarification should become an essential and integral part of the total curriculum. Part III of this book, "Personalizing the Curriculum," provides a number of very specific strategies and procedures for accomplishing this end.

A second means involves doing the Values Clarification strategies described in Part II, "Personalizing Goals in the Classroom," with the whole class or in small groups. This is perhaps the easiest method, especially for those who have been trained to operate more conventional types of classrooms. In the choice-centered classroom, it is very important that a sense of community be developed. Using the Values Clarification strategies with the whole class or a small group is one of the best ways we know of to build a sense of community and at the same time personalize learning. What must be avoided is allowing the strategies to become the sole means of dealing with values in the classroom.

Of course, the act of organizing and managing a choice-centered classroom is a third means of facilitating the Values Clarification process. The teacher in effect conveys the valuing skills to his students by giving them a chance to choose what they will learn, set their own goals, talk with each other about their own interests and concerns, and evaluate their own learning and classroom behavior.

The fourth way of building the valuing process is very consistent with the organization of the choice-centered classroom. It involves creating a "do-it-yourself values center" by turning the group-oriented Values Clarification strategies into self-instructional activity cards. These can then be used by individuals or small groups of students on their own. To transform any of the strategies in this book (or those in *Values Clarification* or *Values and Teaching*) into such a format, follow the procedures below.

A DO-IT-YOURSELF VALUES CENTER

1. Place the name of the activity at the top of the 4 x 6 card or 8½ x 11 sheet of paper. (We suggest that the activity be placed on 8½ x 11 paper and dittoed to prevent loss; or, keep a "master set" of cards.)

2. (*Optional*) Briefly introduce the activity with a statement of purpose or by listing the objectives.

3. Indicate the materials, if any, that will be needed to complete the activity.

4. Write out a set of instructions or steps that the student must follow to complete the activity.

5. (*Optional*) List follow-up activities which the student might wish to explore.

The following are several examples of values strategies which have been written in a self-instructional format.

Making a "Me" Chart[1]

INTRODUCTION

This activity will help you to think about what it's like to be you. You are the only person who really knows this.

INSTRUCTIONS

Think about these questions:

What do I look like? Tall, short, fat, thin, blond hair, green eyes, etc?

What kind of disposition do I have? Quiet, lively, quick to laugh, hot temper, friendly, shy?

What things am I good at?

What things do I like to do? To eat? To wear?

What things or people are important to me?

What would I like to be good at? What would I like to do with my life?

Are there some things in which I believe deeply?

Are there some things I particularly dislike?

Now get a big piece of paper and plan your "me" chart. In the center, put a drawing of yourself. It doesn't need to be artistic, but try to make it show how you look. Then draw a picture, cut words or illustrations out of magazines, or write things that tell about you. You might make one section for things you like, another for your hopes or ambitions, another for your personality, and so on. Use your imagination. For example, one boy drew a bolt of lightning to show a hot temper; another drew a fence to show he felt closed in; another drew a heart around a picture of a crowd of young people to show she had a lot of friends.

Try to make your chart show what makes you the unique person you are. (If you don't know what "unique" means, look it up—that's what you are!)

When you have finished your chart, you might want to put it up in your classroom, and compare it with charts made by other people. Or you might want to take it home and think about it.

A Proud Diary

INTRODUCTION

This activity will help you to think of things you're proud of—all kinds of things.

INSTRUCTIONS

Use a separate place in your notebook for your diary. Or, if you think you might want to keep your diary for a long time, use a small, spiral notebook for it. Either is fine. Begin by writing down all the things you can think of that you're proud of. You may tell about someone in your family who has overcome obstacles, is always cheerful, or who does something very well. You might tell about things you have learned to do, things you're good at, times you have helped others. You might be proud of your school, your nationality or race, your country. Tell briefly why you are proud of each thing.

Then keep a diary for a week, making a separate entry for each day. Write the things you do or think of on the day you do or think of them. Write during the day when you think of things, or at night before you go to bed, but do it every day so you won't forget what happened.

When the week is over, show your diary to your teacher. If you want her to, she will read it and talk to you about it. Otherwise, she will just see that you did what you were asked to do. The diary is yours alone. Keep writing in it if you enjoy doing so. Perhaps you might get an idea for a story you'd like to write from one part of your diary—or a picture you'd like to paint. It's up to you!

What Happened? How Did It Feel?

INTRODUCTION

You will need a partner for this activity. You will practice *really* listening to each other, and learning more than just what the words are telling you.

Did you ever try to tell someone about something that happened to you, or about a problem or fear that you had, and you felt that the other person didn't understand? Maybe he or she didn't really listen. That's hard work sometimes.

INSTRUCTIONS

Find a place where you and your partner can talk without being disturbed—a quiet corner of the room. Each of you think for a while about something that happened to you one time that really made you feel good. Maybe you went somewhere and had a great time; maybe you made something good, or did well in school, or helped someone, or learned something—or maybe someone was very nice to you. It can be anything that felt good to you.

Partner A begins by telling about what happened to him. Partner B is to listen and try to understand what happened, how it made Partner A feel, and why he felt good about it. Then Partner B is to tell Partner A what he has just heard. Try to tell in your own words exactly how the other person felt at the time, and why he felt that way. When Partner A is satisfied that Partner B really understands how he felt, it is Partner B's turn to tell about his event, how it made him feel, and why. When you are satisfied that Partner A really understands, try telling about another event. Don't try to do anything but understand each other.

Notes

1. The following three self-instructional values activities were developed by Mary Hoaglund.

We would encourage anyone who is interested in implementing the ideas and strategies in this book to obtain training by attending workshops in Personalizing Education. For a workshop schedule and a list of humanistic education materials available, please write:

Philadelphia Humanistic Education Center
8504 Germantown Avenue
Philadelphia, Penna. 19118

LELAND W. HOWE
MARY MARTHA HOWE

BIBLIOGRAPHY

Abt, Clark C., *Serious Games.* New York: Viking, 1970.

Allport, G., *Pattern and Growth in Personality.* New York: Holt, Rinehart and Winston, 1961.

Alschuler, Alfred S., Diane Tabor and James McIntyre, *Teaching Achievement Motivation.* Middletown, Conn.: Educational Ventures, 1971.

American Association for Curriculum Development, "Perceiving, Behaving, Becoming: A New Focus for Education" (collected convention proceedings). Copies available from the National Education Association, 1201 Sixteenth St., N.W., Washington, D.C. 20036.

Argyris, C., *Personality and Organization.* New York: Harper & Row, 1957.

Ascheim, Skip (ed.), *Materials for the Open Classroom.* New York: Dell, 1973.

Berger, Evelyn and Bonnie Winters, *Social Studies in the Open Classroom.* New York: Teachers College Press, 1973.

Bessell, Harold and Uvaldo Palomares, *Methods in Human Development.* San Diego, Ca.: Human Development Training Institute, 1973.

Bingham, Margaret, *Learning Dimensions Program: A Series of Concepts and Activities for Teachers and Students.* Printed by the Philadelphia Public Schools, 1968.

Blance, Cook and Mack, *Reading in the Open Classroom: An Individualized Approach.* New York: Community Resources Institute, 1971.

Blitz, Barbara, *The Open Classroom: Making It Work.* Boston: Allyn and Bacon, 1973.

Boocock, S.S., and E.O. Schild, *Simulation Games in Learning.* Beverly Hills, Ca.: Sage, 1968.

Borton, Terry. *Reach, Touch and Teach.* New York: McGraw-Hill, 1970.

_____ (with Oliver Nuse and Jim Morrow), "Prelude" (1966) and "A Lot of Undoing to Do" (1968). Two films about the Philadelphia Cooperative Schools. Films are available through the Audio-Visual Department, Philadelphia Public School Building, Room 327, 21st and Parkway, Philadelphia, Pa.

Bradford, L., J. Gibb, and K. Benne (eds.), *T-group Theory and Laboratory Method: Innovation in Re-education.* New York: John Wiley & Sons, 1964.

Bremer, John and Bremer, Ann, *Open Education: A Beginning.* New York: Holt, Rinehart and Winston, 1972.

Brown, George, *Human Teaching for Human Learning.* New York: Viking, 1972.

Brown, Mary and Precious, Norman, *The Integrated Day in the Primary School,* New York: Agathon, 1970.

Buber, M., *I and Thou.* New York: Charles Scribner's Sons, 1968.

Buckeye, Donald, *Cheap Math Lab Equipment.* Troy, Michigan: Midwest Publications, 1972.

Bugental, J.F.T., *The Search for Authenticity.* New York: Holt, Rinehart and Winston, 1965.

_____ (ed.), *Challenge of Humanistic Psychology.* New York: McGraw-Hill, 1967.

Canfield, John T. and Harold C. Wells, *100 Ways to Enhance Self-Concept in the Classroom* (mimeograph). Amherst, Mass.: New England Center.

Carter, Rachel, *Kit of Learning Center Activities.* Carolina Education Center, P.O. Box 9753, Greensboro, N.C. 27408.

Castillo, Gloria A., *Left-Handed Teaching.* New York: Praeger, 1974.

Cazden, Courtney B., *Infant School.* Newton, Massachusetts: Education Development Center, 1969.

Center for Urban Education, *Open Door.* New York: Center for Urban Education, 1971.

Charbonneau, Manon, *Learning to Think in a Math Lab*. Boston, Mass.: National Association of Independent Schools, Four Liberty Square, 02109.

Cherry, Clare, *Creative Movement for the Developing Child*. Revised edition. Belmont, Calif: Fearon, 1971.

Chesler, Mark and Robert Fox, *Role Playing Methods in the Classroom*. Chicago: Science Research Associates (SRA), 1966.

Childs, Sally B., *Magic Squares*. Cambridge, Massachusetts: Educators Publishing Service, 1965.

Clack and Leitch, *Math Amusements in Developing Skills*. Michigan: Midwest Publications, 1972.

Clegg, Sir Alec, *Revolution in the British Primary Schools*. Washington, D.C.: National Education Association, 1971.

Clure, Beth, *Why Didn't I Think of That?* Glendale, Ca.: Bowmar, 1971.

Combs, Arthus, Chairman of the Committee, ASCD Yearbook, *Perceiving, Behaving, Becoming*. Washington, D.C.: Association for Supervision and Curriculum Development, 1962.

Create Independence: 201 Learning Center Ideas. Phila., Pa.: I Red Co.

Creative Dramatics Handbook. Office of Early Childhood Programs, School District of Philadelphia, 1971.

Creative Moments Investigations. Kits 1 (ages 4-9), 2 (ages 8-12), 3 (ages 10-14). Boston: Creative Studies.

Cullom, Albert, *Push Back the Desks*. New York: Citation, 1967.

Daniels,.Steven, *How 2 Gerbils, 20 Goldfish, 200 Games, 2,000 Books and I Taught Them How to Read*. Philadelphia: Westminster, 1971.

DeKoven, Bernard, *The Interplay Games Catalogue*. Office of Publications, School District of Philadelphia.

Dennison, George, *The Lives of Children*. New York: Vintage, 1969.

Don, Humphrey et. al, *Individualizing Reading Instruction with Learning Stations and Centers*. Riverside Learning Associates, P.O. Box 134, Evansville, Indiana 47701.

Dollar, Barry, *Humanizing Classroom Instruction: A Behavioral Approach*. New York: Harper and Row, 1972.

Dreikurs, Rudolf, *Psychology in the Classroom*. New York: Harper & Row, 1957.

_____, Bernice Grunwald and Floy Pepper, *Maintaining Sanity in the*

Classroom: Illustrated Teaching Techniques. New York: Harper and Row, 1971.

Dunn, Eleanor (director), *Lexikits,* Prolexia, ESEA Title III.

———, *Lexilogs,* Prolexia, ESEA Title III.

Dunn, Rita and Kenneth, *Practical Approaches to Individualizing Instruction.* West Nyack, New York: Parker, 1972.

Early Childhood Education Study, *Building with Cardboard.* Newton, Massachusetts: Education Development Center, 1970.

———, *Building with Tubes.* Newton, Massachusetts: Education Development Center, 1968.

Education Development Center, *Cardboard Carpentry Workshop.* Education Development Center, 1968.

Edwards, Charlotte, *Creative Dramatics.* Dansville, N.Y.: The Instructor Publications, 1972.

Elementary Science Study (EES) Units, *Kitchen Physics: Behavior of Mealworms; Light and Shadows; Brine Shrimp; Crayfish; Eggs and Tadpoles; Mobiles.* New York: McGraw-Hill.

Environmental Study Cards. Packets 1, 2, 3 and 4. Available from Environmental Study, Box 1559, Boulder, Colorado 80302.

Epstein, Charlotte, *Affective Subjects in the Classroom: Exploring Race, Sex, and Drugs.* Scranton, Pa.: Intext, 1972.

ESEA Title I, *Open Education, Theresa, Theater and Terrariums.* Division of Education for the Disadvantaged, The University of the State of New York.

Exploring Moral Values (record-filmstrip sets). Pleasantville, N.Y.: Warren Schloat Productions, Inc.

Fantini, Mario, and Gerald Weinstein, *The Disadvantaged.* New York: Harper and Row, 1968.

———, *Making the Urban School Work.* New York: Holt, Rinehart and Winston, 1968.

Featherstone, Joseph, *Schools Where Children Learn.* New York: Liveright, 1971.

First Things: Values (record filmstrip series). Pleasantville, N.Y.: Guidance Associates.

Focus on Self-Development Kits: Stage One: *Awareness;* Stage Two: *Responding;* Stage Three: *Involvement.* Chicago: Science Research Associates (SRA).

Furth and Wachs, *Thinking Goes to School.* New York: Oxford University Press, 1974.

Gingell, Lesley P., *The ABC's of the Open Classroom.* Homewood, Illinois: ETC Publications, 1973.

Ginther, John L., *Math Experiments with the Tangram.* Troy, Michigan: Midwest Publications, 1972.

Glasser, William, *Schools Without Failure.* New York: Harper and Row, 1969.

Godfrey, Lorraine, *Individualizing Through Learning Stations.* P.O. Box 591, Menlo Park, California 94025: Individualized Books.

_____, *Individualizing with Learning Station Themes.* P.O. Box 591, Menlo Park, California 94025: Individualized Books Publishing Co.

Gordon, Thomas, *Parent Effectiveness Training.* New York: Wyden, 1970.

_____, *Teacher Effectiveness Training.* New York: Wyden, 1974.

Gordon, William J. J., *Synectics: The Development of Creative Capacity.* New York: Harper and Row, 1961.

Greer, Mary and Bonnie Rubinstein, *Will the Real Teacher Please Stand Up.* Pacific Palisades, Ca.: Goodyear, 1972.

Guidelines to Open Education, Bureau of Elementary Curriculum Development, The University of the State of New York, 1974.

Gunther, B., *Sense Relaxation: Below Your Mind.* New York; Collier Books, 1968.

Gurske and Cots, *Learning Center Guide.* CTM (Contract Teaching Method). P.O. Box 1513, Sunnyvale, California 95088.

Handbook of Learning Centers, 4 books, levels 1-4 (grades 1-2, grades 2-3, grades 3-4 and grades 4-5). Order from Board of Education of Howard County, 8045 Route #32, Columbia, Maryland.

Handbook of Staff Development and Human Relations Training: Materials Developed for Use in Africa. National Training Laboratories, Institute for Applied Behavioral Science, associated with NEA, 1201 16th St., N.W., Washington, D.C., 20036.

Harmin, Merrill, *Making Sense of Our Lives* (curriculum materials, grades 7-12). Niles, Ill.: Argus Communications.

_____, *People Projects* (curriculum materials, grades 4-8). Menlo Park, Ca.: Addison-Wesley.

_____, Howard Kirschenbaum, and Sidney B. Simon, *Clarifying*

Values Through Subject Matter. Minneapolis, Minn.: Winston, 1972.

Harris, Thomas A., *I'm OK, You're OK.* New York: Harper & Row, 1967.

Hart, C., L.C. Pogrebin, M. Rodgers, and M. Thomas, *Free to Be . . . You and Me.* New York: McGraw-Hill, 1974.

Hawley, Robert C. and Isabel L. Hawley, *Human Values in the Classroom.* New York: Hart, 1975.

_____, Sidney B. Simon, and D. Britton, *Composition for Personal Growth.* New York: Hart, 1973.

Henderson, George, *Let's Play Games in Metrics.* Skokie, Illinois: National Textbook Company, 1974.

Hertzberg, Alvin and Edward F. Stone, *Schools Are for Children.* New York: Schocken, 1971.

Holt, John, *How Children Fail.* New York: Pitman, 1964.

_____, *How Children Learn.* New York: Pitman, 1967.

_____, *What Do I Do on Monday?* New York: Delta, 1970.

Homme, Lloyd, *How to Use Contingency Contracting in the Classroom.* Research Press, Inc.

Hoover, Kenneth, *A Handbook for Elementary School Teachers.* Boston: Allyn and Bacon, 1973.

Hopkins, Lee B., *Let Them Be Themselves.* New York: Citation, 1969.

Hyquist, Ewald and Gene R. Hawes, eds., *Open Education: A Sourcebook for Parents and Teachers.* New York: Bantam Books, 1972.

Informal Schools in Britain Today. Volume I: Curriculum. New York: Citation Press, 1972.

Institute for Development of Educational Activities, Inc., *The British Infant School,* I/D/E/A's Early Childhood Series, Vol. I. Dayton, Ohio: I/D/E/A, 1969.

_____, *Learning in the Small Group.* Dayton, Ohio: I/D/E/A, 1971.

Instructional Fair (The), *Guess What!* Grand Rapids, Michigan: The Instructional Fair, 1972.

James, Muriel and Dorothy Jongeward, *Born to Win.* Reading, Mass.: Addison-Wesley, 1971.

Jones, W. Ron, *Deschool Primer No. 3: Your City Has Been Kidnapped.* Zephyrus, 1972.

Kaplan, Kaplan et. al., *Change for Children: Ideas and Activities for Individualized Learning.* Pacific Palisades, Cal.: Goodyear, 1974.

Kid's Stuff, Book 1, Kindergarten and Nursery School, Book 2, Primary Level. Tooley Associates, 520 Richley Ave., West Collingswood, N.J.

Kirschenbaum, Howard and Sidney B. Simon, *Readings in Values Clarification.* Minneapolis, Minn.: Winston, 1972.

_____, and Rodney Napier, *Wad-ja-get? The Grading Game.* New York: Hart, 1971.

Kohl, Herbert, *Math, Writing and Games in the Open Classroom.* Vintage, 1973.

_____, *Reading, How To.* Dutton, 1973.

Kohlberg, Lawrence, "The Child As a Moral Philosopher." *Psychology Today.* September, 1969.

Lair, Jess, *I Ain't Much, Baby — But I'm All I've Got.* New York: Doubleday, 1969.

Laliberte, Norman, and Richey Kehl, *100 Ways to Have Fun with an Alligator & 100 Other Involving Art Projects.* Art Education, Inc., 1969.

Laskin, Joyce Novis, *Arts and Crafts Activities Desk Book.* West Nyack, New York: Parker.

Leonard, G., *Education and Ecstasy.* New York: Delacorte, 1968.

Likert, Rensis, *New Patterns of Management.* New York: McGraw-Hill, 1961.

Limbacher, Walter, *The Dimensions of Personality Series.* Dayton, Ohio: Pflaum/Standard Publishers.

Lorton, Mary Baratta, *Workjobs.* Reading, Massachusetts: Addison-Wesley, 1974.

Lyon, Harold C., *Learning To Feel — Feeling To Learn.* Columbus, Ohio: Merrill, 1971.

Maltz, Maxwell, *Psycho-Cybernetics.* Englewood Cliffs, N.J.: Prentice-Hall, 1960.

Maslow, Abraham H., *Eupsychian Management.* Homewood, Ill.: Dorsey Press, 1965.

_____, *Motivation and Personality.* New York: Harper & Brothers, 1954.

_____, "Some Basic Propositions," in *Perceiving, Behaving, Becom-*

ing. Washington, D.C.: Association for Supervision and Curriculum Development, 1962.

_____, *Toward A Psychology of Being.* Princeton, N.J.: Van Nostrand, 1962.

Mattleman, Marciene, *101 Activities For Teaching Reading.* Portland, Maine: J. Weston Walch.

May, Rollo, *Love and Will.* New York: Norton, 1969.

McCaslin, Nellie, *Creative Dramatics in the Classroom,* Second edition. New York: McKay, 1974.

McClelland, David C., *The Achieving Society.* New York: Van Nostrand, 1961.

McCracken, Robert and Marlene McCracken, *Reading Is Only the Tiger's Tail.* San Rafael, Calif.: Leswing Press, 1972.

McGregor, D., *The Human Side of Enterprise.* New York: McGraw-Hill, 1960.

McLuhan, M., *Understanding Media: The Extension of Man.* New York: McGraw-Hill, 1964.

Miles, L.D., *Techniques of Value Analysis and Engineering.* New York: McGraw-Hill, 1961.

Miles, Matthew, *Learning to Work in Groups.* New York: Bureau of Publications, Teachers College, Columbia University, 1959.

Mind Expanders; The American Revolution; Elementary Science and *Social Studies Strategies,* kits from Educational Insights, Inc., Dept. I-42, 211 South Hindry Ave., Inglewood, California, 90301.

Mosston, Muska, *Teaching: From Command to Discovery.* Belmont, Cal.: Wadsworth, 1972.

Moustakus and Perry, *Learning to Be Free.* Englewood Cliffs, N.J.: Prentice-Hall, 1973.

National Association of Elementary School Principals, *The Elementary School: Humanizing? Dehumanizing?* Washington, D.C.: National Education Association, 1972.

National School Public Relations Association, *Informal Education: "Open Classroom" Provokes Change, Controversy.* Arlington, Virginia: National School Public Relations Association, 1972.

Neill, Alexander S., *Summerhill.* New York: Hart, 1960.

Newberg, Norman, "Build Yourself a City" (1968), film about an urban affairs course; "It's Between the Lines" (1968), film about a drama course; "Making Sense" (1968), film about a communications course. All films are available through the Office of Affective Development, Room 329, Philadelphia Public School Building, 21st and Parkway, Philadelphia, Pa.

Notes on Mathematics in Primary Schools. London: Cambridge University Press, 1969.

Nuffield Mathematics Project, *I Do and I Understand; Pictorial Representation; Beginnings; Mathematics Begins; Shape and Size; Computation and Structure; Probability and Statistics; Checking Up; Graphs Leading to Algebra; Logic.* London: Newgate Press.

NTL, *Group Development.* Washington, D.C.: National Training Laboratories, 1961.

Ojemann, Ralph, *A Teaching Program in Human Behavior and Mental Health,* Handbooks 1-6 (first-sixth grade). Cleveland, Ohio: Educational Research Council of America, Rockefeller Building, 44113.

Otto, H.A., *A Guide to Developing Your Potential.* New York: Charles Scribner's Sons, 1967.

_____ (ed.) , *Explorations in Human Potentialities.* Springfield, Ill.: Charles C. Thomas, 1966.

_____ , *Group Methods Designed to Actualize Human Potential: A Handbook.* Chicago: Achievement Motivation Systems, 1967.

Patterson and Gullion, *Living with Children, Revised Edition.* Champaign, Illinois: Research Press.

Pence, Helen E., *Personalizing Reading.* New York: Young Readers Press, 1973.

Perls, Frederick, Ralph F. Hefferline and Paul Goodman, *Gestalt Therapy.* New York: Julian Press, 1951.

Perls, Frederick, *Gestalt Therapy Verbatim.* Lafayette, California: Real People Press, 1969.

Pfeiffer, J. William and John E. Jones, *A Handbook of Structured Experiences for Human Relations Training* (3 Vols.). Iowa City, Iowa: University Associates, 1971.

Piaget, Jean, *The Moral Judgement of the Child.* New York: MacMillan, 1965.

Platts, Mary E., *Anchor: A Handbook of Games, Activities, and Ideas for Vocabulary Enrichment.* Stevensville, Michigan: Educational Service, 1970.

_____, *Spice: Suggested Activities to Motivate the Teaching of the Language Arts.* Stevensville, Michigan: Educational Service, 1960.

Pluckrose, Henry, *Art.* New York: Citation Press, 1972.

Postman, Neil and Charles Weingartner, *Teaching As a Subversive Activity.* New York: Delta, 1969.

Queens College, *Open Education Newsletter.* Flushing, New York: City University of New York, October/November, 1972.

Rathbone, Charles H., ed. *Open Education: The Informal Classroom.* New York: Citation Press, 1971.

Raths, Louis, Selma Wasserman, et. al., *Teaching for Thinking: Theory and Application.* Columbus, Ohio: Merrill, 1967.

_____, Merrill Harmin and Sidney B. Simon, *Values and Teaching.* Columbus, Ohio: Merrill, 1964.

Ridgway, Lorna and Irene Lawton, *Family Grouping in the Primary School.* New York: Agathon Press, 1965.

Rogers, Carl R., *Freedom to Learn.* Columbus, Ohio: Merrill, 1969.

_____, *On Becoming a Person.* Boston: Houghton Mifflin, 1961.

_____, "Toward A Modern Approach To Values," *Journal of Abnormal and Social Psychology,* Vol. 68, No. 2, 1964.

Roy, Mary M. (ed.), *Probe: A Handbook for Teachers of Elementary Science.* Stevensville, Michigan: Educational Service, 1962.

Sargent, Betsye, *The Integrated Day in an American School.* Boston, Mass.: National Association of Independent Schools, Four Liberty Square, 02109.

Sax, Saville and Sandra Hollander, *Reality Games.* New York: Popular Library, 1972.

Schein, E. and W. Bennis, *Personal and Organizational Change Through Group Methods.* New York: John Wiley & Sons, 1965.

Schmuck, Richard A. and Patricia A. Schmuck, *Group Processes in the Classroom.* Dubuque, Iowa: Brown, 1971.

Schrank, Jeffrey, *Teaching Human Beings.* Boston: Beacon.

Schultz, et. al., *Pain and Joy in School.* Champaign, Illinois: Research Press, 1973.

Schultz, W. C., *FIRO: A three-dimensional theory of interpersonal behavior.* New York: Holt, Rinehart, & Winston, 1958.

Schultz, William, *Joy*. New York: Grove Press, 1968.

Sciara and Walter, *Reading Activities with the Tape Recorder*. The Instructor Curriculum Materials #318, The Instructor Publications, Dansville, New York 14437.

Science 5/13 Series, *Working with Wood; Time; Early Experiences; Structures and Forces; Science from Toys; Minibeasts; Holes, Gaps and Cavities; Change; Metals; Trees; Ourselves; Like and Unlike; Coloured Things*. MacDonald Educational, 49-50 Poland Street, London.

Seif, Elliott, *Open Education: A Manual for Administrators, Parents, Teachers, and Students* (mimeographed copy). Temple University, Philadelphia, Pa.

Severin, F. T. (ed.), *Humanistic Viewpoints in Psychology*. New York: McGraw-Hill, 1965.

Shaftel, Fannie and George Shaftel, *Role Playing for Social Values*. Englewood Cliffs, N.J.: Prentice-Hall, 1966.

Shiman, Culver and Lieberman, (eds.), *Teachers on Individualization: The Way We Do It*. New York: McGraw-Hill, 1974.

Silberman, Charles E., *Crisis in the Classroom*. New York: Random House, 1970.

_____, *The Open Classroom Reader*. New York: Vintage, 1973.

Simon, Sidney B., *The IALAC Story*. Niles, Ill.: Argus Communications.

_____, Leland W. Howe and Howard Kirschenbaum, *Values Clarification: A Handbook of Practical Strategies*. New York: Hart, 1972.

Skinner, B. F., Esalen tapes on Affective Education which include interviews with Maslow, Skinner, Rogers, etc. Available through Esalen, Big Sur Hot Springs, Big Sur, California.

_____, *Walden Two*. New York: Macmillan, 1962.

Smith, James, *Creative Teaching Series*. Boston: Allyn and Bacon, 1967.

Spache, Evelyn B., *Reading Activities for Child Involvement*, Boston, Massachusetts: Allyn and Bacon, 1972.

Spolin, Viola, *Improvisation for the Theatre*. Evanston, Ill.: Northwestern University Press, 1963.

Stanford, Gene and Barbara Stanford, *Learning Discussion Skills Through Games*. New York: Citation, 1969.

Starch, Daniel and Edward C. Elliott, "Reliability of the Grading of High School Work in English," *School Review*, 1912.

Steve Caney's Toy Book. New York: Workman, 1972.

Taylor, Joy, *Organizing the Open Classroom: A Teachers' Guide to the Integrated Day*. New York: Schocken, 1972.

The Crafts Center; Creating Learning Centers; Projects for a Math Lab. Creative Teaching Press, 514 Hermosa Vista Ave., Monterey Park, California, 91754.

Thelen, Herbert A., *Dynamics of Groups at Work*. Chicago: University of Chicago Press, 1954.

Torrance, E. Raul and R. E. Myers, *Creative Learning and Teaching*. New York: Dodd, Mead, 1972.

Van Allen, Roach, *Language Experiences in Reading I, II,III*. Chicago: Illinois: Encyclopedia Britannica Press, 1970.

Voigt, Ralph, *Invitation to Learning: The Learning Center Handbook*. Washington, D.C.: Acropolis, 1971.

_____, *Invitation to Learning: The Learning Center Handbook 2*. Washington, D.C.: Acropolis, 1974.

Warner, Sylvia-Ashton, *Teacher*. New York: Bantam, 1964.

Watson, Goodwin (ed.), *Change in School Systems*. NEA, 1967. Available through National Training Laboratories, 1201 16th St., Washington, D.C. 20036.

_____, *Concepts for Social Change*. NEA, 1967. Available through National Training Laboratories, 1201 16th St., Washington, D.C., 20036.

Wayne, William, *Two Hundred Plus Art Ideas for Teachers*. Yorkville, Illinois: Art Ideas, Box 54. Revised edition, 1972.

Weber, Lillian, *The English Infant School: A Model for Informal Education*. New York: Agathon Press, 1969.

Weinstein, Gerald and Mario Fantini, *Toward a Contact Curriculum*. New York: B'nai B'rith Anti-Defamation League.

_____, *Toward Humanistic Education: A Curriculum of Affect*. New York: Praeger, 1970.

Williams, Rosemary, *Reading in the Informal Classroom*. Newton, Massachusetts: EDC.

Wurman, Richard Saul (ed.), *Yellow Pages of Learning Resources*. Cambridge, Massachusetts: The MIT Press, 1972.

Yanes, Samuel (ed.), *Big Rock Candy Mountain: Education and Classroom Materials.* Menlo Park, California: Portola Institute, 1971.

_____, and Cia Holdorf (eds.), *Big Rock Candy Mountain: Resources for our Education.* New York: Dell, 1971.

INDEX

INDEX OF STRATEGIES

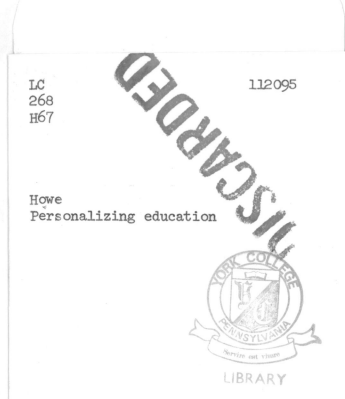